Obedient Servants?

Obedient Servants?

Management Freedoms and Accountabilities in the New Zealand Public Sector

Richard Norman

Victoria University Press

VICTORIA UNIVERSITY PRESS
Victoria University of Wellington
PO Box 600 Wellington

ISBN 0 86473 467 0

First published 2003

National Library of New Zealand Cataloguing-in-Publication Data
Norman, Richard (Edmund John Richard)
Obedient servants? : management freedoms and accountabilities
in the New Zealand public sector / Richard Norman.
Includes bibliographical references and index.
ISBN 0-86473-467-0
1. Administrative agencies—New Zealand—Management.
2. Civil service reform—New Zealand. 3. Public administration—
New Zealand. I. Title.
352.30993—dc 21

Printed by Astra Print, Wellington

Contents

Figures

Tables

Preface

Every Friday the chief executives of the central agencies, the control centre of the public service, meet to eat lunch together, talk over the problems of the past week, and what might come up during the coming week. Chatting over the sausage rolls one day, shortly after I became Secretary to the Treasury, the conversation turned to occupations. What did each of us write down on our arrival cards when we entered a country?

I called myself 'economist'. Everybody else present, all longer experienced than me, said they wrote down 'civil servant'. 'Did they really consider themselves servants?' I asked, surprised. 'And be in the service of Ministers who at times were not even civil?'

Together they answered that they thought of themselves as servants of the people, they felt privileged to be so, and that this traditional view was quite consistent with working in what in some ways was the most modern public sector in the world.

New Zealand was one of the first countries to throw open its public sector and challenge it to perform better. It is very timely to have a study like Richard Norman's to test how we have done and challenge us to improve. In any modern economy, how well off people are depends on how organisations fare, and that depends on how well they are managed. Private sector management is cajoled, bullied, and incentivised by all sorts of market disciplines. We cannot assume the same for public sector management. Instead, a good public management system relies on a series of best practice models, codes of behaviour, benchmarks, and contracts. Fundamentally, however, following the rules is easy. Judgement and decision-making are much more difficult.

Many managers outside Wellington see public sector management as uni-dimensional: a matter of using taxpayers' revenue wisely. But experienced public sector managers know that there is much more complexity and subtlety in their work. In doing this, they can expect to be confronted with tradeoffs and tensions, argument and ambiguity. That is what this book is all about.

Dr Alan Bollard, Governor, Reserve Bank of New Zealand,
Secretary to The Treasury, 1998–2002.

Acknowledgements

The creation of this book has been assisted considerably by the following people:

Associate Professor Bob Gregory, for his encouragement to draw conclusions from empirical data about new realities experienced by New Zealand public sector managers rather than use preconceived ideas.

Professor Pat Walsh, currently Dean of the Faculty of Commerce, who provided funding for my attendance at conferences which stimulated my thinking and broadened my understanding of academic debates in this topic area.

The 91 interviewees, for their perspectives on how New Zealand public sector control systems work in practice.

Two excellent research assistants, Barbara Van der Geest and Jennifer Dickie.

Eight senior public servants who provided helpful feedback on the draft book.

My wife, Janice Wilson, and teenage son, Michael, for their support during this long project.

The publisher, Fergus Barrowman, for his verdict that the PhD thesis which is the basis for this book was 'surprisingly readable' and publishable; Daphne Brasell for helping transform a thesis into a publishable book; Sue Brown for detailed editing and production and Heather McKenzie for marketing.

Foreword

'Societies get the public services they expect. If people
believe that government is bumbling and bureaucratic,
then that is what it will be. If, in contrast, they recognise
public service for the noble calling it is, then they will
end up with strong government' (Mintzberg, 1996: 83).

Questions about public sector performance have provided a central focus
for a diverse range of work roles in Wellington, New Zealand's capital, a
city which has been well described as a 'village with skyscrapers'.[1] My
experience as a journalist during the 1970s, coupled with study for a
multi-disciplinary Master of Public Policy degree, established an enduring
personal interest in the ways in which systems affect organisational
performance. This interest was sharpened and tested by the revolution
in the public sector which began with a new government and a foreign
exchange crisis in 1984, and moved on to a rapid and comprehensive
adoption of the theories described subsequently as New Public
Management or NPM (Hood, 1991).

The introductory quotation from Henry Mintzberg encapsulates two
aspects of a period that saw a questioning of every aspect of public service
delivery in New Zealand. Faced with an economic crisis, the Labour
Government of the late 1980s set about reinventing the way public
services were delivered. This reinvention promised a way of moving
beyond the 'bureaucratic and bumbling' delivery of public services.
Changes that removed red tape, freed public servants to manage, and
expected them to achieve results, provided hope of a reinvigorated public
service. But alongside such change came rhetoric about public service as
a dead weight on overall economic performance – an overhead which
needed drastic trimming. Cutbacks to public services, an agenda

---

1   An allusion made in an interview in *North and South*, March 1999, by Raymond
    Thompson, a British film producer and founder of Cloud Nine, a company based
    in Wellington until 2003, when it shifted to Brisbane.

summarised by Lane (1997b: 1) as 'deregulation, privatisation and marketisation', meant that during the 1980s and early 1990s, public service came to be experienced as working in an 'industry in long-term decline' (Corrigan and Joyce, 1997: 418).

Mintzberg's statement is a helpful antidote to the fervour for private sector techniques that has been a dominant feature of the New Zealand public sector revolution. Techniques such as accrual accounting and strategic planning have certainly helped to bring rapid change to tradition-encrusted bureaucracies. As a consequence, the challenge is to redefine the 'noble calling' so that it can be more than a pale imitation of private sector systems. These business-like systems have shown, particularly since the late 1990s, that they can create different forms of bumbling, such as excessive remuneration for executives, inflated valuations for companies, the destruction of shareholder wealth, and corporate collapse.

Mark Moore (1995) developed the concept of 'creating public value' as a way of stating the distinctive contribution of effective public services. While private sector organisations create 'private value' for their owners, public organisations have a wider brief. The effectiveness of public services increasingly defines the effectiveness of the economies of countries and cities. Management of the environment, law and order, social welfare systems, education and health, and the supervision of industries such as telecommunications, transport, electricity and water, affect the individual's quality of life in more fundamental ways than most private sector products or services. International travel provides a salutary reminder of the extent to which public services define whether a visit is a pleasure or a nightmare. Through the management of customs, airport security, public transport, health services, town planning, food and hotel standards, the provision of museums or art galleries, or the quality of the air and drinking water, public services have a disproportionate impact on the experience of travelling. On returning from overseas travel to New Zealand, I am always thankful for the privilege of being a citizen in a country that, despite the budgetary limitations of a small economy, takes the provision of public services seriously. A thorough examination of how control systems in a practical way affect the delivery of these services will, I hope, make a practical contribution towards the maintenance of a noble calling and strong government.

Experiences which have influenced the book are briefly outlined below, to demonstrate the ways in which I have been encouraged or forced to think about the complex questions raised by the systems through which public services are defined, delivered and evaluated.

Reporting on the 'unelected government'

Working as a journalist for most of the 10 years until 1982, and gathering news stories about central and local government issues, I gained insights into a growing level of frustration with the closed systems of that era's public service. The institutions of the public service seemed to be timeless, with an ability to operate seemingly unchanged amidst an increasingly turbulent economic and political environment. Politicians complained that permanent heads of government departments behaved as though they really ran the country, while political leaders came and went. Administrators within the public service complained about navigating red tape to achieve results in a system where appeal procedures made it almost impossible to appoint outsiders. Appointments to top roles seemed to be largely reserved for men within three years of their retirement age.

This was a solid, conformist public service, where playing it safe appeared to be the most important among the many rules within which it operated.

After a time, rather than reporting on the shortcomings of these systems, I wanted to play a constructive role in developing new systems and sought a role in an organisation that appeared to be doing so.

Managerial freedom and risk in a government corporation

In 1983, I joined an organisation that was a newly created mix of public purpose and private sector management methods. The Development Finance Corporation (DFC), a government-owned development bank, was a niche lender to small and medium-sized businesses, employing about 200 staff. DFC was using the 'latest' techniques of strategic planning and financial analysis to chart its own directions. It was staffed with people from a range of mainly private sector backgrounds, who prided themselves on their ability to support the growth of small and medium-sized enterprises, while also trading profitably as a lending business.

As it turned out, DFC's success was more dependent on wider government policies than independent management action. The 1984 Labour Government, which was expected to be a supporter of organisations such as DFC, opted instead to reduce support for business development in pursuit of budget savings. Government funding for the Small Business Agency[2] was removed and lending staff of DFC were told their new mission was to be a successful business rather than a means for implementing a government goal of diversifying the economy. Along with other DFC staff, I learned some painful lessons about the consequences of too much entrepreneurial zeal and too little control. Until 1986, DFC had been chaired by a retired banker whose aversion to risk was summed up in a favourite saying that 'any fool can lend money, the trick is to get it back'. After his departure, and in response to the injunction from the Government to be fully commercial, DFC management increased targets sharply for lending and linked remuneration to the achievement of these targets. Head office lifted its controls on the types of businesses that could be loaned money. A research division that had previously provided corporate advice on the risks of lending to particular sectors was expected to earn its keep by charging regional lending staff, who unsurprisingly were reluctant to pay for such advice. Profits from foreign exchange dealings increased dramatically and staff numbers doubled during a period of unrestrained growth. The October 1987 share market crash proved fatal to DFC as the value of companies and land against which it had loaned plummeted. Two years later, it was placed in statutory management to enable an orderly selling of assets to pay back its largely foreign investors.

From being an example of the power of managerial freedom to create a new form of government agency, DFC became an example of the perils of too few controls. I had left DFC before it crashed into statutory management, to take up work that was about to become as turbulent as the finance sector.

Restructuring of the public service

In early 1988, I began working with the Training Unit of the State Services Commission (SSC), just ahead of the introduction of a State Sector Bill which would create far-reaching changes for the public sector. The State Services Commission (SSC) would face radical change, with a planned reduction of its 300 staff positions to less than half that. The Training

---

2   A division of DFC that was receiving government funding to provide advice and counselling for small businesses.

Unit, established 25 years earlier to provide centrally funded training for public service organisations, was told initially to recover half of its costs and six months later to recover all its costs. The unit was no longer a central government service, but a competitor for the training budgets of government organisations that were seeking to demonstrate their new found independence from SSC. Between 1988 and 1994, work life was constantly accompanied by a question mark over whether the Training Unit would still exist in three month's time.

The uncertainty also created opportunities. The Treasury, which had on the one hand taken away financial support for the Training Unit, had introduced the 1989 Public Finance Act reforms that created enormous demand among public servants for knowledge about outputs-based budgeting and accrual accounting. I developed a number of training programmes that became strong earners, experience which led to an invitation in 1991 to manage the SSC unit, now renamed Training Works. In hindsight, this was a doomed effort. Training Works was expected to recover its costs from other public sector organisations, many of which were happy to buy from anywhere other than the control agency from which they had just been freed.

Two determined years of marketing and the launch of new programmes still failed to lift performance higher than 75 percent of full cost recovery. In 1994, after other efforts to save the training function, SSC decided to stop its involvement in training delivery. By this time, I had learned about the amount of time and effort required to prepare plans and reports to satisfy corporate planners, central agencies and the Audit Office. Such work came to occupy almost more energy than seeking and serving new clients, and gave an insight into the problems that might arise from the systems our training efforts were helping to establish.

Experience with managing a contestable fund

During this period of working for SSC, I had a part-time role as a member of the Wellington Region Employment and Access Council that provided me with practical insights into the problems of allocating public money. Access Councils were established as a way of devolving responsibility for allocating funds for employment-related training to communities around New Zealand. Councils consisting of employer, union and community representatives were established to allocate funding which had previously been distributed by officials of the Department of Labour.

Devolution proved to mean Council members taking responsibility for unpopular cuts to the budgets of training providers, as we discovered that funds had already been overcommitted by decisions of Department of Labour officials. In order to ration funds the Council had to determine the relative merits of the different training programmes. The Access programme was an early example of contestable funding for outputs and in microcosm it demonstrated the difficulties of comparing between one or another output. How, for instance, was the Council to choose between:

- Short programmes from commercial providers with a relatively high per week cost, but also high rates of success with work placements, compared with lengthy programmes from community providers who had low per week costs and an ability to relate to students, but lacked strong links to employers.
- Tertiary education institutions providing educational qualifications compared with community organisations that found jobs for trainees.
- Programmes which had high success rates for placements into jobs compared with those that mainly prepared trainees for further study.

Statistics and rational analysis proved inadequate for the task of comparing the cost-effectiveness of different organisations. The outputs framework suggested that the Council could buy a course which related to its current priorities in one period and drop that output a year later. In reality any decision to drop an 'output' could be guaranteed to provoke public recrimination from those affected. Frequently, the Council found it could not stop purchasing a single course from a provider without jeopardising the viability of the whole training organisation. Outputs were inextricably linked with the capability and viability of the organisations providing the training. The experience at a local level provided insights into the vastly more complex trade-offs involved in government-wide budgeting.

Experience as a university researcher and teacher

As a senior lecturer at Victoria University since 1994 I have been able to convert the experiences described above into a programme of research into the costs and benefits of the public management model established between 1987 and 1993. This focus has been prompted by personal experience, an awareness of the extent to which such change has affected many people in the capital city, and as a response to challenging questions from international visitors.

Initially I invited a sample of public sector managers to reflect on their experience through the anonymity of Decision Support software, which enables a group to discuss issues via a suite of computers, typing in ideas anonymously and voting on the merits of the ideas. A scorecard developed from this input concluded that accrual accounting was the major success of the new system, with outputs contributing positively but not without their problems. Successes were most evident in the 'hard', visible areas of organisational life, while the greatest problems lay in 'soft', people-related issues such as the management of change (Stace and Norman, 1997).

This conclusion prompted me to record lessons learned by managers from specific examples of public sector change. A number of writers helped complete a series of studies about public sector innovations (Norman, 1997a, 1997b, Smith and Norman, 1997, 1998, VictoriaLink series, 1997–2000).

From each case study emerged different questions about the New Zealand public management model. From one study came the question of the applicability of business solutions to a service that was funded by near-monopoly purchasers from other parts of the public sector. Faced with decreasing budgets, these purchasers merely passed on the pressure to their sub-contractor, creating a stress-filled environment for this 'business-like' agency. A private sector solution may have been to pursue more profitable markets, but public ownership meant this was not a feasible option. From another organisation came insights about the limitations of private sector strategic planning techniques. The organis-ation had hired someone with private sector experience to facilitate its planning, only to find the facilitator lacked understanding of legislative restraints and the degree to which public agencies must interact with the whole public sector system rather than operate independently as in the private sector.

In teaching the topic of strategic human resource management, I ask postgraduate students, many from public organisations, to assess how well the organisational and human resource strategies of their organisations are aligned. Frequently, students working for multi-national businesses, for whom New Zealand is no more than a small branch office, have reported that they see their organisations taking a strategic and long-term perspective on how they integrate the human and business issues. Disturbingly, students from public sector organisations have found it difficult to point to any links between organisational and human resource strategies. Repeatedly, staff from major public service organisations would describe their organisations as short-term in focus, showing few links between outputs required and human resource management strategies adopted. The impression gained, to use an extreme metaphor, was of a 'hypodermic needle approach to human resources strategy' – a use and dispose approach to people. Too many students from central government units would convey a sense of helplessness in what they would see as a spider's web of controls and the risk of job loss amidst frequent restructuring.

Such recurring comments contributed to my thinking that the systems for funding and assessing public sector work may have created a new form of bureaucracy, in its own way as unresponsive as the centralised structures of the 1970s.

Perspectives gained from international comparisons

Overseas observers have been particularly interested in a number of themes relating to the New Zealand experience. They have commented on the speed and scale of change, the decentralisation of management authority, the radical change in the nature of central agencies, the use of contracting to specify the outputs sought from public organisations, and the extensive use made of business terms and techniques.

This book provides a response to public and international interest in the important issue of how public services can best be delivered. It is a response based on the experiences of a representative sample of people whose working lives have been significantly altered by an important experiment. The book discusses the extent to which public sector reform is a cyclical process and how rhetoric, the art of argument, plays a major role in the government's adoption of different strategies for improving the delivery of the public's business. The book provides insights into the impact of a powerful set of ideas on practical issues of performance.

Introduction

Manager: Achieving change in this public sector organisation is like turning around a supertanker.
Colleague: No, it's more like trying to turn around a convoy in which each member of the organisation is on an individual jet ski.[3]

The art of progress is to preserve order amid change and to preserve change amid order.
—Alfred North Whitehead [4]

This book is about change and order in New Zealand's public sector. It aims to capture some of the drama behind official processes described in bland and technical ways such as 'statement of intent', 'strategic plan' and 'estimates of expenditure'.

Beginning in the second half of the 1980s the New Zealand public sector underwent radical change. Structures, employment practices and systems for reporting on performance were substantially modified in pursuit of improved efficiency and effectiveness.

A set of administrative 'doctrines' later given the label of New Public Management (NPM) were introduced in a comprehensive way, at greater speed than in any other country. These changes created a new order that in 2003 is itself subject to change. In the familiar pattern of revolutions, radical changes have become a new status quo.

Two images and a concept sum up the experiences of those interviewed for this book. The first image is that of the thermostat, an image that usefully summarises the systems adopted in the late 1980s to break up a public service organised as a monolithic pyramid. The cycle for planning and reporting adopted has thermostat-like qualities in the way standards

3 Anecdote provided to the author by a senior public sector manager, June 2002.
4 Quoted in Bridges 1995: From Gilbert Seldes, ed., *The Great Quotations* Secaucus, NJ, The Citadel Press, 1983: 738.

are set and reported against. The elements of this thermostat provide the basis for the chapter headings of the book. The second image is that of a pendulum, used to consider changes in organisational strategies. An extreme swing is followed by smaller swings as the pendulum moves towards a new equilibrium. The concept of paradox – the existence of opposing values or realities, each of which is valid – helps summarise the experience of managers interviewed for this book.

This is a study of how rhetoric has translated into organisational routines. Inevitably the realities of the NPM recipe for organisational control are more complex than suggested in the rhetoric that prompted their introduction. These systems replaced the pyramid of traditional bureaucratic hierarchy with the business metaphor of contracts for performance. The result, in the experience of those interviewed for this study, is a new set of paradoxes, in the tradition of the contradictory pairs of proverbs identified by Simon (1946) as core elements of traditional, scientific management approaches to the design of bureaucracies.

The key characteristic of a paradox is the 'simultaneous presence of contradictory, even mutually exclusive elements' (Cameron and Quinn, 1988: 2). As subsequent chapters elaborate, the doctrines used to create the control systems of the New Zealand model seek to give greater freedom for managers, while also providing politicians with greater authority to set strategic directions and to allocate resources. Clear objectives are sought in a political environment in which the consequences of non-delivery are so severe that the logical management response is to minimise clarity or set easily achievable objectives. Assessment of performance is based on flows of information that are unavoidably distorted by the use of that information for assessment. The focus on accountability for performance and results can narrow the perspective of managers to visible and predictable outputs. This is at the expense of taking responsibility for less easily predicted and controlled outcomes. Structures and systems that emphasise accountability and the delivery of performance can provide focus at the expense of coordination.

Later chapters examine how public sector managers and Members of Parliament (MPs) respond to and cope with such paradoxes. The search for public sector performance has the dynamic of a pendulum as solutions for one set of problems create unintended or undesirable consequences that then become the challenges for the next period. The implementation of a comprehensive set of NPM doctrines in the late 1980s was designed to tackle the dominant problems of that time. Efforts duing that period of reform, to ignore paradox in favour of an analytical, rational approach, have created a groundswell of frustration – encouraging a pendulum swing towards a new set of doctrines that has been taking shape since 2001.

In 2003, it is clear that the political pendulum in New Zealand has swung away from enthusiasm for the prescriptions of the reformers of the late 1980s and early 1990s.[5] Nonetheless there has been no move away from the essential principles of those reforms, which were to free managers from detailed rules about inputs, and hold them accountable for achieving results. The two major pieces of legislation which underpin the New Zealand public management model, the State Sector Act 1988, and the Public Finance Act 1989, remain in place although change is planned. The Minister told the annual meeting of the Institute of Public Administration of New Zealand on 30 June 2003, that he plans to introduce a Public Management Bill which will change reporting arrangements for crown entities, and extend the State Services Commissioner's mandate on ethics, values and standards to the wider state sector. Part of the Bill is likely to amend the Public Finance Act to make it easier for departments to work together on cross government projects. The Bill is expected to be introduced in late 2003 or 2004.

The reforms of the 1980s and 1990s focused to an unusual extent on the 'how' of government. Reformers sought to introduce rational, business-like efficiency to decisions about the use of public resources. They sought to deregulate government, privatise as much as possible and use markets to create ongoing pressures for efficiency. Ultimately, however, techniques are means to political ends and NPM techniques have suffered from a 'one best way' fervour rather than an ability to

5   A Labour Government, consisting largely of sceptics and opponents of NPM techniques, received 41 percent of the party vote in the 2002 election, almost double the 21 percent support for the National Party, the governing party for nine years during the 1990s. The ACT Party, the political party which most closely subscribes to NPM prescriptions for reduced state activity and greater use of market solutions, retained 7 percent support, leaving its representation in Parliament unchanged from the previous election. In a 120-seat Parliament, 74 Members of Parliament (MPs) belong to parties that have opposed NPM strategies, and 36 to parties that have strongly supported them.

create a balance between contradictory, yet equally necessary, elements of the delivery of public services.

An emphasis on market-like mechanisms and competition has led to perceptions of narrowly based decision-making focused on price, rather than distinctively public sector issues such as equity in resource allocation and the creation of inter-generational assets. Examples of changes that have occurred since the election of the Labour-Alliance Coalition Government in 1999 include:

- A major change in the health sector, where local democratic input and decision-making has replaced a national system for allocating health funds on the basis of competition and contracting.

- A change in tertiary education away from funding purely on the basis of student demand, towards greater emphasis on national priorities and collaboration between institutions.

- A move back to income-related rents for state housing, and away from funding market-related rents through the social welfare benefit system.

- Some reduction in the numbers of special purpose agencies, particularly with the remerging of special education and early childhood education with the Ministry of Education and the remerging of the Ministry of Justice and Department for Courts.

A single-minded focus on performance and efficiency has given way to concerns about resource allocation, achievement of results that are beyond the capacity of any one public organisation to deliver and concerns about the longer-term capability of public organisations.

NPM techniques provided a major shake-up for an entrenched bureaucratic system. By 1999, after nearly 12 years of structural changes and focus on the short term, the public sector and politicians were ready for a more incremental and pragmatic approach to public management.

But, while major elements of the NPM model are being reconsidered, core questions about how best to deliver public performance remain. At the heart of the techniques adopted lies a set of contradictory realities connected with the control systems that provide the daily, monthly and annual routines through which organisational performance is monitored and controlled. These paradoxes are discussed in following chapters, and are briefly summarised here.

Freedom to manage

- Giving public sector chief executives freedom to manage resources encourages initiative and client-focused delivery.
- Giving chief executives freedom to manage inputs encourages politicians, particularly members of opposition parties, to seek to rein in that freedom, and in so doing create a climate of fear in which initiative is stifled.

Clear objectives

- Clear statements of performance provide an effective way of improving performance.
- Clear statements of performance encourage chief executives to focus on reporting the safe, measurable, trivial and readily achievable.
- Outputs are an effective means for holding public organisations to account for results.
- Outputs promote focus at the expense of coordination, narrowing the breadth of activity to the safe and predictable, crowding out innovation and risk-taking.

Quality information

- Quality information is that which enables external parties to assess whether performance is delivered.
- Quality information is that which most assists 'doing' rather than 'reporting'. Such information is tacit and rarely fully expressable through formal conventions which emphasise historic, auditable information.
- Accrual accounting provides high quality information about both 'purchase' and ownership dimensions of organisations.
- Accrual accounting provides only historic information, segmented into short-term periods, providing most information about immediate purchases of services rather than longer-term organisational capability.
- The more information that is available, the more effective assessments of performance can become.
- The more information that is available, the less knowledge is provided, leading to decision-makers in central agencies and Parliament relying more on informal knowledge than formal reporting.

Accountability and effective assessment

- Accountability systems spur improved performance from chief executives.
- Accountability systems divert chief executives from real work to focus on reporting formalities and image cultivation.
- Central agencies are important checks for quality and coordination.
- Central agencies cannot get sufficiently close to information about what is really happening in operational agencies to make sufficiently informed judgements.

Obtaining objectives efficiently

- A focus on efficiency gives an appropriate focus for managers in the public sector, enabling politicians to make the larger strategic decisions.
- Limiting public managers to a focus on efficient delivery leads to a reduction of emphasis on outcomes, effectiveness and a range of democratic values.

Paradoxes arise where opposite truths coexist. Effective management lies in the ability to strike a balance between paradoxes rather than follow a one-dimensional set of prescriptions. One useful model for seeking balance is that developed by Simons (1995), described in Chapters 2 and 11. This portrays organisational control as a balance between centrally driven controls for the achievement of results and the motivation that comes from empowering staff and managers to explore different paths to performance. In using the yin-yang symbol, it takes a similar approach to that of Collins and Porras (1994), who see effective management as a 'both and' challenge, rather than a 'tyranny' of 'either or' choices.

The essence of paradox is that opposite perspectives are equally valid. Management involves reconciling the paradox that organisations require efficiency, discipline and order, while also having the ability to change and grow on the basis of staff commitment and trust. The competing values framework of Quinn (1988), described in Chapter 11, provides an additional framework for interpreting the challenge faced by public managers. As noted in that chapter, NPM techniques have drawn very heavily on the 'rational goal' quadrant of this model and, in doing so, have underemphasised desirable and opposite characteristics.

Understanding management, as an art of balancing a series of necessary and irreconcilable opposites, lacks the resonance of rhetoric that declares that a best way is possible. But it is a realistic approach to public sector tasks that require a high tolerance for ambiguity and intellectual ability (Lynn, 1996: 100). If public sector executives lack such intellectual ability, 'performance may become disorganized or desultory or reactive. Public executives with inadequate mental preparation may be driven to seeking paths of least resistance through the daily morass of claims, irritants, and frustrations, to making snap judgements, deferring to someone else, procrastinating, or simply screwing up' (Lynn, 1996: 111).

Competence in the public sector means 'having confidence in one's ability to think and act sensibly in the face of uncertainty, incomplete information, multiple and competing objectives, value conflicts, and irresolvable disagreements over what should be done' (ibid).

This is a more realistic description of public management tasks than the 'either/or' strategies that dominate the techniques of NPM. This NPM tide of public sector reform sought to impose order on a series of paradoxes. Tasks became either outputs or outcomes, in order to tighten the definition of accountability. The New Zealand public sector was subdivided into purchase and ownership interests, rather than being seen as an integrated whole, replete with paradoxes. Public servants were either policy or operational, rather than interactive learners who move relatively easily between the two. Public servants and politicians were categorised as either principals or agents, rather than seen as parties who can share a common interest in long-term stewardship of resources and institutions.

A new agenda

Having worked through a cycle which has sought to separate and subdivide, the New Zealand public sector now enters a more ambiguous period in which performance gains depend on a reconciling of opposites and the practice of 'both/and' strategies of management. The performance challenge is to find a constructive balance between:
- Focus and coordination, retaining the benefits of clear objectives, while developing ways of sharing across organisational boundaries.
- Results and capability building, in which the artificial distinction between purchase and ownership interests is replaced with a realism that performance requires both delivery in a current year and

preparation for future performance.

- Accountability and responsibility, in which externally driven demands for performance and reporting do not undermine the drive that can come from individual commitment to a set of standards.

One of the major challenges of tides of reforms is to ensure that strong features of past systems are not swept aside amidst enthusiasm for new ways. This book records lessons from a major experiment, in the process of a shift. It focuses particularly on the frequently invisible recurring processes involved in organisational control as a way of expressing daily realities.

Major benefits have been gained from the public sector revolution of the 1980s and 1990s. The challenge is to retain both the hard-edged focus on describable performance, a useful import from private sector experience, while not diminishing the distinctive features of public services.

PART ONE

Public Sector Performance

Challenging the conventions

CHAPTER I

Public sector reform – choices for change

The performance challenges described in the previous chapter arise from an ongoing debate about how best to translate political strategies into delivered performance. This question is a central preoccupation of the fields of public administration and public management.

Should governments deliver services directly through their own organisations or buy performance from other sectors? Should they control public spending on the basis of inputs and procedures, or outputs and outcomes? Such debates about how to organise government services have occurred throughout recorded history with at least 99 'doctrines' being developed to advise on the what, how and who aspects of delivering public services (Hood and Jackson, 1991).[6]

The New Zealand public management model is strongly based on a set of choices about change made in the late 1980s. The 'doctrines' adopted drew on business experience to reshape New Zealand's public sector, with the intention of achieving improved performance from 'the public's business'. New structures and systems were introduced to create a thermostat-like cycle of goal setting, feedback and correction – making transparent the information and decisions about resources that had previously been the province of career public servants. As an early and comprehensive adopter of these techniques, New Zealand has played a role out of proportion to its size in an international debate about methods that are described as managerialism or New Public Management (NPM) (Pollitt, 1990; Hood, 1991; Aucoin, 1995). Governments that have adopted this model of public management have sought to shift from funding organisations and institutions to funding performance. Public services, previously delivered through government-owned bureaucracies, are now delivered through a 'mixed economy' (Gray, 1998) of public

6   Hood and Jackson collected 99 doctrines to illustrate the variety of approaches. Doctrines are defined as ideas that lie half way between theory and policy and are presented as 'revealed truth' rather than the 'tentative hypothesising of theory' (Dunsire, 1973: 39).

and private organisations competing for available funds. Government bureaucracies have been 'reinvented' in attempts to reduce costs to taxpayers and increase responsiveness to clients and citizens (Osborne and Gaebler, 1992; Gore, 1993; Osborne and Plastrik, 1997).

New Zealand's reorganisation was more comprehensive and occurred more quickly than in most countries, adopting proposals from *Government Management* (The Treasury, 1987), a report which Hood (1990: 210) describes as an 'NPM manifesto'. Private-sector accounting, outputs budgeting and contracts for performance have been used to replace a traditional inputs-oriented bureaucracy. The changes have earned for New Zealand a reputation which has been variously described as: an example worth studying (Aucoin, 1995); a radical outlier (Ferlie et al, 1996: 250); an experiment not to be recommended for most developing countries (Schick, 1998); a system which is 'getting better but feeling worse' (Gregory, 2000); and the 'world's most advanced performance system' (Kettl, 2000: 7).

Amidst the controversy generated about NPM methods, there has been surprisingly little in-depth information about how these methods work in practice. As Peters and Savoie (1998) comment, most literature focuses on describing rather than evaluating changes that have occurred. Pollitt (1995: 135) believes that it is paradoxical that while public services have been expected to develop measurable outputs, fundamental aspects of NPM have been almost immune from such requirements. For one commentator on the New Zealand reforms, it is a matter of amazement that 'massive upheavals with their many repercussions' have occurred with 'little or no attempt to find out the results, the price paid, by whom and whether it was worth it' (Rhodes, 1999: 123).

This book contributes insights into the ongoing contribution of the managing for performance revolution. The essence of the New Zealand model is a set of control systems that provide public service managers with greater freedoms to manage, while concurrently holding them accountable for achieving results. This system of management has continued largely unaltered in the face of shifts away from other features of the NPM agenda, particularly privatisation and the use of market mechanisms for delivering public services. After a period of 'massive upheaval', change in the New Zealand public sector has been gradual and incremental since 1999.

While some structural changes have occurred, notably in health, housing and education, core thinking about organisational control, established by the State Sector Act 1988 and Public Finance Act 1989, has remained. Managing for performance has proved to be as popular a recipe for a government of the political left as it has been for the political right

Control systems are defined as the 'formal, information-based routines and procedures managers use to maintain or alter patterns in organisational activities' (Simons, 1995: 5). The New Zealand public sector has sought to let managers manage, while holding them accountable for results. Managers are advised through formal, information-based routines about the extent to which they are succeeding in the delivery of results. This book explores the realities of these new control systems, focusing on this question:

> How do control systems that seek to provide managers with autonomy and hold them accountable for results, work in practice?

Perceptions of the practical realities of control systems have been gained in three ways, each designed to test and triangulate information from the other sources. First, during 2000, interviews were carried out with 41 Wellington-based senior executives and consultants, for whom control systems are a major part of their work. This group provided a 'horizontal' sample of opinion, taking in a wide cross-section of organisations and occupations. Interviews were followed by a survey that established areas of strongest agreement and disagreement. Secondly, interviews were carried out during 2001 with 50 people working at different hierarchical levels on the delivery of four outputs, chosen to illustrate the diversity of public sector tasks. This round of interviews provided a 'vertical' sample of perceptions, from frontline staff, chief executives, central agency analysts and members of Parliamentary select committees. Thirdly, a wide range of official reports and newspaper articles has been used as a cross-check on the memories of interviewees, and to provide historical information about trends in financial and human resource management.

The process by which these sources of information have been analysed is described in full in Chapter 3, Research Methodology.

The focus for the research

The book is limited in scope with its focus on one segment of New Zealand public organisations: tax-funded central government departments and ministries. This segment of the New Zealand public service employs 31,440 of 234,340 central government staff, with local government employing an additional 31,100.[7] These organisations have been less affected by market-like mechanisms than trading organisations or institutions that must compete for 'contestable' funds. While subject to 'business-like' practices, they deliver services that have few if any private sector equivalents. They do, however, operate within a structure of purchasing, ownership, contracting and accountability, that has sought to introduce business-like mechanisms into the core public service.

The study has attempted to gain 'business as usual' views by seeking comments from individuals and organisations whose work lives, during 2000 and 2001, were not subject to organisational restructuring. Health restructuring during this period meant that views from this sector have been under-represented.

Re-evaluation of the NPM doctrines adopted in New Zealand in the late 1980s has been an important backdrop to the interview-based research, but in the area of control systems, there has been more continuity than change.

The election of a centre-left Labour-Alliance Coalition Government in 1999 brought a shift in political philosophy after 15 years during which governing parties had focused on reducing the size of the public sector, and reducing differences between public and private sectors. The 2002 election confirmed this shift away from the strategies adopted in the late 1980s. Symbolically, the most public example of change in emphasis away from business-like methods was seen in criticism of the performance of the Chief Executive of the Department of Work and Income, Christine Rankin. In 1999, the department had chartered an aircraft to take managers to a corporate conference at a central North Island tourist resort, provoking pre-election controversy about the imitation of private sector practices within a core government agency. In government, Labour Ministers found it considerably more difficult than in pre-election rhetoric to remove a Chief Executive whose spending they had used to symbolise managerial

---

7   Statistics obtained at 30 June 2001, from the Quarterly Employment Survey of Statistics New Zealand.

Garrick Tremain, *Otago Daily Times,* 9 April 2001

extravagance. A Ministerial Review first recommended tighter controls on the department, and then in early 2001 the State Services Commissioner decided not to renew Ms Rankin's employment contract. Ms Rankin responded to this decision with a much-publicised appeal to the Employment Court. The case ended in August 2001 with a decision by the Employment Court that the State Services Commissioner had a right not to renew the Chief Executive's contract. This high profile case was fresh in the minds of interviewees as they considered how public sector control systems affected their performance.

Public sector reform and the New Zealand context

Located at the southern edge of the world, New Zealand is 'a test tube whose glass sides are 2000 kilometres thick, in which some of the grand themes of world history are played out more discernibly than elsewhere'.[8]

8   A comment made by Auckland University history professor, James Belich, cited in *North and South* magazine, August 1997: 95.

Changes to New Zealand's system of public management, particularly during the early and mid-1990s, attracted many visitors to a country whose population, at 4 million, is no larger than many cities in more populated countries. During the mid-1990s, for instance, the financial management group of the New Zealand Treasury was receiving on average one delegation a week (Norman 1997a: 1).

Such interest was sparked by the radical nature of the market and business-oriented solutions adopted by governments in the late 1980s and first half of the 1990s. Since the 1999 election, this overseas interest in the New Zealand experiment has waned markedly as the more radical market-oriented experiments in the redesign of public services have fallen from political favour.

The book revisits the promises and prospects of the major changes of the late 1980s and early 1990s. It is the author's hope that the insights such reflection can provide will make a constructive contribution to those who are now grappling with the question that sooner or later occurs with any organisational or public sector change – where next?

Public management reform and reorganisation is 'a long, hard and frequently futile endeavour' (Kaufman, 1978: 418). It has also been likened to a series of tides coming in and out, each leaving a mark on the foreshore (Light, 1997). As with all cycles of change, the challenge is to keep the best from a previous era while grafting on systems appropriate to a new era. This book aims to contribute towards making these distinctions.

The New Zealand experience of reform has added significantly to a world debate about ways in which business-like practices can be used to deliver public services. Knowledge about how such techniques either assist or impede the delivery of public services is important for ensuring that as one tide ebbs and another gathers strength, the more effective contributions remain, while the ineffective drift back to sea.

CHAPTER 2

Managing for performance – an overview

'I obeyed every order with which I agreed.'
—Admiral Hyman Rickover[9]

'Tell a performer they were wonderful and they will tell you of the tiny mistakes. That's what makes them great. They are never satisfied.'[10]

New Public Management (NPM) prescriptions for reform have provided a radical challenge to the bureaucratic model of organisation that dominated public service delivery during most of the twentieth century.

The traditional model, *managing for process*, used rules and regulations to maintain centralised authority over the process through which government services would be delivered. It has been challenged by a *managing for results* model, which seeks centralised control of results but decentralising of decisions about service delivery (Feldman and Khademian, 2000). NPM ideas have sought to replace the presumed inefficiency of hierarchical bureaucracy with the presumed efficiency of markets (Power, 1997: 43). NPM prescriptions have been presented as a means for 'breaking through bureaucracy' (Barzelay, 1992) or 'banishing bureaucracy' (Osborne and Plastrik, 1997). They are more realistically defined as a set of techniques for replacing procedural bureaucracy with corporate, market or network forms of bureaucracy (Considine and Lewis, 1999). Results- and performance-oriented public sector systems are still 'bureaucracies' in the sense that they are rational, legal creations not organisations based on personal charisma or inherited position.

Procedural bureaucracy had a distinct advantage of simplicity, a factor in its longevity. As befitting a system originating during an era in which railways were the dominant mode of transport, traditional public

---

9 Quoted in Downs and Larkey (1986: 239).
10 A poster on a wall in the foyer of the Westpac Trust St James Theatre, Courtenay Place, Wellington, 2001.

administration could be likened to 'a railway signal person faced with one lever operated precisely according to a rule book' (Gray, 1998: 2).

The extent to which centralised control can deliver desired results is an enduring challenge of management and leadership. President Harry S Truman expressed his frustration that not even presidents could manage through command, contemplating what General Eisenhower was likely to face if he became president. The general would say 'Do This! Do that!' Truman is reported as commenting. 'And nothing will happen. Poor Ike – it won't be a bit like the Army. He'll find it very frustrating' (Neustadt, 1990: 10).

Any organisation is a balancing act between a desire for central control and pressure for individual autonomy. At the top of a hierarchy, managers try to develop a unified mission or strategy, using commands and rules and other means to create 'centripetal forces'. By contrast, middle managers can be expected to use autonomy to create centrifugal forces that pull an organisation towards 'balkanisation' (Bolman and Deal, 1997: 71). Too much control at the centre can undermine motivation among those who are furthest from the source of power and result in the passivity, lack of initiative and acceptance of rule-bound behaviour that is seen as a failing of traditional bureaucracies, and a rationale for public sector reform. Overly centralised controls will reduce the discretionary effort of those who have most contact with citizens and clients – resulting in problems being passed up the hierarchy, slow response times and the comment that 'it is not my responsibility'. However, too much autonomy and too little control can undermine coordination and prevent the delivery of a consistent service or product. Too little control over financial management can result in the overspending of budgets and threats to financial viability. Too much autonomy in the setting of employment standards may result in publicly embarrassing lapses in service delivery or legal action over personal grievances.

Finding a balance between sufficient central control for a coordinated strategy and sufficient local autonomy to foster initiative and responsiveness is undoubtedly the organisational equivalent of efforts of medieval alchemists to manufacture gold. The challenge is magnified in public sector organisations where two steps of delegated authority are involved, from political to administrative leaders, and then from organisational leaders to their staff. While similar delegation occurs with private sector or not-for-profit boards, the public sector is distinctive because of the extent to which organisational strategies are created in public.

Control is a central preoccupation in the delivery of public services, because public agencies are 'invested with awesome powers of compulsion – to tax, regulate, inspect, arrest – and attractive powers of reward – to subsidise, purchase and protect. Typically they (public agencies) exercise these powers as monopolists, immune from competition. To make them accountable, we enshroud them in a maze of laws, regulations, and court rulings; to keep them responsive, we expose them to access by endless reporters, lawyers, committees, and investigators' (Wilson, 1994: 672).

The solution to this problem of public sector control for much of a century was to deliver services through hierarchical bureaucracies, responsible directly to elected representatives. In the British Westminster system, adopted by New Zealand, Cabinet Ministers had 'ministerial responsibility' for the work of the departments that reported to them. Performance of public servants was constrained by procedures designed to maintain a separation between political decision-making and administrative delivery. The hierarchical, bureaucratic approach to service delivery led to the creation of distinctive public service organisations. These were set apart from the private sector by employment procedures that created self contained life-time careers. The traditional British civil service, for instance, has been described as a 'great rock on the tide line' of politics (Hennessey, 1989: 628), and has been caricatured by the popular and influential British television series *Yes, [Prime] Minister* for the ways in which departmental heads could influence political decision-making (Borins, 1988). In pre-Communist China, the Mandarins were the class apart; in France, the graduates of Les Grandes Écoles; while the Ottoman Empire had the most distinctive group of public servants, its eunuchs. The culture of a career apart, reinforced by central controls and careful attention to cultural symbols, is well described in the classic study of the United States Forest Service of the 1950s by Kaufman (1967).

Control prescriptions of the New Public Management recipe

The strength of procedural bureaucracy lies in its ability to create 'centripetal' forces to deliver standardised services. But centralised control means there is limited autonomy for staff to respond to change or to vary service delivery. Problems with the bureaucratic model, which led to pressure for change, are described later in this chapter and in Chapter 4 where the specifics of New Zealand change are discussed.

The NPM prescription for the delivery of public services differs fundamentally from the hierarchical, bureaucratic model. In essence, it offers a seemingly straightforward proposition that governments should seek to buy performance instead of funding institutions. Governments should 'steer rather than row' (Osborne and Gaebler, 1992: 25–48), and seek to buy the best performance possible rather than assume that established government organisations are the best means for providing services.

Traditional bureaucracy draws strongly on military traditions of command and control, and religious traditions of vocation and service. The NPM recipe favours the model of organisation used in the business sector, in which activist managers mobilise resources to meet the needs of clients and customers, while delivering profits to shareholders (Hood and Jackson, 1991).

In seeking to provide an alternative to traditional procedural bureaucracy, NPM theory can be seen to consist of a number of 'antiphons' or contradictory pairs of proverbs (Peters, 1998: 89). The following antiphons highlight the tensions involved in maintaining a balance between the autonomy of managers, and control by elected representatives.

A. 'The principal goal of reform is to empower public employees, create autonomous and effective public managers and make government a more attractive employer.
B. Effective government will only work by reducing the power of the civil service and empowering their nominal political masters.'

As Peters (1998) points out, the use of contradictory proverbs in the process of administrative reform has a long tradition (eg Simon, 1946 and Kaufman, 1978). Identifying and understanding contradictions is an established method for understanding the dynamics of administrative change. Contradictions are plentiful among the different tides of reform that created near continuous efforts to change the United States Federal Government during the 20th century (Light, 1997). Three of the tides (scientific management, 'war on waste' and 'watchful eye') emphasised control located outside the public service, while liberation management, the most recent, focused on the need to free managers from controls created by the other tides. See Appendix 1 for more detail about these tides and other aspects of control systems.

The importance of control systems

Control is the ability of one person to direct others to do things they would not otherwise do or to refrain from doing things which they would otherwise do (Pollitt et al, 1998: 11). Control is an exhibition of power, 'the potential ability to influence behaviour, to change the course of events, to overcome resistance, and to get people to do things they would not otherwise do' (Pfeffer, 1992: 30). Organisations face a common problem of how to gain cooperation between individuals or units that share only partially congruent objectives. The problem of organisation design is to discover the balance of socialisation and measurement that best enables a particular organisation to achieve cooperation among its members (Ouchi, 1979: 845). The primary means by which managers can achieve this is through the use of effective control systems, already defined in Chapter 1 as 'the formal, information-based routines and procedures managers use to maintain or alter patterns in organisational activities' (Simons, 1995: 5). Control systems are the means by which hierarchical authority is established and maintained, and a balance attained between organisational focus and individual initiative. Information and procedures provide the basis from which managers exercise power to direct or restrain action.

An understanding of control systems requires perspectives from a range of disciplines. While the principles of economics guide the allocation of resources, and accounting provides techniques for implementing management controls, a grasp of social psychology is necessary for understanding the effect of reporting systems on people's behaviour (Anthony and Young, 1994: 5).

A tension running through the literature about control is that accountants tend to see it as a solution and sociologists see it as a problem (Hofstede, 1981: 209). The accounting discipline focuses on conventions and standards that are intended to increase the reliability of reported information. Sociology, by contrast, makes a distinctive intellectual contribution through the study of unintended and unanticipated consequences of social practices (Merton, 1957: 66). One discipline proposes solutions while the other queries whether the result of the solution might be a 'fatal remedy' (Sieber, 1981).

The standardised reports of accounting have become virtually synonymous with organisational control systems, but a restriction of focus to accounting would narrow the understanding of that control. Hofstede (1978, 1981) and Ouchi (1979) provide frameworks for taking into account the wider psychological and sociological dimensions involved in the creation of effective control.

Hofstede (1978, 1981) distinguishes between cybernetic and judgement-based controls. Cybernetic control usually involves a division of labour in which staff of a control department monitor standards set by higher management. The essence of the cybernetic approach is setting a standard which can be monitored so unwanted differences can be eliminated.

Judgement-based controls, by contrast, are needed for situations where standards are difficult to define. Intuitive control might be needed for activities that are not repetitive, judgement control needed to assess suitable indicators where outputs are not measurable, and political control needed when objectives are ambiguous.

A major drawback of cybernetic or thermostat-like control is that organisations will collect and use only the information that fits against existing standards. A self-correcting system may work efficiently in times of stability but not provide sufficient information to allow innovation during more ambiguous periods. It may result in single loop learning in which results are compared only with the standard. Double loop learning, by contrast, occurs when questioning and changing of basic assumptions and policies follows a match or mismatch with expected results. This is the equivalent of a thermostat questioning why it is set at 20 degrees centigrade (Argyris, 1980: 207).

Hofstede's (1981) analysis raises questions relevant to the performance feedback frameworks advocated by NPM theorists as an alternative to hierarchical, bureaucratic control. These are essentially cybernetic, or thermostat-like in design, in a sector where decisions are frequently based on processes of judgement, intuition and politics.

While Hofstede's (1981) model of control emphasises the process of decision-making, Ouchi (1979) provides a typology of organisational cultures that addresses the question of which mechanisms an organisation can use to move towards its objectives.

Bureaucratic mechanisms use close personal surveillance and direction of subordinates by superiors. The information necessary for the task is contained in rules about processes or standards of outputs to be achieved. Rules are essentially arbitrary standards against which later comparisons will be made, and convey less complete information than prices used in market mechanisms.

Market mechanisms simplify decision-making by using price as the only or dominant element in decision-making. Work is put out for competitive quotes and the market process defines what is a fair price. Markets require reciprocity based on the assurance that comes from legal safeguards that other parties will act honestly.

Clan mechanisms involve a deep commitment to the objectives of the organisation among people who have been chosen and socialised into a culture or profession, in which more informal and implicit controls can be used. Reciprocity between the organisation and its members is based on more complex exchanges related to group membership, status and belonging.

Ouchi's analysis provides a way of categorising the control solutions of NPM prescriptions for government reform. The NPM approach is to increase the emphasis on market mechanisms for control, and so reduce the range of social elements involved in control. At its extreme, control is based on information about price, with Government, by buying performance, acting as a steering mechanism. Such thinking assumes a marketplace of willing sellers, in which social interactions are minimised and mediated by contractual arrangements based on price. Advocates for NPM strategies emphasised the harmful effects of bureaucracy's rules and the ability of traditional ways to frustrate political strategies or reduce service to clients/citizens.

Building on the work of Ouchi (1979) and Hofstede (1981), among other researchers, Simons (1990, 1991, 1995, 2000) emphasises controls as a means for implementing strategy. A model developed by Simons (1995) integrates the cybernetic approach to control with a broader picture of strategy and organisational purpose. This model provides a way of overcoming Hofstede's objections to overemphasis on cybernetic control by showing cybernetic feedback as one of four important forms of control. Feedback against pre-set standards makes an important contribution, in Simons' model, as a way of using an organisation's most limited asset – the time that senior managers have available to pay attention to any particular issue. Effective diagnostic reporting against standards improves the 'return on management'.

Simons' particular contribution is to demonstrate how control systems can contribute to implementing different aspects of strategy, categorised in the following ways:

1. **Beliefs systems** relate to strategy as perspective. Strategy develops from ways of viewing the world that are ingrained in organisational members. Commitment to purpose provides inspiration for implementation.
2. **Boundary systems** relate to an organisation's strategies about the niches in which it operates. A company may differentiate itself on the basis of distinctive products, low cost or specific customer groups (Porter, 1985). On the other hand, the niche of a public agency is likely to be largely defined through legislation and political mandate. Boundaries set limits to the territory in which the organisation will operate and how it will relate with its stakeholders.
3. **Diagnostic control systems** are a cybernetic form of feedback, similar to that of a thermostat that assesses progress against pre-set standards. This is strategy as planning, in which progress is checked against clear objectives and indicators.
4. **Interactive control systems** are those used to detect patterns from experience. Strategy is 'emergent' as the organisation interacts with its environment and discovers new opportunities or responds to threats. Interactive controls stimulate organisational learning, and the emergence of new ideas and strategies.

These four levers of control represent opposing forces – the yin and yang – of effective strategy implementation. In Chinese philosophy, positive and negative forces are opposing principles into which creative energy divides, and whose fusion creates the world. Two of these control levers – beliefs systems and interactive control systems – create positive and inspirational forces. These are the yang: forces representing sun, warmth and light. The other two levers, boundary systems and diagnostic control systems, create constraints and ensure compliance with orders. These are the yin: forces representing darkness and cold (Simons, 1995: 7–8).

Figure 2.1: Levers of control model

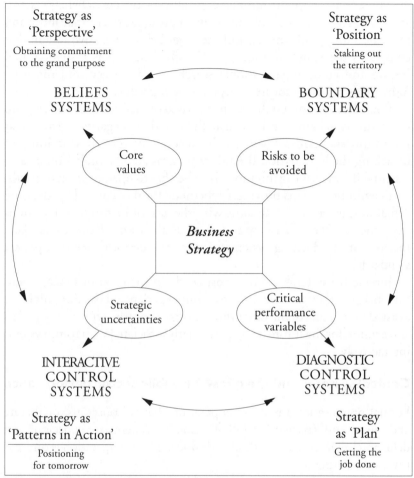

Source: Simons, 1995: 159, Figure 7.3.

Implementation of strategy requires a balance between the four quadrants. The levers described in each corner are a means for understanding the neglected process of implementation. Effective implementation requires more than monitoring of a plan. Control systems should be used selectively to balance the tensions between unlimited opportunity and limited attention (the role of boundary systems), the plan as intended (diagnostics) and emergent strategy (interactive controls), and between self-interest (requiring control) and the desire to contribute (requiring empowerment) (Simons, 1995: 28).

The search for opportunities is controlled by the use of beliefs systems and boundary systems, with one being a positive system that motivates the search for opportunities, and the other being a negative system that constrains the search (Simons, 1995: 33). The beliefs system should inspire and guide organisational search and discovery, and motivate individuals to search for new ways of creating value.

Boundary systems establish limits, based on defined business risks, to opportunity-seeking and are usually stated in negative terms or as minimum standards. They will be accompanied with sanctions for breaching the boundaries. Boundary systems are like brakes on a car – essential if a car (or organisation) is to be able to operate at high speeds.

Diagnostic systems provide a cybernetic form of control by assessing actual outputs against standards with the aim of identifying deviations from the standard. At its most automatic the form of control is like a thermostat of a heating system that controls performance to a pre-set standard.

Interactive systems are the most costly in their use of management time because they involve learning from experience. Learning might be assisted by any one of the other three forms of control, with strong beliefs and a vision for the future being particularly associated with using systems interactively.

Control systems and the quest for public sector performance

Formal organisation involves cooperation that is 'conscious, deliberate and purposeful' (Barnard, 1968: 4). Control systems are conscious and deliberately constructed methods for ensuring that cooperation is directed towards a purpose.

The effect of the messages conveyed by organisations and their control systems is profound. One 'does not live for months or years in a particular position in an organisation, exposed to some streams of communication, shielded from others, without the most profound effects upon what he (she) knows, believes, attends to, hopes, wishes, emphasises, fears, and proposes' (Simon, 1976: xvi).

Dissatisfaction during the 1980s and 1990s, led to political interest in business-like systems of control for public services. The marketplace became an appealing new symbol for control, to supersede traditional bureaucracy. The market emphasis on price mechanisms, and a semi-automatic and cybernetic feedback system, appeared to promise rapid responses based on price signals – as an alternative to rule-based bureaucracy or socially determined clan behaviour.

At the heart of the systems for control adopted for the New Zealand public sector are some deceptively simple propositions about the nature of effective management. A founding document of the New Zealand system (The Treasury, 1987) lays out the foundations for an alternative to the bureaucratic method. The report proposed that government organisations should be managed through a cycle consisting of:

- clarity of objectives
- freedom to manage
- accountability
- adequate information flows
- effective assessment of performance.

The logic through which these principles connect has subsequently been described this way:

> If managers are clear about what is expected of them (clarity of objectives) and are given the power to achieve their specified objectives (freedom to manage) and then made accountable for achieving the objectives by being judged (accountability) with quality information (adequate information flows) on how well they met their stated objectives (effective assessment of performance), managers will make efficient resource allocation decisions and obtain objectives in the most efficient way (SSC10, 1999: 13).

In drawing on theory from New Institutional Economics and management literature, this New Zealand NPM prescription for control takes a distinctly cybernetic or thermostat-like view of organisations. Clear objectives are designed to make it possible for an external monitor, the accountability thermostat for the system, to assess progress against a set of standards. Organisations are machine-like systems through which resources (inputs) are managed to produce goods or services (outputs) that contribute towards outcomes. The economic purpose of the organisation, and particularly its price signals, are emphasised almost to the exclusion of the social factors inherent in clan control or the restrictions of traditional bureaucratic rules. The model of management envisaged can be expressed diagrammatically as follows:

Figure 2.2. Inputs-outputs model of management

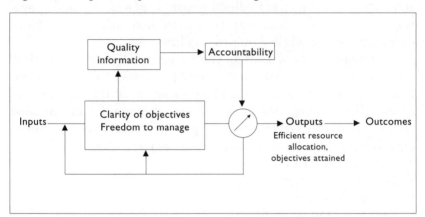

Source: Norman, 2003.

Any model of management necessarily simplifies the complexity of reality, but mental models also shape realities by limiting the focus of decision makers.

Just as the pyramid is an expressive symbol for traditional bureaucracy, the thermostat is a useful symbol for the arms-length, market-like decision-making envisaged in NPM prescriptions. Markets are thermostat-like feedback mechanisms, in which prices are the primary means by which consumers hold producers accountable. The thermostat encapsulates the concept of governments as steering organisations that can use planning, purchasing and feedback systems to achieve government goals.

The thermostat in Figure 2.2 is a much-simplified representation of a system of planning and feedback that necessarily involves much decision-making based on intuition, judgement and politics. But it provides a way of crystallising the management system envisaged by reformers of the late 1980s and early 1990s, as a radical alternative to bureaucracy. Examination of each of the elements of the thermostat in subsequent chapters helps identify how this form of organisation, just like traditional bureaucracy, creates contradictory proverbs or paradoxes to test the will and creativity of those who manage public services.

CHAPTER 3

Research methodology

'If I have seen further it is by standing on the shoulders of giants.'
—*Sir Isaac Newton, (1642–1727)*[11]

'Show me a man who claims to be objective, and I'll show you a man with illusions.'
—*Henry Luce (1898–1967)*[12]

Research which seeks to distinguish reality from rhetoric in the creation of performance-oriented public services inevitably raises questions of 'whose rhetoric' and 'whose reality'. Differences between rhetoric and reality are captured visually in a cartoon drawn shortly after Bill Clinton was elected president of the United States in 1992. The saxophone-playing president is depicted having to shift his attention from the clear flowing lines of a rhetoric waltz to begin playing a complex score entitled 'reality fugue'.[13]

Reality is a subjective concept and this chapter briefly identifies the lenses through which reality has been defined and interpreted for this book.

Findings are derived from:

- public administration and management research
- consideration of the usefulness of management knowledge for practice
- fieldwork based on a series of questions rather than an hypothesis
- interviews, a survey, case-study-based data collection and official reports.

11 *Oxford Dictionary of Quotations*, fifth edition, Oxford University Press, Oxford, 1999: 543.
12 *New York Times*, 1 March 1967: 33.
13 *Time*, 21 November 1992.

The field of public administration and management

The subject matter of public administration and the more recently developed 'public management' is unavoidably multi-disciplinary and applied in nature. These subjects have developed in response to a need for professional education for public sector employees. Public administration originated largely with the drive to professionalise public services in the United States in the late nineteenth century. Public management has developed as a response to the recent use by the public sector of techniques drawn from the private sector. Whether the focus is on political context or managerial performance, public administration and management are subjects that face a constant challenge from their public sector 'clients' to respond to practical problems and challenges.

The issues raised by the experience of public sector employees cannot be tackled effectively by using the frameworks of single disciplines. Depending on the reality being studied, useful techniques can come from subjects as diverse as political science, law, strategy, organisation behaviour, economics, statistics, anthropology, psychology, sociology or accounting. Such diversity reflects the breadth of public sector services, from routine clerical tasks to the complex exercise of professional judgement about issues that have an impact across generations.

The origins of public administration and management are thoroughly explored in a book by Lynn (1996), whose title *Public Management as Art, Science and Profession* sums up the breadth of perspectives of those working in this field. Public management is more akin to engineering than science, Behn (1996) argues. Engineers work with projects or problems in which the major question usually begins with a 'how'. Scientists are more likely to focus on questions beginning with 'why'. While engineering draws on scientific knowledge, its applied nature means that practitioners sometimes get ahead of theory as they seek solutions for practical problems. For engineers, as with managers, case studies are important as a means for establishing wisdom that derives from the rules of thumb, built up from experience (ibid, 115).

During the past 20 years, the subject matter of public administration and management has been strongly driven by project-oriented practitioners, in search of 'how' answers, ready to try ideas supported by anecdote and ideology as much as by systematic evidence. The intellectual agendas of managerialism and NPM result more from the initiatives of politicians, public servants and consultants, than academics and researchers. Indeed, reformers sought to sideline an 'old public administration' which emphasises process, bureaucratic delivery and the distinctiveness of public sector organisations. In contrast there is 'new public management' (NPM), which puts the emphasis on getting things done using techniques borrowed from the private sector. The focus of public management depends on whether emphasis is placed on the word 'public', and the political context, or the word 'management', and executive action (Eliassen and Kooiman, 1993: 4). If the accent is on public, as has frequently occurred with public administration, elements such as equity, fairness and the rule of law are likely to be stressed. If the emphasis is on management, as with NPM ideas, the focus is likely to be on effectiveness, efficiency, and analysis of costs and benefits.

Traditional public administration interests are highly relevant to this study because of the subject's focus on interaction between the political and administrative domains, an arena that is increasingly referred to as 'governance'. Control systems are the means by which political strategies are translated into managerial or administrative practices.

The research in this book is in the tradition of scholars who have sought to describe and explain issues faced by public administrators or managers in implementing politically derived strategies. Kaufman (1967), in *The Forest Ranger,* provides an explanation of how the United States Forest Service sought to balance regional autonomy with national oversight. Aaron Wildavsky anchored his analysis in practical experience with budgeting or implementation (Pressman and Wildavsky, 1973; Wildavsky, 1979, 1986, 1992). In their study of *The Private Government of Public Money,* Heclo and Wildavsky (1981) shed light on the closed world of British Treasury officers. Ban (1995) illustrates the value of qualitative research with a systematic examination of bureaucratic constraints and organisational culture in the context of the impending reinvention of United States federal agencies, in the early 1990s. The work of Hood et al (1998) in identifying the costs of regulatory explosion in the British public service is an exemplar of the value of systematic enquiry and builds on the considerable theoretical contribution that Hood has made in categorising and critiquing 'new public management' (eg Hood, 1991; Hood and Jackson, 1991; Hood, 1998a). Also in this British tradition is the work of Pollitt (1990, 1998) and Pollitt and Bouckaert, (2000), which assesses performance management, and monitoring systems, in different organisational and national contexts.

The single most useful springboard for this research has been the work of Wilson (1989), whose case-based generalisations provide enduring insights into realities that confront public managers, whether they work in traditional bureaucracies or 'reinvented' systems. Wilson (1989: xi) doubts that a 'simple, elegant, comprehensive theory of bureaucratic behaviour' is possible. In the absence of such theory, an important contribution of research into public organisations is to describe as accurately as possible what government agencies actually do and how they do it. He calls for bottom up approaches to research (Wilson, 1989: 11). This book is a response to Wilson's exhortation.

A field of questions rather than answers

If two words could be used to sum up the recurring themes of public administration and management research they would be complexity and ambiguity. Organisational action in the public sector occurs within a context of contested ideologies, the arena of politics. As the power of particular political ideologies waxes and wanes, the definition of effective performance shifts. What may be outstanding managerial performance seen through one political lens can be seen as obstructive and unresponsive by a different group of politicians. At one point results might be all that matter; in another political climate the methods used to gain the results may be viewed as paramount. While private sector organisations pride themselves on the ability to focus on the creation of 'bottom line' results, public sector organisations work with multiple constituencies that vary in their impact over time. Their bottom line equivalent is to avoid 'learned vulnerabilities', episodes of high political cost that have entered the organisation's memory as legendary horror stories (Wilson, 1989: 191).

A useful approach to public management enquiry is to adopt the proposition advocated by Behn (1995) of focusing on 'big questions' rather than narrow methodologies. Behn makes the case that science develops in this way, with physics, for example, developing in response to a big question of 'how did the universe begin?' and palaeontology developing from the question of 'why did the dinosaurs die out?'.

The following questions have been proposed as a stimulus to research by Behn (1995: 315):

1. **Micromanagement:** How can public managers break the micro-management cycle – an excess of procedural rules, which prevents public agencies from producing results, which leads to more procedural rules, which leads to . . . ?
2. **Motivation:** How can public managers motivate people (public employees as well as those outside the formal authority of government) to work energetically and intelligently towards achieving public purposes?
3. **Measurement:** How can public managers measure the achievements of their agencies in ways that help to increase those achievements?

These three questions focus on enduring 'how' questions about how best to organise for public sector performance.

Evaluating New Public Management reforms

The difficulties of evaluating system-wide changes such as those unleashed by NPM reformers have been thoroughly identified (Pollitt, 1995; Rainey, 1998; Boston, 2000). Even a limited effort to evaluate efficiency gains in a small sample of New Zealand organisations struck considerable difficulties in proving the case one way or another (Brumby et al, 1996).

Such reforms are particularly difficult to evaluate because of their multi-faceted nature, as Pollitt (1995) points out in an article entitled *Justification by Works or by Faith?* The following types of issues arise. Are changes a result of a structural reform or a concurrent budget cut? What baseline for evaluation can be used if the essence of the reform has been to change organisational structures and descriptions of the outputs produced? How long-term are the consequences? Or is there perhaps a 'Hawthorne effect' (Roethlisberger and Dickson, 1939) in which short-term improvements in performance stem from the attention paid to an organisation or group rather than the strength of a particular change strategy. Even evaluation against pre-set goals can be difficult. This may miss unintended effects and in any case struggle with a lack of precision in the setting of the original goals.

Reformers in any case have little incentive to encourage rigorous evaluation, as Behn (1991) points out in contrasting the perspectives of initiators and evaluators. Implementation depends often on simple faith. Rigorous evaluation is biased against proof of faith, particularly where it starts by seeking to disprove a null hypothesis that the policy has no effect unless a comparison with a control group proves otherwise (Behn, 1991: 160). Where the manager is passionate about achieving change, the evaluator is patient. For the implementer, there is only a down side to evaluation – the evaluator will never confirm all the claims that have been made. In any case the cost of patient evaluation may be such that it outweighs the benefit of the information gained (ibid, 166).

As described in Chapter 4, the introduction of NPM methods in New Zealand was driven at top speed by a small group of committed reformers, both politicians and public servants, who had little interest in patient or rigorous evaluation.

Mindful of such difficulties of evaluation, the writer has taken a different route, seeking a snapshot of realities as perceived by a representative group. The focus is on organisational routines which have been relatively unaffected by political change. The focus is firmly on enduring 'how' questions of public management.

Researching management and organisations

The influence of formal organisations is so pervasive that their impact can easily be taken as a reality rather than as a social construct. We are born into health organisations, educated through schools and universities, work in organisations, trust organisations to manage our finances, food, transport, and provide entertainment and communication. Informal family and community relationships which characterised life before the Industrial Revolution have been replaced by formal organisations, each requiring formal management. This trend has given rise, during the past 50 years, to an explosion of research and education, focused on organisations and management.

Researching organisational constructs such as control systems is an interactive process which creates complexities not present in the study of most physical and biological phenomena. A defining feature of organisational and management research is that people are participants – not subjects – in the sense that animals, neutrons and chemical substances can be viewed as subjects. Organisational participants are an active part of the research process, and influence its progress (Lawler et al, 1986).

Data gathered for the research in this book included:
• A review of the literature, canvassing approximately 500 references.

- Transcripts of interviews with 41 capital city informants, chosen to provide a horizontal sample of people with experience at senior levels with public sector control systems.
- A survey completed by 90 percent of the 41 interviewees, in which 95 statements were rated on a scale of 'strongly agree' to 'strongly disagree'. This provided a quantitative base for assessing which views were widely and strongly held, and which were minority opinions.
- Interviews with 50 people in a vertical sampling focused on four outputs.
- Data from published documents, including annual reports, special reviews, government budget statements, and decisions by the State Services Commission about the appointment and reappointment of chief executives.

Ultimately the research in this book has a pragmatic aim, well expressed by Zifcak (1994: 2), who researched British and Australian responses to financial management reforms, using an approach which sought 'to understand and record the changes . . . as far as possible, through the eyes of the participants'.

Choice of case studies

The selection of case studies was designed to provide theory-oriented insights rather than provide a statistical sample.

A sample of four outputs was chosen to assess the extent to which control systems vary with the context and the nature of the task. The typology proposed by Wilson (1989), and further developed by Gregory (1995), suggests that managerial information will differ considerably depending on how observable the outcomes and outputs are, and that organisations can be categorised as examples of 'production, procedure, craft and coping' styles.

Studies were chosen to provide examples of these four different types of organisation, and perspectives were sought about democratic and organisational accountability at different levels in the hierarchy:
- elected representatives who were members of select committees to which estimates for expenditure and annual reports were presented
- central agencies and policy agencies which monitor the output of the organisation
- senior executives

- operational managers
- 'operators' in the delivery agency.

Access to the case study organisation was sought initially through the chief executive or general manager of each output.

Particular emphasis was placed on gaining perspectives from staff and middle managers whose outputs and outcomes are the end result of the control systems, and whose work is the rationale for the existence of the agency. These are the people whom Wilson (1989) terms 'operators' and Lipsky (1980) terms 'street level bureaucrats'. They are a group whose views have seldom been heard in the debate about the theories of NPM and whose unfiltered views are the most difficult to obtain, given the ways in which hierarchical organisations control employment conditions and the flow of information.

The outputs chosen for detailed analysis were designed to be illustrative of different types of public sector tasks. Factors involved in the researcher choosing the particular outputs were:

- **A reasonably stable organisational environment.** It was considered important to gain views not influenced by recent or impending organisational restructuring.
- **Outputs which lack easy comparability with the private sector.** The outputs represent core government activities producing community results which can only be achieved through the collective action of government intervention.
- **Access through key decision-makers** who had demonstrated their interest in and commitment to the study. Organisational case study work is critically dependent on senior decision-makers providing access. This reality biases studies towards those organisations led by people who are least concerned about public exposure. This means that studies tend to be carried out within better performing organisations.

Interviews

Interviews are the major source of data for the information in this book. Interviews provide a way for the writer to gain perceptions from a cross-section of people that is considerably more economical than observation and more flexible than structured questionnaires. They provide a way of avoiding the low response rates and potential for superficial answers that can occur with survey research. For the first phase, the emphasis was gathering open-ended, exploratory information. The second phase targetted people connected with the four case example outputs, and employed more structured interviews, seeking context-specific insights.

A frequent question about interviews as a source of information is 'how do you know if the informant is telling the truth?' (Dean and Whyte, 1970: 119). This raises the issue of whether an interviewer can tell what someone really believes on the basis of a few questions put during an interview. Dean and Whyte's response is 'No', accompanied by the wry comment that such questioning implies that if interviewers could develop shrewd enough techniques they could make people 'spill the beans' and reveal what their basic attitudes really are. The interviewer is better advised to take an informant's statement as 'merely the perception of the informant, filtered and modified by his cognitive and emotional reactions and reported through his personal verbal usages' (Dean and Whyte, 1970: 120).

Rather than asking 'is the informant telling the truth', the interviewer should ask what the informant's statements reveal about his feelings and perceptions, and what inferences can be made about the actual environment or events experienced. Findings from interviews are limited to the vagaries of informants' interpretations and presentation of reality (Minichiello et al, 1995: 72). Interviews are a pragmatic and more economical way of gaining information than direct observation, which could provide a richer understanding of the informant's perspective.

In line with the advice of Dexter (1970), the template used for interviews in both phases was limited to a series of major headings. These headings created 'semi-structured' interviews and effectively provided platforms from which interviewees would explain their unique perspectives, as unencumbered as possible by the views of the interviewer. In many interviews, answers were given 'out of sequence' and questions needed to be rephrased to ensure a flow of discussion that allowed informants to fully convey their impressions.

Conclusion

This book provides empirical information about experiences with a new model for the control of public services. It summarises qualitative, exploratory research, which uses quantitative results from a survey as a means for assessing whether views are widely held or not. Rather than prejudging results by starting with an hypothesis, the writer has used an open-minded approach to data gathering. Data has been interpreted through a variety of theoretical lenses drawn from traditions of scholarship in public administration and management. The book adds to the development of theory-based understanding as well as being a foundation from which practitioners can derive ideas for improving practice.

CHAPTER 4

Introducing business-like controls – a public sector revolution in New Zealand

'There can hardly be a doubt, I think, that New Zealand is over governed, over legislated for, over provided with officials, and overburdened with debt.'
—Anthony Trollope, (1815–88), writing in 1873[14]

'I had the impression that New Zealand was the best governed country in the world, and the most easily governed.'
—Sir Karl Popper, 1902–94 (Popper, 1976: 112).

New Zealand's adoption of NPM techniques was part of a much wider programme of economic and social change unleashed by the Labour Government, elected in July 1984, and continued with an initial fervour by the National Government elected in 1990. For an isolated and peaceable country, this was a period of upheaval and controversy, as is reflected in the titles of books written about the process of change. Authors have variously seen change as: *New Territory – the transformation of New Zealand, 1984–92* (James, 1992), *Rolling Back the State. Privatisation of Power in Aotearoa/New Zealand* (Kelsey, 1993), *The New Zealand Experiment – A world model for structural adjustment?* (Kelsey, 1995), *Revolution: New Zealand from fortress to free market* (Russell, 1996), *New Zealand's Remarkable Reforms* (Brash, 1996) and *Only Their Purpose is Mad. The money men take over New Zealand* (Jesson, 1999).

Following the election of the Labour Government in 1984, a considerable change occurred in rhetoric about the role and art of the state. A country that had used strongly collectivist strategies to create the world's first welfare state in the late 1930s suddenly gave birth to radically 'individualist' public-management designs (Hood, 1998a: 191). A nation-

---

14 From *Australia and New Zealand*, Vol 11, by Anthony Trollope, 1873: 340, cited in Weir (1998: 297).

building state changed its mind (Pusey, 1991) and set about using 'the market' instead of government intervention as the dominant means for fostering economic development and delivering public services.

In large part, this revolution was the result of a sudden generational shift in political leadership. In 1984, a Labour Government Cabinet with an average age of 41 replaced a National Government Cabinet whose average age was closer to 60. The National Government, led by Robert Muldoon, was dominated by men who had direct experience of the hardships of the 1930s depression and military service in the Second World War. They had also benefited from an activist government which started with the election of the first Labour Government in 1935. Members of the 1984 Labour Cabinet, brought up during a period of postwar prosperity and collectivist uniformity, had very different life experiences. Whereas a generation affected by depression and war had looked to the state as a 'friend' and shield from economic difficulties, a new generation of politicians thought a 'nanny' state was stifling initiative and holding back development in the face of economic difficulties that had become increasingly pressing since 1974 (James, 1992). Policies adopted by Prime Minister Muldoon, for instance, have been characterised by a leader of the NPM reforms as an 'Eastern European regime of economic controls and state sponsored investment in heavy industry' (Scott, 2001: 363).

The comprehensive programme of economic liberalisation and public sector reform undertaken by the 1984 Labour Government has been extensively recorded and debated elsewhere (Bollard and Buckle, 1987; Boston et al, 1996; Chatterjee et al, 1999). Economic changes included the lifting of controls on foreign exchange, the abolition of subsidies for farming, removal of import licensing and reduction of tariffs.

Rising public debt forced the Government to rethink the delivery of public services. Government net debt as a proportion of GDP had risen from 9 percent in 1976 to 41 percent by 1985, and was forecast to rise much higher because of budget deficits. Actions taken by the Government after 1984 managed to contain the rise, resulting in the public debt ratio peaking at 52 percent in 1992 (Scott, 1996).[15]

15 Total debt reached its highest level in 1992, at $37.67 billion. By 2002, foreign debt had been repaid, leaving $19.2 billion remaining in New Zealand based debt. Source: website of the Debt Management Office of the Treasury: http://www.nzdmo.govt.nz/govtdebt/historytable.asp Accessed 9 June 2003.

Business techniques and the methods of the market were seized on as an alternative to a bureaucratic model of public service that had become increasingly cumbersome since its basic structures were established in 1912. The conversion of State Owned Enterprises (SOEs) from departmental structures to businesses controlled by boards of directors with private sector experience provided the impetus for wholesale reform of the public service. In 1986 government trading operations in areas such as electricity, post and telecommunications, forestry, coal mining and rail were valued at $20 billion but the return to the Government on these assets was zero (The Treasury, 1987: 74). Within months of the 1987 change, as a result of actions taken by the new commercially oriented boards, State Owned Enterprises were generating profits for the Government.[16] These profits came at the expense of significant staff reductions and resulting problems with unemployment, particularly in more remote rural regions.[17] However, for a government concerned about persistent deficits and the scale of borrowing, the financial turnaround achieved by the methods of private sector directors provided a spur to use similar techniques in core public services perceived to be inefficient and suffering from bureaucratic inertia.

Designing a results-focused public sector

The rationale for radical change in the structures and control systems of New Zealand's public sector is most completely contained in a report entitled *Government Management,* prepared by the Treasury (1987) as a briefing for the incoming Government. Written at a time when the financial turnaround of SOEs had boosted the Government appetite for further change, this 472-page book is remarkable for the breadth of its coverage and the extent to which its theoretical perspectives were subsequently turned into government action. Nothing 'remotely comparable in quality or quantity to this NPM manifesto' was produced

16 By 1992, the SOEs were paying $537 million in dividends and a similar amount in taxation (Scott, 1996). Spicer et al (1996) provide a case-study based assessment of the issues involved in the use of SOEs as a means for gaining efficiencies.

17 The creation of the Forestry Corporation for example led to redundancies for 3640 staff and wage workers, many in small rural communities established by the Forest Services in the 1930s. Electricorp, the corporatised successor of the Electricity Department, reduced staff by 1100, to 4889, and the postal and banking companies created from the Post Office laid off 2700 staff (Lister et al, 1991).

in either Canberra or Whitehall (Hood, 1990: 210). The report is also remarkable for a near-complete lack of referencing for propositions which are presented as received, fact-based wisdom about management practices.[18] The propositions derive from a set of theories collectively known as New Institutional Economics (NIE). The components of NIE derive from public choice theory, agency theory and transaction-cost economics. Alongside these are propositions based on private sector experience, about decentralisation of management authority, described as 'managerialism'. As is clear from a critique of these theories in Boston et al (1996: 16–40), these are anything but value free or commonly accepted principles of management.

The fiscal problem was understandably uppermost in the minds of the Treasury (1987: 5–6). Despite efforts to curb the growth of government expenditure, there had still been a 'relentless increase in outlays and corresponding increase in the tax burden'. The answer to this problem was seen by the authors of the Treasury report to lie in the nature of the incentives for public sector managers and those seeking government assistance. Combined advisory, regulatory and operating functions of public sector agencies were seen to create the regulatory or producer 'capture' where agencies tended to take greater account of the interests of their sector than society overall. A lack of clear lines of accountability diffused responsibility for management decisions and permitted poor management practices. A rigid public sector labour market made it difficult to employ professionals with the technical skills needed by the public sector. The solution was to draw on experience of market mechanisms to create the right incentives for the achievement of desired results.

The report concluded that the pervasive influence of the public sector and its effect on the rest of the economy through tax meant that reform should clearly be 'the single most important item on the Government's agenda for the next three years' (The Treasury, 1987: 8).

For the Prime Minister of the time, David Lange, simple inefficiency was the major reason for public sector change. The public sector could not do what the new government wanted. 'Sometimes the government could not even find out whether or not it had done what it wanted'

18 A Treasury commentator on the draft of the book points out that references would
    have been included in earlier draft papers but omitted from the report for the in-
    coming government.

(Lange, 1998: 14). The Post Office,[19] for instance, had a business plan approved, and a year later reported that it had spent $100 million more and employed 2000 people more than planned.

As Education Minister, Lange found that schools had to get approval from the Department of Education to paint their buildings a particular colour. He was asked to sign approvals for the installation of temporary classrooms. 'It was maddening because nobody was actually responsible for anything' (ibid, 17). 'Politicians, me included, began the process of restructuring because we wanted control. We wanted to be free from the trivia of administration so we could make the big decisions' (Lange, 1998: 18).

Cabinet unease about the management of the public service was heightened by unanticipated budget blowouts, which called into question the reliability of financial management (Norman, 1997a: 5).[20] Other pressing reasons for reform are listed by Scott (2001: 2–3). Departmental heads were frustrated by inputs-based controls that restricted the use of common sense in pursuit of efficiency or effectiveness. The heads then tended to blame poor performance on policies and controls of the Treasury and SSC. Wage-fixing systems effectively tied the public service to changes in private sector pay, and led to a 26 percent increase in pay, a $2 billion budget item. Ministers saw the budget process as a game in which the winner was the one who extracted the biggest expenditure increases. Ministers were also concerned about restrictions on appointments of suitable people from outside the public service and a lack of effective input into the appointment of department heads (Scott, 2001: 2–3).

Simon Upton, National Party MP and Cabinet Minister, noted a lack of openness in the delivery of public services. He would later recall his first select committee encounter with the Department of Scientific and Industrial Research as a new opposition spokesman in 1985. The department's annual report provided 'acres of information on the resources deployed . . . but no comprehensive account of exactly what research was being conducted with what end in view. That was assumed to be so

19 The Post Office, which in 1987 employed 40,000 people, was split into three State Owned Enterprises, Telecom (subsequently privatised), PostBank (sold to the ANZ Banking Group) and New Zealand Post, retained as a State Owned Enterprise.

20 One such blowout was announced on 29 June 1988, where the estimate of a deficit was raised from $1 billion to $1.8 billion, increasing the determination of Cabinet to introduce major financial reform.

self-evident that no elaboration was required.' Upton wrote that he would never forget the avuncular smile with which the Director General greeted his request for such information when commenting that 'we don't gather information in that way'. 'And yet what could have been of greater interest to someone concerned with making the case for publicly funded science? If politicians couldn't tell taxpayers what research their funds were supporting, why should taxpayers continue to support all that effort?' (Upton, 1995: 2).

The appointment of key public servants, closer in age and thinking to the Labour Cabinet, paved the way for a radical overhaul of public service structures. In 1986, 44-year-old Roderick Deane, a PhD in economics and Deputy Governor of the Reserve Bank, was appointed State Services Commissioner, and 43-year-old Graham Scott, also a PhD in economics, was appointed as Secretary to the Treasury. Both men would be major contributors to the change agenda sought by the Labour Government.

The level of distrust in, and perceived shortcomings of, traditional public service methods is illustrated in this summary by the Treasury (1987: 82). Departments, it was claimed, could be expected to:

- underestimate the cost of programmes and overstate the benefits
- argue for an incremental approach to expenditure allocation rather than evaluate the efficiency and effectiveness of the resources already at their disposal
- disregard the cost of the funds raised either through taxation or borrowing
- present expenditure proposals in terms of a macro objective (for example creating employment) rather than analysing the investment itself
- monitor inputs not outputs
- advocate other interventions, the costs of which are not included in their budgets (for example tax expenditures and increased regulation)
- encourage the use of non-cash resources, or resources which are underpriced
- enter into commitments for future years
- spend their full allocation for the year regardless of whether the expenditure is justified because unspent allocations are typically not carried forward

- ignore the second and third year of three-year forecasts, and the associated financial monitoring of these limits.

In late 1987 and early 1988, with advice from officials, a core group of Cabinet Ministers[21] worked out the frameworks that were to become the State Sector Act 1988 and Public Finance Act 1989. This legislation created the thermostat-like feedback system that is central to the control systems of the New Zealand model. The traditional system of ministerial responsibility for public service actions, and a unified public service bureaucracy, were about to be replaced by a market-like constellation of organisations accountable for performance – for the delivery of outputs.

The rapid adoption of NPM doctrines in New Zealand was the result of a unique combination of political and economic circumstances. A small and determined group of decision-makers in a party of the Left was willing and able to implement at top speed policies more normally associated with a right-wing agenda. The ideas were introduced during a period of economic crisis that included a devaluation of the currency in 1984, high inflation, high budget deficits, increasing levels of government debt and a share market crash in 1987.[22] With a parliamentary system which provided few checks on the potential power of a small number of determined Cabinet Ministers, this was a process of comprehensive, 'frame-breaking change' (Tushman et al, 1986).

The speed with which change was introduced was a deliberate strategy of the Finance Minister between 1984 and 1988, Roger Douglas, who later described his change philosophy as being to:

> implement reform by quantum leaps. Moving step by step lets vested interests mobilise. Big packages neutralise them. Speed is essential. It is impossible to move too fast. Once you start the momentum, never let it stop.[23]

Public sector reorganisation was a second stage of reform, building

---

21 Deputy Prime Minister, Geoffrey Palmer; Finance Minister, Roger Douglas; Minister of State Services, Stan Rodger; and the Minister of State Owned Enterprises, Richard Prebble.

22 The New Zealand share market rose by 140 percent between 1985 and 1987. In September 1987, just before the October crash, market capitalisation was $42.8 billion. By December it had plunged to $24.2 billion (Kelsey, 1995: 89).

23 Roger Douglas, in a speech to the Australian Education Council Conference, Adelaide, December 6, 1990 (reported in the *Evening Post*, October 24, 1991).

on the creation of State Owned Enterprises and following the re-election of the Labour Government in 1987. The State Sector Act 1988 was passed into law in the face of strenuous opposition from public sector unions. By contrast, the financial framework created by the Public Finance Act 1989, attracted bi-partisan support. This legislation laid the base for 'the most fundamental changes to financial management practices seen in New Zealand's history', reforms which were 'enormous, ambitious, and, in large part, unprecedented anywhere in the world'.[24]

Economic and public sector change at such speed carried a heavy political price. Both the Labour and National Governments carried out policies of privatising public services in the face of strong public opposition. A result of frustration with the near dictatorial power of these First-Past-the-Post (FPP) governments was public support for the establishment of a Mixed Member Proportional representation system (MMP) for electing MPs to Parliament. The first MMP government was elected in 1996. For the Labour Party, the tensions of reform led to a splintering of the party, with left wing members leaving to create the Alliance party and Roger Douglas and other former Labour Party Cabinet Ministers creating the Association of Consumers and Taxpayers (ACT) party on the right of the political spectrum.

Doctrines for public sector reform

The control systems adopted in the New Zealand public sector are most usefully understood as a series of doctrines (Hood and Jackson, 1991). Acceptance of a doctrine does not rest on objective proof. Doctrines are articles of faith, subject to review with changing political circumstances. Winning administrative ideas, Hood and Jackson argue, are 'rarely very profound'. Often they are repackaged and relabelled versions of old ideas, based on 'some banal notion of "human nature" coupled with a contestable view about links between cause and effect' with proof typically consisting of 'no more than a few colourful examples' (ibid, 11). Indeed, one group of academic commentators has characterised NPM doctrines as *Something Old, Something Borrowed, Little New* in the title used for a critical article (Dixon et al, 1998).

---

24 Brian Tyler, Controller and Auditor-General, *Annual Report of the Controller and Auditor-General*, 1988–89.

The adoption of a set of doctrines is a process similar to finding the right combination with which to open a lock (Hood and Jackson, 1991). The door opens when the rhetoric for a set of ideas convinces a particular audience at a particular time about how to act on an issue. Support is 'achieved mainly by timing, packaging, presentation; not by objective, conclusive demonstration of the superiority of one doctrine over its rivals' (ibid, 17). Administrative doctrines are often contradictory and unstable, and are like 'clothing and automobiles', in which there is a constant search for 'new styles, fashions and fads' (ibid, 18).

Doctrines about 'how to organise' differ markedly depending on whether they originate with military, religious or business experience. From the military comes a belief in command structures which ensure that orders are carried out and that lines of responsibility are held under fire, enabling organisations to 'adapt and to function reliably even in worst-case conditions'. From religious tradition comes the belief that the best motivation is that which comes from within, tempered by the scrutiny of peers also involved in a life-time vocation. The test of good organisation is seen as 'fairness, mutuality, the avoidance of corruption or error'. From business experience comes a focus on the bottom line and material rewards. Good wages are used to keep good people, non-performers are fired, and paperwork is kept to a minimum as part of keeping costs down amidst a search for innovation. The test of good organisation is the ability to 'marshal the resources needed to perform a particular task competently, without waste, contradiction or muddle' (Hood and Jackson, 1991: 4).

The combination of doctrines chosen by the Labour Government in 1984, and continued largely unchallenged by the 1990–1999 National Government, originates distinctly from business experience. Indeed the choice of these doctrines was a deliberate rejection of military and religious traditions that were present in the New Zealand public service prior to 1984. Centralised bureaucracy had mirrored the command and control wartime experiences of the generation that had fought in World War Two. The public service offered quasi-religious commitment to an ideal of detached, non-partisan service within the structure of a life-time career and included a ritual known colloquially as the 'College of Cardinals'. This was the means by which a conclave of existing permanent heads appointed a new head – a ritual as 'in-house' and shielded from the public's gaze as the selection of a new Pope by existing cardinals.

Business-like efficiency was to be the new doctrine for the delivery of public services. A new system of the what, who, and how of administration followed these broad patterns.

Table 4.1 Doctrines for New Public Management changes

	From (pre 1984)	To (1986–99)
What	Large bureaucracies with long hierarchies	A variety of smaller organisations with flat structures
What	Consolidated organisations advising and delivering	Separation of policy and delivery
What	A self-contained system of services	Contracting of support
Who	Life-time vocation	Employment variety
Who	Permanent heads of departments	Chief executives on fixed-term contracts
Who	Technical skills for senior roles	Managerial skills for senior roles
How	Management by rule book	Let managers manage and hold them accountable for results
How	Accountability for inputs	Accountability for outputs
How	Cash accounting	Accrual accounting

A thermostat-like model of control

In this new combination of doctrines, the traditional pyramid of bureaucracy is replaced with the image of a thermostat-like marketplace of transactions, in which Government and its closest advisers make their preferences known by their purchases. Government organisations are increasingly like 'a transparent universe of subcontractors, organised around statements of goals and strategic plans, concerned not with some nebulous public good but with meeting performance indicators set out in an agency agreement' (Davis, 1997: 226).

Traditional hierarchical, bureaucratic forms of control have been replaced by a system of accountability 'patterned on the relationship of buyers and sellers in commercial transactions' (Schick, 1996: 1). The doctrines adopted shift the focus from the institutions of bureaucracy, to seeing public agencies as problem-solving and programme delivery mechanisms; production units within which 'inputs' are used to produce measurable 'outputs' that generate 'outcomes' (Breton, 1974). The system sets out to create the 'self correcting, dynamic feedback loop' (Dixon et al, 1998: 169) that is characteristic of the individual firm constantly subject to the feedback of price signals from the market. While the traditional bureaucratic model of public service delivery placed institutions at the centre of administration, the NPM model puts more focus on performance and transactions between economic units (Coase, 1937; Williamson, 1985).

The extent to which the doctrines adopted for reorganisation of the New Zealand public sector are seen as ideological or pragmatic depends on the viewpoint of the analyst. In the process of reform, the Treasury moved 'beyond its normal brief of economic advice and management to becoming the model builder for the entire government machine. It acted as a 'think-tank' for the neo-Liberal movement, using its authority as the top government department to influence political leaders and secure implementation of its blueprint' (Wistrich, 1992: 121).

Boston et al (1996) provide the most complete analysis of the use of transaction cost, agency theory and public choice theory, as foundations for the system constructed from Treasury advice. An additional critique of the use of economics-based theory is contained in Shaw (1999), with the most complete defence of the model provided by Scott (2001).

Scott (1997) seeks to de-emphasise the role played by New Institutional Economics, describing steps taken in the late 1980s as a 'practical response to identified problems'. While many reforms could be viewed as practical applications of NIE concepts, they could equally be seen as ways of implementing better management practices (Scott, 1997: 163).

Matheson (1997) echoes the emphasis on 'practical management', in commenting on an observation by a United Kingdom colleague that New Zealanders seemed to have become 'mad-dog public choicers' overnight. The visitor to Wellington, in Matheson's view, was more likely to be impressed not by the legal formality of interactions in the public service but by the 'ease and informality with which our small, somewhat incestuous, community continues to operate' (ibid, 168).

In public choice theory, government is described as being a series of economics-like transactions in which parliamentarians provide publicly financed goods and services to constituents in exchange for votes. The theory applies the economics model of rational utility-seeking individual behaviour to the analysis of politics and public institutions. From this perspective comes concern about 'provider capture' of public resources. Agency theory focuses on techniques such as contracts and incentives to align the interests of agents to those of principals. The theory focuses on information asymmetry, the situation in which an agent can be expected to know more about a work role than the principal. Transaction cost theory links closely to the principal agent approach. It tackles the question raised by Coase (1937) about why organisations exist rather than all transactions being carried out in a transparent way through markets. Within this perspective, the old-style public sector can be seen as an extreme case of the large vertically integrated organisation with costs arising from lack of transparency and competitive pressure on transactions.

As an agenda for redesign of public administration, such propositions have been 'covert politics' Gregory (1998b) contends: the prescriptions in *Government Management* (The Treasury, 1987) provided a recipe for a dramatic shift toward technocratic government in which a 'coherent body of theoretical knowledge' was used at the expense of 'political bargaining and negotiation'. The result was that power was concentrated in the hands of a 'small group of policy advisers and decision makers'. The approach denigrated political processes and was preoccupied with enhancing the 'productive efficiency and managerial competence of the economy' (Gregory, 1998b: 107). For Easton (1997: 98) *Government Management* reads like a treatise proposing rule by Plato's philosopher kings, who would use their expertise to rule over the rest of society in a kindly, but undemocratic way. The writers favoured rule using a pure, flawless ideal of the market, 'untainted by the practicalities which they suffer as working public sector bureaucrats'.

The creation of the system involved major change to the language of public service, harnessing words designed to 'name the set of ills to be cured'. For instance, the term *purchase* was used to emphasise that 'resources are scarce, that priorities change and that ministers should have a choice' (Matheson, 1997: 167). Another major change was the replacement of the term 'Permanent Head' by 'Chief Executive', emphasising a shift towards managerialism.

The significance of the combination of doctrines was that for a period of time they provided a coherent agenda for action at great speed. Consequences of the doctrines have also created the ingredients for a pendulum swing in thinking since 2001, a change described in Chapter 10.

Doctrines for change

The 'what' doctrines of public service delivery

Structural solutions featured strongly in the creation of the New Zealand model. In the design of the 'what' of public service delivery, the logic of the thermostat can be seen at work in an institutional framework which sought to:

- separate ownership and purchase responsibilities
- separate policy and operations
- separate funding, purchasing and provision of services
- create competition between service providers (Scott, 1997: 158).

Structural separation is the means for creating the elements of thermostat-like feedback. It emphasises focus rather than coordination, a major rationale for the previously unified public service. The new doctrines favoured small, focused organisations, which, with few layers of management, were seen as a means for achieving timely results. Creation of these organisations involved breaking up large bureaucracies that lacked clear objectives because they carried out a 'mixture of commercial, social, regulatory and policy advisory roles' (Deane, 1986).

The purchase and ownership distinction is a simple and powerful analytical distinction. It embeds a central concept of the marketplace in government control systems, controversially replacing traditional notions about ministerial responsibility for the actions of their departments with a more arms-length, market-like relationship.

The principle of steering and rowing, prescribed by Osborne and Gaebler (1992), is evident in the structure; the core public service reporting to political leaders responsible for directing activity, while second and third tier structures are responsible for delivery of services. Particular use has been made of what Stewart (1996: 33) terms the 'elixir' of separating policy and delivery organisations, to reduce the potential for provider capture of public services. This concern was expressed by the Treasury (1987: 433) as the need to design institutions for a 'world with few saints'. It is a 'disbelief in the proposition that organisations, either private or public, can always safely be assumed to act selflessly in the interests of shareholders or citizens' (Scott, 2001: 27).

The most complete current examples of structural separation are in the areas of science and research, transport and broadcasting. In each sector, where activities were once carried out by a single organisation, different organisations provide policy, funding, regulation and service delivery. In broadcasting for example, policy is provided by the Ministry of Culture and Heritage, funding by New Zealand on Air and the Maori Broadcasting agency Te Mangai Paho, regulation by the Broadcasting Standards Authority and delivery by the publicly owned Radio New Zealand and Television New Zealand, but also through a range of funded programmes broadcast by private stations.

In keeping with the belief in separating policy, ownership, funding and delivery, a three-tier state mechanism was created. At the centre is a 'core' public service of policy ministries and departments delivering public services that cannot be readily subject to competition. These organisations report directly to Ministers and their chief executives work for Ministers but are employed by the State Services Commission and employ 32,838 staff, or 13 percent of the total central government workforce of about 260,000.[25]

The second tier is a set of service delivery public organisations (termed Crown agencies) that report to Ministers through policy ministries and can be subject to competition. These organisations are intended to be more distant from the political process, responsible to boards appointed by the Government or elected by local constituencies. The sector consists of 217 Crown Entities, including health boards, tertiary education institutions and research institutes and 2664 schools.[26] Crown agencies

25 Source: SSC Human Resource Capability Survey of Government Departments, June 2002. http://www.ssc.govt.nz/display/document.asp?navid=124&docid=2621&pageno=3#P26_3065 Accessed 9 June 2003.
26 Source: Budget Economic and Fiscal Update. Reporting entities as at May 10, 2002. http://www.treasury.govt.nz/forecasts/befu/2002/befu02-gaap.pdf. Pages 142–3. Accessed 17 September 2002.

deliver services predominantly in the areas of education, health, transport and science research. The most independent agencies are the State Owned Enterprises, of which the most significant are New Zealand Post, Television New Zealand and since 2002 Air New Zealand.

The third tier consists of privately owned or not-for-profit organisations which compete for government contracts to provide services. This sector has expanded with the contracting out of significant areas of tertiary education, health and social services, a process termed by Rhodes (1994) as 'hollowing out'. Sub contract services also include property management, information technology, purchasing, engineering, architectural services, staff training and a range of consulting activities, which prior to 1988 were part of a largely self contained public service.

The 'who' doctrines of public service delivery

The major intention of reform relating to the people of the public sector was to open up a previously closed labour market. Systems designed to protect the merit principle in appointments and to maintain a coordinated life-time career service were seen as obstacles to managing for results. In the previously unified public service, all public servants had a single employer, the State Services Commission, which was primarily concerned about the maintenance of relativities and fairness. Appeal procedures virtually ensured that no outside applicants could be considered for senior public service roles.

Using business-like doctrines of pay-for-performance and recruitment of the best person for the job, the reforms broke apart the centralised personnel bureaucracy. Instead of permanent heads, there would be chief executives, appointed on fixed-term contracts and responsible for employing staff in their organisations, subject only to the general principle that government organisations should be 'good employers'. Pay rates for chief executives were increased to bring them, at least initially, more into line with comparable private sector positions.

With managerial efficiency as the major aim of the system change, the primary skills sought in those who would fill top management roles underwent a considerable shift. Whereas emphasis had previously been placed on technical or specialist administrative skills managerial skills now came to the forefront. Work already underway within the public service on this change was accelerated.

The 'how' doctrines of public service delivery

'How' public services should be controlled is summarised in the prescription that managers should be freed to manage, while being held accountable for results. Results and performance are seen as more important than procedures. In place of controls over inputs is a cycle of planning and reporting, and performance contracts. As Lane (1999: 180) puts it, the NPM approach envisages contracts as more important than the traditional tools of Government – law, regulations and budgets. Schick (2001: xvii) observed that 'no country has been as bold as New Zealand in managing by contract'.

For Matheson (1997: 170–1) contracting has the effect of causing 'relationships to be clarified and services to be more carefully described' and to an 'unscrambling of muddle purposes and a clarification of hitherto unclear roles'. The move to contracting was cathartic, he argues, 'not because of the intrinsic merits of contracting but because the public management system was seriously muddled in what it was doing and why, and in who was responsible'.

Contracting might sound coercive, but according to Matheson, it was in 'most cases empowering and liberating' in contrast to centralised input and process controls. The critical idea was that 'public servants would be given the freedom to produce certain services in exchange for reporting on how they had done so' (ibid). 'The threat to traditional shared public service values and trust comes not from contracting per se, but from bad contracting' (Matheson, 1997: 178).

Accrual accounting, the language of business, became the logical form of accounting for the reformed system because it enables a decentralisation of authority based on financial measures, and provides periodic information about the ownership interests of the Government through the statement of financial position – the balance sheet. Accrual accounting is also important for comparing the cost of government delivery with what it might cost a private sector or not-for-profit provider. The convention of depreciation is used to allocate the cost of long-term assets to current outputs, and the process of 'accruals' matches cash transactions to the outputs delivered.

A cycle of strategic plans and annual reports is the core of the process of accountability. Organisations must set out their performance targets (ex ante reporting) and report on results (ex post reporting). All public organisations must report on the year to June 30 with information being provided to the Audit Office by the end of August, after which Audit has 30 days to issue an opinion with the release of the report.

The term output plays a major role in the redesign of the 'how' of delivery, providing a contract-based format for describing accountability. Outputs describe services that a single chief executive can be held accountable for delivering and provide the legal basis for appropriations from Parliament. The adoption of outputs as the method for appropriating was a response to limitations of the programme budgeting system which existed before 1989. Then, appropriations were made for a set of services designed to achieve a specific outcome or policy objective. Budgeting was based on organisational units, resulting in most departments having a programme labelled 'administration' (Scott, 2001: 175).

With outputs-based appropriations, departments have considerable freedom to vary the mix of spending between staff and other costs such as travel or computing. The major restriction of output budgeting is the limited ability to transfer funds between outputs.[27] The larger the size of an output, the greater the freedom a department has in transferring financial resources.

In the language of the model, outputs contribute towards outcomes. However, a connection between the two has been much harder to achieve in practice than theory, as Chapters 6 and 10 discuss.

Critiques of New Public Management methods

The comprehensiveness of the New Zealand model and the speed of its introduction have attracted considerable international attention. Aspects of the model, particularly accrual accounting, performance measurement and decentralisation of authority to managers have been adopted by other countries, but 'few countries, and none of the most developed ones, have modelled their public sector along the lines of the New Zealand version' (Schick, 2001a: 2).

As seen in Chapter 10, the doctrines for change are currently subject to a swing of the pendulum of political and public sector opinion. Also, after 15 years, as predicted by Wistrich (1992: 126) 'perpetual

27 Up to 5 percent of funds can be moved with approval from a Minister.

revolutionary zeal is hard to sustain,' and with the passing of the 'first flush of enthusiasm . . . older habits of inertia' have arisen.

Critiques of NPM techniques internationally can be seen to cluster under the following headings, each relevant to the establishment of the New Zealand model:

A distrust of political decision-making and excess faith in 'rationalism'

The techniques of NPM emphasise rational planning, analytical decision-making, clarity of purpose and client or customer service as ways of solving political problems. The 'sotto voce' implication, Pollitt (1998: 47) contends, is that management is or should be expanding, while the sphere of politics should be limited. 'Politics is a realm of disorder, amateurism, conflict and drama, while management is a realm of order, professionalism, dynamism and strategic thinking' (ibid).

By using the 'customer' metaphor, the NPM approach sees individual satisfaction as more important than 'achieving collective democratic consensus' (Frederickson, 1996: 265). Jervis and Richards (1997: 9) argue that the NPM recipe in Britain produced substantial gains in economy and efficiency, but was found to be increasingly unsuitable for the pursuit of effectiveness. The systems worked against the effective tackling of 'complex problems requiring coordinated multi-disciplinary, multi-organizational responses' (ibid).

Denhardt (1992: 9) saw the rational ideas of managerialism as most vulnerable in their lack of ethical content. In common with earlier theorists the focus of NPM is on one paramount value, efficiency, overlooking criteria such as liberty, justice, equity, equality and responsiveness that might also be used to gauge the work of public organisations (ibid, 12).

Simplistic understanding of the nature of public services

Ranson and Stewart (1994: 4) challenge the extent to which the values of the private sector have come to dominate thinking about management issues. 'If public organisations were only private, it is contended, then problems of efficiency and bureaucracy would disappear.' But management in the 'public domain' necessarily involves a process of balancing interests and assessing results by multiple criteria (ibid, 97). 'Public pressure and protest are part of public discourse (ibid, 98), while the delivery of public services involves responding to political processes that 'operate through 'voice' as opposed to the option of 'exit' in the market' (ibid, 177); that is, a democratic process rather then an individualistic one.

Management in the public domain requires a culture of stewardship, which means that power is exercised not in its own right, but on behalf of the citizens from whom the power is derived (ibid, 237).

Rather than a marketing culture, a public service orientation is needed – a service 'for' the public, not just 'to' members of the public. The strategic challenge is different from that in the private sector, where rational analyses about wealth accumulation and efficiency can be used. For public organisations, strategy has to come from a political process of 'mediating and reconciling in a judgement of common purpose for the public good' (ibid, 271).

Allison (1983) has described the public and private sectors as 'fundamentally alike in all *unimportant* respects'. Pollitt (1990: 119–22) pursues this theme in analysing differences between the accountability of elected representatives, chosen through democratic processes, and boards of directors in the private sector. In the public sector, elected representatives have a range of agendas, with some paid to be an organised

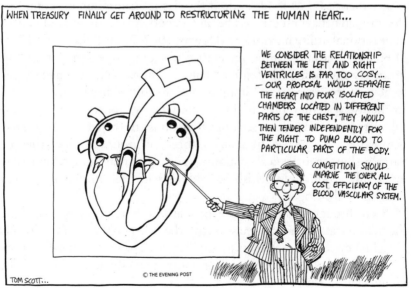

Tom Scott, *Evening Post*, 23 October 1990

opposition. Multiple and conflicting goals are reconciled by elected representatives by avoiding being too explicit at the level of legislation and political intent. Most government functions have no competition, unless artificially created. The source of public sector funding is the Government's ability to compel citizens to pay taxes, and the rewards for service delivery are fundamentally different for the public and private sectors. The aim in the public sector is to deliver as much service as possible to the general population for a capped budget, compared with a private sector search for profits by growing markets and restraining costs.

Public organisations may be able to be business-like but they are not a business (Gray, 1998). Customers and citizens frequently have differing expectations. For example, town planners work both with a customer who pays to gain approval for a house extension, and the applicant's neighbours, who expect citizens' rights to 'due process, participation and deliberation'. Most public organisations are unable to reject service users, and 'must regard the means of delivery as being as important as its substance' (Gray, 1998: 11).

Misunderstanding the motivation of public sector employees

In their use of theories based on economics, and in particular public choice theory, NPM models adopt the classic assumption of economics that human behaviour can best be understood by considering individuals to be rational utility maximisers (Downs, 1967: 2). As Fukuyama (1995: 18) puts it, 'the entire imposing edifice' of economic theory rests on this 'relatively simple model of human nature'. Humans are assumed to seek to 'acquire the largest possible amount of the things they think are useful to themselves, they do this in a rational way, and they make these calculations as individuals seeking to maximise the benefit to themselves before they seek the benefit of any of the larger groups of which they are part. In short, neoclassical economics postulates that human beings are essentially rational but selfish individuals who seek to maximise their material well-being.'

Seen through this model, the 'people who finance, operate and use the welfare state are no longer assumed to be either public-spirited altruists (knights) or passive recipients of state largesse (pawns). Instead they are all considered to be in one way or another self-interested knaves' (Le Grand, 1997: 149).

Pollitt (1990: 115) writes that the vision of the 'new right' of efficient management lacks a 'coherent model of the highly motivated, productive public servant'. 'If it had one at all it was a clockwork model that ran on targets and bonus pay, not a flesh and blood figure that needed public recognition and self-respect.' During the period of Margaret Thatcher's reforms in Britain (1979–90), for instance, 'all of the best lessons' were seen to have come from the private sector (Corrigan and Joyce, 1997: 418).

The tendency of many reformers to treat all government employees as incompetents and laggards not only reduces their energy and enthusiasm but also all too frequently disenfranchises them from the entire reform process (Downs and Larkey, 1986: 243). An alternative approach to explaining the distinctiveness of public sector work is provided by Denhardt (1992: 272–6) who concludes that it is the 'pursuit of significance' than drives the best public servants. 'They are concerned about others, they are concerned about their programs, they are concerned about the public interest but most of all, they are concerned about making a difference. They want their lives and their careers to be meaningful . . . in terms of . . . how they have changed the world for the better, and how they have helped to meet the democratic bottom line.'

Conclusion

As rhetoric, NPM ideas have achieved significant success in challenging the conventions of public service delivery in place since the late nineteenth century. These focused on impartial and politically neutral delivery of services by career public servants, accountable to elected representatives. NPM doctrines provided a rallying point for modernising bureaucratic structures which had come to be seen as inflexible and unresponsive in a market dominated world, in which citizens have become used to choice and responsiveness.

At their broadest level, NPM doctrines adopted in New Zealand in the 1980s and 1990s reshaped the structures of the state. In their effect on the central control systems of the public service, the focus for this study, they have had a lasting effect on the routines through which performance is defined and delivered.

The logic of the prescription is appealing and difficult to argue with. Who for instance could be against clear objectives, well focused managers, quality information, and a feedback loop of accountability? The lines of the rhetoric waltz are clear, flowing and highly persuasive.

The rapid adoption of NPM techniques in New Zealand in the late 1980s and in the 1990s resulted from a convergence of several economic and political forces. The set of doctrines used to open the doors to major reform during this period quickly became a new established order. As will be discussed subsequently, the system has created a set of paradoxes that have helped lead to a pendulum swing in thinking about how best to organise for performance.

PART TWO

Realities of Reforms

Perspectives from public servants
and politicians

CHAPTER 5

Limits to freedom

'Freedom is not worth having if it does not connote freedom to err.'
—Mohandas K Gandhi[28]

Freedom to manage is a distinctive feature of the New Zealand public management model. Action-oriented managers, free to allocate resources in pursuit of goals and accountable for delivering results, are the cornerstone of a model in which 'managerial discretion is less constrained ... than in any other country which has reformed its State sector' (Schick, 1996: 2). Within budget limits and the law, managers have flexibility in how they hire and pay staff, obtain office accommodation, and purchase supplies and services. 'Robust, entrepreneurial, risk-taking managers' are expected to revamp operations, reallocate resources and point organisations in new directions. These top managers are expected to 'actively recruit others who are willing and able to take charge' and 'shed workers who shirk responsibility or are unproductive' (ibid, 41).

However, risk-taking management occurs within a political arena in which Opposition politicians can be expected to probe for management weaknesses and politicians have concerns about the extent to which they delegate power and authority.

The freedom provided in the New Zealand model is freedom of choice over means rather than ends. It provides operational autonomy – the freedom, 'once a problem has been set, to attack it by means determined by oneself', as opposed to strategic autonomy – the freedom to set one's own agenda (Bailyn, 1985: 129).

To some extent, freedom to manage has been a deliberate exchange of the appearance of control for the substance of control. Worried that the previous system did not make it possible to impose restrictions on

---

28 *Young India*, 1931, cited in *The Moral and Political Thought of Mahatma Gandhi* by Raghavan N Iyer, Oxford University Press, New York, 1973: 350.

the total resources used by a government agency, the Treasury sought to 'give away control of small numbers in exchange for control of large numbers' (Scott, 1996: 89). Freedom is available within the boundaries of incentives and sanctions intended to 'modify the behaviour of managers to ensure that they *do* act to meet established objectives rather than pursuing independent goals of their own' (The Treasury, 1987: 55–6).

For managers, freedom was largely associated with the removal of large manuals which governed the lives of public servants prior to 1988. The State Services Commission's manual of rules about appointments, appeals, classifications and grading restricted the human resources authority of local managers in the interests of the whole service. The Treasury's manual specified limits on authority for spending on inputs and a range of finance-related issues.[29] In addition, centralised arrangements for purchasing stores, computers and accommodation further narrowed the area of freedom for a local manager.

Rather than being an exercise in 'banishing bureaucracy' (Osborne and Plastrik, 1997), the move towards managerial freedom is better understood as a move away from procedural bureaucracy, bound by laws and rules, to a corporate bureaucracy based on goal-driven plans, carried out by managers in the interests of particular target groups (Considine and Lewis, 1999: 468). For service deliverers outside the core public service, the move was to a 'market bureaucracy' controlled by contracts and competition with reduced costs being a primary virtue.

Freedom to manage within a corporate bureaucracy

The structures and systems adopted for the New Zealand public sector follow a path well travelled by large businesses since the 1920s. Major United States companies then began adopting decentralised, divisional structures as alternatives to the centralised, functional structures (Chandler, 1962). The subsequent success of the divisional structure of General Motors in particular, and publicity given to it by Drucker (1964), meant that by the 1970s, the 'corporate bureaucracy' of multi-division structures had become a new organisational orthodoxy.

Divisionalising is a way of striking a balance between the centralising or centripetal forces of the centre and the centrifugal forces of the

---

29 Instructions had become so detailed that they included rules about how to park cars on Wellington's hilly streets and what could be spent on refreshments.

periphery. Divisions are held responsible for operational decisions while group headquarters retains control over setting long-term strategy and allocating capital. Divisionalising involves shifting from a focus on task, characteristic of traditional organisations, to management by performance, particularly financial performance (Sisson, 1995: 70). Arms-length reporting systems, described in this thesis as 'thermostat-like', are central to the success of such decentralisation of authority.

The control exercised through corporate bureaucracy can vary significantly, depending on the style adopted by the centre. The following typology, developed by Goold and Campbell (1987: 10),[30] provides a way of understanding the impact of the choice of 'financial control' as a dominant style for the New Zealand public sector.

Strategic planning companies build portfolios around a small number of 'core' businesses, often with coordinated, global strategies. They search widely for the best strategy options, and pursue ambitious long-term goals. In comparison with the other two models, decisions tend to be slower, reaction to poor performance less decisive, and managers and business units given time to improve. There is less ownership of strategy at the business unit level.

Financial control companies focus more on financial performance than competitive position. A focus on financial results provides clear success criteria, prompt reaction to events, and strong motivation at the business level resulting in strong profit performance. But the style can cause risk aversion, reduce concern for underlying competitive advantage, and limit investment where the payoff is long-term.

Strategic control companies balance competitive and financial ambitions, adopting a style in between strategic planning and financial control. These companies support growth in strategically sound businesses, but rationalise their portfolios by closing down or divesting other businesses. This style permits businesses to adopt long-term strategies, and fuels the motivation of business unit managers. But there is a danger that planning processes can become superficial and bureaucratic, and that ambiguous objectives can cause confusion, risk aversion and 'political' manoeuvring.

---

30 The typology was developed from a study of the control styles of 10 diversified British companies.

While issues of market share, competition, profit and portfolios have no direct counterparts in the public sector, strategic concepts from the private sector provide useful analogies. With its emphasis on budget control and specifications for appropriations based on outputs, the New Zealand system is a strong example of the financial control style. This approach has the advantage of clarity, simplicity, and cost control, because all the centre needs to do is to refer to the 'bottom line' of the budget, and performance against specified indicators. Thermostat-like controls are based on the use of financial or similarly numeric information.

But the clarity and simplicity of the bottom line is more elusive in the public sector than in the private sector because there are a variety of bottom lines. Governments must deal with issues that transcend the accounting entities created by the structures of financial control. Issues are frequently in the 'public domain' (Ranson and Stewart, 1994) because they are not manageable through a private sector in which independent entities compete for customers, each focusing on their own bottom line accountabilities, unwilling and unable to move far from the outputs that ensure financial survival. Governments instead must deal with 'wicked problems' (Rittel and Weber, 1973): those that are complex, deep-rooted, intractable and multi-faceted, and tend to fall between organisational boundaries.

Rather than financial control, a more appropriate model may be its opposite – the strategic planning style (Jervis and Richards, 1997: 14). This recognises that freedom is less definable in the public sector context and overall performance depends on interactions between organisational units as much as within a single unit. The fragmentation and incoherence that is a feature of private sector organisations (Hart, 1998) is not necessarily an ideal model for public sector tasks that require collaboration and boundary crossing.

Freedom to manage – the New Zealand experience

Among interviewees for this book, freedom from rulebook control was undoubtedly the most strongly welcomed feature of the New Zealand public management model. The survey group[31] summed up the balancing

---

31 The 41 initial interviewees who were surveyed to establish levels of group support for individual comments.

act of freedom and accountability with these two statements, among the most agreed in the survey.

Clearer lines of accountability are central to providing greater management freedoms. These have empowered people to be better managers.

The extent to which you are given trust and advised that you are going to be held accountable acts as a very strong incentive.

Most members of the survey group had experience of pre-1988 controls, enabling them to compare present and past freedoms, and to chart the changing nature of those freedoms during the 1990s. A number of these interviewees had anecdotes about the effort required for public servants to respond to the centralised rules of the pre-1988 system and in particular the restrictions of the appointments and appeals processes that maintained an internal labour market and life-time career structures.[32]

The effect on managers of the freedom to make decisions about staffing and to transfer funds between budget line items was experienced in a variety of ways. For one general manager, it has been 'empowering and enabling'. For one chief executive (CE), the freedom was 'infinite, constrained by expec-ted standards of behaviour, ethics, public service, public expectations about how things should be done and the scrutiny of Parliament and the media'.

Interviewees with experience of other organisations compared relative levels of freedom. A policy manager, comparing colleagues in similar work, concluded that New Zealand public servants knew more about management issues and were more concerned about sources of funding than more specialised counterparts in other countries. A CE with private sector experience thought the freedoms of the public sector compared favourably with those of large companies. Provided policies, rules and guidelines were followed, chief executives, the equivalent of divisional managers, had considerable freedom. 'Within a corporate group, the corporate finance guy can basically say that is the way it is going to be and you do not have any right of reply. In the public sector, Treasury can

---

32 One interviewee recalled how the manual forbade the purchase of the chocolate drink Milo, and how staff would exchange two spoons of instant coffee for one of milo with staff from a private business on the same floor. The practice placed a higher value on the drink than if it had been purchased directly.

only go so far. They cannot tell you what to do; they cannot take over your responsibility.'

For the survey group, the achievement of the right amount of freedom was a matter of balance, as shown in this agreed statement:

Managers will achieve more if they are given more freedom and responsibility. They are also likely to make more mistakes, but these will be well offset by the achievement. Organisation achievement can only really be influenced by focusing on the achievement side, not by attempting negative controls.

Constraints on freedoms

Freedom is a relative concept and has changed in definition during nearly 15 years of experience in the New Zealand public sector. While members of the survey group and other interviewees believed they have significant managerial freedoms, they were also conscious of the limits to these freedoms, and the growth of restraints. Some constraints on freedom have been inherent in the model, and others have resulted from accretions of control in response to politically embarrassing incidents. The survey group agreed with the view that:

Public management in New Zealand has been strongly control oriented and at odds with trends in management theory and philosophy, which have emphasised motivation and coaching strategies.

Representative of widely held scepticism about constraints on managerial freedom was the view from a policy manager that it was debatable whether the reforms had resulted in much real change in the nature of freedom. Freedom was, in this manager's view, more than the ability to manage inputs and resources. Freedom was also the ability to generate new ideas, put forward advice and see things happen. Current freedom was constrained within organisational silos and the relative political influence of the chief executive.

One CE thought the Treasury had never really loosened the apron strings, continuing to take a line-by-line interest in budgets. After discussing the accountability requirements surrounding the agency, the CE commented 'you would wonder if there was any freedom left'. This feeling of being surrounded by accountability pressures was echoed by a policy manager, who commented that freedom was tinged with a 'fair amount of looking over your shoulder'.

One CE thought freedom had to be constantly guarded against the tendency of central agencies to seek more controls than were provided for in legislation. Weaker chief executives were more likely to be targeted than strong chief executives and lose their freedom to act.

The change of Government in 1999 had heightened concerns about the balance between control and freedom. The Labour Government had campaigned about corporate excess in the public service, highlighting failed Information Technology (IT) projects, the cost of external consultants, bonuses, and the chartering, by the Department of Work and Income, of an aircraft so that managers could attend a conference at a tourist resort. The boundaries of the freedoms established in the late 1980s had become unclear, with the group agreeing on the following:

When there is a sign of an input performance failure a first instinct has been to go back to an across-the-board control. This has resulted in implicit delegation changes which are ad hoc and non-systematic.

Bit by bit since the late 1980s, there has been a chipping away at management freedoms over inputs and to a lesser extent management systems.

The boundaries of the freedoms to manage have become unclear during the past year. We have had to be careful in undertaking expenditure on items funded through depreciation, for example, building refurbishment.

Interviewees commented that in retrospect there had been some early 'heady days of empowerment'. This had included what a policy manager described as 'militant independence' as a reaction to the previously overly centralised system. According to a corporate services manager, managers recruited from the private sector had, in particular, regarded any central interference as inherently bad and to be resisted.

A consultant observed that chief executives appeared to 'go hell for leather' after the State Sector Act 1988 provided them with freedoms for decision-making, but then drew back quite quickly – most likely because of 'quite sensible' Audit Office controls.

Amidst a climate in which embarrassment in the media is a major control, risk minimisation is an understandable response. For one CE, the solution was to be a 'beer rather than champagne' department. By being flexible, but not flamboyant, and remaining relatively cautious, the department had avoided being reined back in.

The change in New Zealand's political system from First-Past-the-

Post (FPP) to Mixed Member Proportional (MMP) representation was seen to have significantly increased the amount of scrutiny of public service activity. In the view of a CE, under FPP, select committees had been insignificant as a form of accountability because public sector chief executives had been able to ask Ministers to 'fix a troublesome select committee'. With six political parties in Parliament, and coalition governments, such stifling of select committees is no longer possible.

The instability of MMP politics between 1996 and 1999[33] had certainly reduced the degree of freedom for at least one CE, who had experienced a rapid turnover of Ministers. Formally, the CE had the authority to implement a programme of restructuring, but chose not to move until a political sign-off was gained. Each Minister had wanted to be briefed and had delayed signing. The net result for the CE had been that 'I have lost the knack of moving quickly'.

'Learned vulnerabilities' and reduced freedoms

High profile disasters and embarrassments have played their part in a gradual reduction of the freedoms envisaged in the late 1980s. Wilson (1989) describes the effect of such episodes as 'learned vulnerabilities'. When something goes wrong at high political cost, the incident can be expected to enter an agency's memory as a legendary horror story. The result is that a great deal of time and energy is spent creating mechanisms designed to insure that the horror never recurs (Wilson, 1989: 191). Avoiding such vulnerabilities is the equivalent of the bottom line for public managers.

Throughout the study, interviewees were certainly aware of the lessons from three high profile learned vulnerabilities. These, coupled with lesser events, had played a significant part in building up a web of 'case law' about just how much freedom managers perceived they had.

Public safety and risk management have been seared into the consciousness of New Zealand public managers since 28 April 1995, when 14 people were killed in the collapse of a Department of Conservation viewing platform at Cave Creek, on the West Coast of the South Island. In an entrepreneurial effort to show results within a constrained budget, staff of the Department of Conservation had built the platform

---

33 A result of an uneasy coalition between the National Party and the New Zealand First Party, an arrangement which was broken after a change in the leadership of the National Party in the election year of 1999.

with insufficient engineering supervision. No longer subject to the traditional oversight of engineers of the Ministry of Works and Development, local staff used nails rather than bolts to anchor a viewing platform over a deep ravine. The platform collapsed under the weight of students from an outdoors education course, killing most of the group on the rocks at the bottom of the 30-metre drop.

The freedom exercised by staff of the Department of Conservation to build the platform provided the first real test of accountability within a decentralised system. Initially both the chief executive and Minister of the department argued that they should demonstrate responsibility by continuing in their roles to tighten up the systems that lay behind the collapse. Subsequently, however, both resigned in the face of public determination that blame should be apportioned (Gregory, 1998a, has a full analysis). Risk management became a new, centrally mandated concern. Faith in letting managers manage took a severe blow.

Cave Creek was a turning point in thinking about managerial freedom, a central agency manager believed. Up until the tragedy, the emphasis had been on looking at different ways to do business, including the contracting out of functions. Since then officials have become

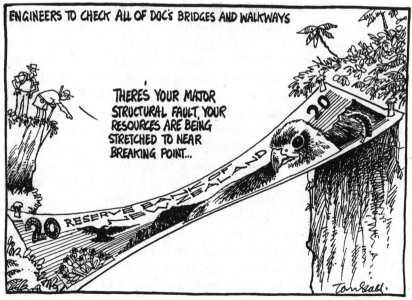

Tom Scott, *Evening Post,* 3 May 1995

risk averse, rather than seeking to manage risk.

A policy manager took a different lesson from Cave Creek, that of refusing to be pressured by Ministers to deliver more outputs than those contracted and funded for. This meant having a purchase agreement that was clear about what could not be delivered. 'I gave the minister a list of what we will and will not do. To get a different output the Minister will have to contract for it.' This response was the exception among interviewees, who mostly acknowledged they were essentially pressured by Ministers to juggle priorities.

A different challenge to managerial freedom occurred in 1994, when the Controller and Auditor-General, Jeff Chapman, was found to have used credit cards to spend lavishly on personal luxuries. In March 1997, Chapman was found guilty of fraud and sentenced to 18 months jail. A conviction of this nature for the officer charged with upholding financial integrity of the public service had a powerful symbolic effect. It was previously thought inconceivable that an officer charged with maintaining the integrity of the system could be so vulnerable to temptation. The use of credit cards became a new learned vulnerability, with some organisations making the checking of payments a chief executive responsibility. The amount of time this came to involve for chief executives was described by one consultant as 'astounding'.

The horror story mentioned most frequently by interviewees during 2000 and 2001 was the chartering of a plane in 1999, by the newly formed Department of Work and Income, to take managers to a team-building event at a tourist resort. An organisation that served the least well-off in the community apparently aspired to the style of a well-funded corporate. The chief executive of the department, Christine Rankin, already highly visible in the media because of her style of dress and long dangling earrings, became a target for an Opposition Labour Party keen to make an election issue out of corporate excess in the public sector. In office, the Labour Government commissioned a ministerial review which recommended changes in the department but fell short of recommending the dismissal of Ms Rankin. In early 2001, however, the State Services Commissioner, Michael Wintringham, decided not to renew the contract of the CE, scheduled to end midyear. Ms Rankin appealed the decision to the Employment Court, seeking damages. Ms Rankin's case failed, but only after weeks of media coverage about the inner workings of the public service. The effect was one about which the State Services

Commissioner, Michael Wintringham, later wrote: '. . . I do not think our system of public management could stand more than one such case without seriously undermining the ability of the Government and Public Service to operate effectively' (Wintringham, 2001a: 4).

For interviewees, the immediate learned vulnerability of the 'Rankin affair' was to be particularly wary about spending on conference venues and team building activities. As one CE put it, 'I sit here now and fret about every little travel sign-off and choice of venue.'

Other controversies, about accommodation costs, failures of IT projects, spending on consultants and bonuses for staff and even the cost of coffee making facilities[34] have also contributed to a reduction in the implied or actual freedoms given to public managers. One private sector manager, brought in for a fixed-term contract to establish the Health Funding Agency, attracted public criticism and a rebuke from an independent audit report for procedures used to buy imported ergonomic chairs with a $1000 price tag.[35] Payments to directors and executives departing from the Tourism Board and Solid Energy (formerly Coal Corporation), and bonuses to staff of the New Zealand Qualifications Authority further fuelled political controversy during 1999 and 2000.

At the beginning of the 1990s, goal-oriented, hard-driving managers were seen as a way of changing sluggish bureaucracies. By the end of the 1990s, such managers had come to be characterised as recipients of largesse at the expense of taxpayers.

Despite considerable publicity about limits to freedom, chief executives continue to have wide discretion over the most important of resources – the deployment of staff and allocation of budgets. One clear result of public criticism has been the adoption of elaborate systems to justify spending. While the statutory focus is on output delivery, the reality of political enquiries is what one CE described as an 'obsession on inputs'. Chief executives have come to expect regular 'trawling' expeditions by opposition MPs seeking to find how much has been spent on consultants, severance pay to staff, or information technology. For example, one Opposition MP is noted for regularly using the Official Information Act

34 A campaign conducted by ACT MP, Rodney Hide, during April 2002, focused on the purchase of $3000 coffee making equipment by a number of Wellington ministries, including the Treasury, Ministry of Economic Development and the Ministry of Health.

35 The *Evening Post*, Wellington, 9 July 1999: 15.

1982 to 'fish' for information about payouts for terminations of employment contracts. Indeed MPs and their research units have come to lodge almost a quarter of all enquiries using the Official Information Act 1982.[36] Ironically, the creation of a system based on outputs may have encouraged politicians to seek more information about inputs.

Managerial freedom to spend on inputs

Staff

Freedoms associated with the role of chief executives as employers remain as a central feature of the control model. Before 1988, organisations had been constrained by central policies about staff numbers and occupational classifications. These were replaced by the delegation of authority to chief executives to employ staff as needed, within budgets, to meet results. Public sector-wide rules were replaced by what a policy manager described as 'some sensible internal rules'.

The State Sector Act 1988 requires public sector organisations to operate as 'good employers', a requirement for due process and fairness that restricts flexibility compared with the private sector. A central agency manager provided an example of selecting a staff member. One person had been clearly suited for the role, but fairness required a full selection, and a second person who was almost as good as the first was found. The first person was still hired. 'We just went through a big process to get there. In a private sector firm we would have just hired that person without even bothering to interview because we knew them and there was a very strong CV.'

The major brake on freedom for staffing decisions comes through State Services Commission (SSC) oversight of wage bargaining, in which the predominant concern is the setting of sector-wide precedents. These limits to freedom had been experienced by one CE who had negotiated with staff and their union for pay rises that were within budget, and provided a means for an occupational group to regain relativity with other occupations. At the last minute, SSC recommended that the settlement not go ahead for fear of setting a precedent. Given the SSC's

---

36 For the year ending 30 June 2001, MPs and political party research units lodged 273 of 1128 new enquiries. From the *Annual Report of the Office of the Ombudsman*, Part V, Analysis and Statistics, http://www.ombudsmen.govt.nz/part5.htm #Official%20Information%20Act. Accessed 13 September 2002.

role as manager of the chief executive's performance contract, the recommendation was interpreted as an order.

The size and budgetary impact of salaries means that freedom is effectively constrained, despite the formal budgeting for outputs. One corporate services manager was unable to win a case for increasing pay to a group of graduates who tended to stay for five years and then move to the private sector for considerably higher salaries. The department's overall staff turnover wasn't sufficiently high to warrant concern, the manager was told.

Consultants

As well as the freedom to decide whom to employ, chief executives were given the authority to choose the balance between long-term staff and short-term consultancy. Under the outputs model, in theory it should make no difference how people are engaged for the work, provided the result is achieved. In practice, the use of consultants has been a matter of debate from the outset of reforms, and particularly during the election campaign of 1999. Consulting contracts provide flexibility in a labour market – but often at the cost of high daily rates that have become the subject of political controversy. Re-employment of redundant public sector staff as consultants had also attracted scrutiny.

Strong attacks by the Labour Party in opposition before 1999, led to expectations within the public service, and fears among consultancy organisations, that new restraints would be imposed on consultant spending. Opposition anger was particularly directed at the use of consultants for core public service roles, such as preparing strategic recommendations for incoming Ministers, something that occurred at the Department of Work and Income. Pre-election rhetoric, however, has given way to a quiet acceptance that hiring consultancy expertise for time-limited, specialist projects can be more cost-effective than maintaining permanent staff.[37]

37 For example, the Minister of Social Services, Steve Maharey, who before the 1999 election described the establishment of the Department of Work and Income as a 'gravy train for consultants', commented in July 2000 that the use of consultants would never be stamped out altogether. 'We are not keen on having a public service that runs all the time on consultants. But where there are exceptions, that's fine – we have to hire people for short-term work' (*New Zealand Herald*, 8 July 2000).

Interviewees in both the survey group and case studies noted little change in practice. If a skill is needed only periodically and it costs too much to support internally, the freedom still exists to buy it externally. The only difference, noted one CE, is that organisations now might think about whether it is possible to borrow the skill from another part of the public service.

On the receiving end of a new nervousness about hiring consultants was the consultant who started an interview by exclaiming 'they've gone bananas'. A ministry that wanted a single day of facilitation had sought three quotes for the event, a process that almost certainly cost as much in staff time as the total external contract.

Information technology

The failure of a small number of large Information Technology (IT) projects, particularly an ambitious Police project, the Integrated Crime Information System (INCIS), has made information technology an area for particular risk aversion.[38]

The survey group agreed that the following result had occurred:

Limited understanding of information technology issues among SSC and Treasury staff has made them become extraordinarily risk averse and [to] try to impose additional controls for IT projects.

For one CE, a lack of understanding of the detail of systems resulted in central agencies calling for reports from private sector consultants. The CE thought involvement of central agencies in more than broad-level policies and funding allocations could jeopardise project success.

On the other hand, a corporate services manager thought technology changes made central agency involvement logical and desirable. Moves towards Electronic Government (E-Government), with the need for communication protocols and the ability to exchange secure documents, could be expected to drag the public service in the direction of collaboration. Departments had perhaps been in denial about being public service organisations and both political leadership and technology

38 INCIS was started in 1994 with the intention of using computerised information to free up more Police hours for frontline policing and allow reductions in the number of sworn personnel. After continued delays in implementation because of problems with software design and changing specifications, the project was abandoned in 1998.

were bringing this back into prominence. The manager indicated the technology trends meant that there wasn't the same freedom to act in this area as four or five years previously. 'It's (a matter of) waking up to being part of a government organisation, that our needs are subsidiary to the greater good of the government systems.'

This viewpoint has subsequently been translated into government practice, with the SSC re-emerging as a force in the delivery of information technology after having exited that area in 1986 with the corporatising and subsequent sale of Government Computing Services. SSC now has the lead role in the development of E-Government strategies that require consistency and coordination across government, employing 50 full-time and contract staff to carry out this work (SSC, 2001a).

Freedom to innovate?

The challenges to would-be innovators, seeking to use managerial freedoms to develop new processes and services in the public sector are daunting, as demonstrated by this statement from the survey group.

With public service work, you can build your reputation on 99 outstanding things and destroy it all overnight with one. It's a very harsh environment.

The difficulties of being an innovator in a public sector environment are well documented. The authors of a follow-up study of innovation award winners in the United States conclude that it is 'probably not an accident' that several innovative executives were subsequently not re-employed in public sector roles (Levin and Sanger, 1994). Another United States writer colourfully describes common conditions in a public sector environment that contribute to the worst possible circumstances for sustaining innovation. These are 'unrelenting turbulence in the external environment, public cynicism, a media concerned with failures rather than successes, funding programmes which pit organisations against each other and reduce funds available for experimentation, impermeable internal structures of small fiefdoms protecting their turf, high turnover among staff except those who most value security, frequent reorganisation, fostering of leaders who are rewarded for self promotion and an environment in which mistakes are punished and information treated as secret'. There are also complex internal management systems, budget systems that do not deliver real time information and funders with short-term horizons (Light, 1998: 30–1).

For the decentralised New Zealand public sector, a dilemma for innovators observed by Sapolsky (1967: 509) is a significant issue. Decentralised management systems that foster a diversity of approaches help with innovation. But such diversity also frustrates the implementation of these proposals. A conflict exists between the conditions that foster a search for innovation and conditions that foster adoption. As noted in Chapter 9, about central agencies, preserving space for innovation while also fostering its transfer, is a major feature of the tension between control (or guardian) agencies, and service providing, spending agencies.

Conclusion

Freedom within a public sector environment is necessarily constrained. Freedom for managers potentially means less freedom for politicians to drive their strategies. The early assumptions of the New Zealand model about private sector style freedoms have proved to be unrealistic. The early result was a flurry of initiatives by empowered managers, and celebration of risk taking. This changed during the 1990s as freedom came to be reinterpreted as leading to excessive spending or political embarrassment. The emphasis on focused action has come to be associated with an undermining of coordination.

The tension between the ideals of 'financial style' independence and the reality of interdependent 'strategic planning' of the public sector environment is well captured in a comment from a review of the Department of Work and Income's controversial decision to charter an aircraft (Hunn, 2000: 6). 'The corporate approach tends to emphasise the importance of the single organisation as it strives to compete in an unforgiving world. It stresses difference, taking charge of one's own destiny, a unique mission, vision and strategy – all of which are aimed at the bottom line. There is less emphasis on collegiality, the collective interest and a shared set of values across many organisations, which are essential to the running of the Public Service.'

While important elements of the 'freedom to manage' model remain, freedom has less of the heady independence that was experienced in the late 1980s and early 1990s. Freedom to hire and fire staff within broad delegations, given to chief executives, remains a distinctive feature of the model. So does the ability to vary the range of inputs, although this is constrained by heightened awareness of the potential for criticism by the media or MPs.

In seeking to give politicians less control over inputs while putting their focus more on strategic directions, the model ironically has made politicians – particularly minority Opposition parties – even more interested in learning about inputs. New freedoms to manage can be seen to have triggered stronger interest among politicians to enquire into the input costs that lie behind the publicly presented output information.

One of the 'big questions' that Behn (1995) poses as an agenda for public management research relates to a tendency towards micro-management. Behn asks how public sector organisations can avoid a cycle in which politicians create increasingly complex controls in response to failure in public service delivery, thus making it increasingly difficult for public agencies to perform. Following the axing of detailed, input-focused controls from the Treasury and the State Services Commission in the late 1980s, high expectations were created for managerial freedom. Nearly 15 years of experience has seen a different form of constraint emerge. This time, instead of detailed manuals, a web of case-based experience creates the new boundaries. Core freedoms remain, but surrounded by many hard lessons about spending and actions likely to generate controversy.

CHAPTER 6

Clarity of objectives – an elusive ideal

Once the whole is divided, the parts need names.
There are already enough names.
One must know when to stop.
—Taoist Proverb by Lao Tsu
(Overman and Loraine, 1994: 196)

The need for clarity of objectives seems at first glance to be an unexceptional principle for effective management. Clear objectives have been virtually a cornerstone in the discipline of management since the concept 'management by objectives' (MBO) was codified and promoted by Peter Drucker's influential book, *The Practice of Management* (1958). Objectives – short, measurable statements of intended results – provide a means for clarifying and aligning organisational and individual goals. They are a spur to achievement and a means of using performance rather than procedures as the basis for accountability.

The quest for clarity has been a central feature of public management reforms. For Osborne and Plastrik (1997: 91–108), clarity of purpose sets the stage for improved performance, enabling 'reinvention' to clear away functions that no longer contribute to core goals. Clarity of role through the separation of functions helps organisations concentrate on achieving clear purposes. Clarity of direction comes from using performance information to constantly redefine the core purposes of government agencies. For the Treasury (1987: 55), clarity is an initial element of a management process that aims to create objective performance targets where possible and avoid 'multiple, conflicting objectives'.

Examined more closely, advocacy for clear objectives contains a paradox, with 'elements that seem logical in isolation but absurd and irrational when appearing simultaneously' (Lewis, 2000: 760). On the one hand organisations use information to encourage commitment, trust and creativity, and see self-management and development as a spur for achievement. On the other hand, information is also a means to create efficiency, discipline and order through the imposition of performance requirements by an external party (Rogers, 1999: 1–2). The same data might enable a promoter to proclaim that 'fully 75 percent of targets' have been met while a detractor can sigh that 'only 75 percent of the targets' have been met (Hogwood, 1993).[39] As a motivator, clear objectives can spur achievement; as a coercive force and a means for enhancing accountability, clear objectives can foster a variety of defensive routines (Argyris, 1990: 504). The tensions created by this paradox were evident throughout the 91 interviews, with informants tending to support the principle of clear objectives, while explaining almost conspiratorially, the lengths they feel they need to go to avoid the potential consequences of too much clarity.

Clarity of objectives is the 'ex ante' phase of thermostat control, the stage at which standards are set for assessing subsequent performance. The process is affected by whether managers anticipate the standards will be used for motivation or control. Budgets, the most common form of thermostat-like feedback, are instruments for both planning and for control. A number of research studies (Parker et al, 1989: 66–70) conclude that the most effective performance results are achieved when budgets are set at levels that, on average, will not be achieved. Stretch targets motivate more achievement from staff than might otherwise occur. Budgets that are not fully achieved are in fact a sign that the system is working. However, if variances from budgets are used as instruments for control rather than planning, and adverse outcomes are criticised, the predictable result is that safer budgets will be set and performance will be reduced.

Interviewees showed a clear understanding of the difference between clear objectives as a significant management theory, and the practices they carried out. Members of the survey group readily agreed with the principle of clear objectives, voting that 'clarity of roles and responsibilities' is a major benefit of reform and that 'clearer lines of accountability' are central to providing greater management freedoms that have 'empowered people to be better managers'.

---

39 A form of response which Hogwood observed occurring in Britain, in 1991–92, following the release of the first information from Next Steps agencies in which a considerable amount of data was available for interpretation.

When it came to the practice of responding to external monitoring, the group's reality was that:

The things you tend to report formally are those you have real confidence about being able to measure and prove to an auditor. These often may not be the things you most want to worry about in your organisation – the softer indicators that really tell you how well the organisation is doing.

The potential for loss of flexibility and compartmentalising that comes with clarity was noted in this statement:

Overly detailed performance agreements result in the same problem that occurs with overly tight job descriptions – people refuse to do certain work because 'it's not in my job description'. Important activities can fall between the cracks.

The paradox of clear objectives is starkly put. Clarity is an important concept but managerial survival requires the restriction of its impact. Through the process of interviewing members of the survey group and case study outputs, it became clear that for managers, a high priority task is to minimise the risks of too much clarity.

Before considering in more detail how clarity-creating techniques work in practice, it is useful to review a short history of performance management. Enthusiasts see the development of clear and measurable objectives as challenges to be overcome while critics see the measurement of public sector activities as involving deeply seated problems.

Making performance explicit – a history of advocacy

The quest by an industrial engineer, Frederick Taylor, in the United States, for one best way of organising has had a major impact on thinking about the design of work and the management of performance. In the late nineteenth and early twentieth centuries, Taylor promoted 'scientific management' as a way of obtaining with 'absolute regularity' the hard work, goodwill and ingenuity of workers, which previous craft forms of organisation could only obtain 'spasmodically and somewhat irregularly' (Taylor, 1964: 39). Spectacular gains in productivity and efficiency in factory work created enthusiasm for the application of scientific management in government organisations. Consequently, it became the dominant tide of government reform in the United States during the first half of the twentieth century (Light, 1997: 196). Scientific management dovetailed with the bureaucratic structures considered by Weber (1947) to be the preferred alternative to the unpredictable rule by charismatic leaders. With scientific management and bureaucracy, the emphasis is on authority and control, based on clear, narrowly specified tasks.

For bureaucracies, the use of comparative statistics is a favoured technique of control. Statistics can be used to make visible the differences between units and to highlight deficiencies in performance, setting in motion attempts to overcome shortcomings (Blau, 1963: 50).

Support for clarity of objectives comes from research into the effect of goal setting on performance. Extensive research indicates that goal setting can lead to improvements in performance, but that goals must be specific, meaningful and perceived by the subordinate as difficult but attainable (Locke and Latham, 1990). For instance, in one early study, performance requirements that were translated into specific goals brought improvement in 65 percent of cases, compared with 27 percent improvement for non-specific goals (Meyer et al, 1965).

Goal-setting research provides support for Management by Objectives (MBO), formulated by Drucker (1958) from observations of large company practices and General Motors in particular. MBO in organisation-wide application involves defining, in quantitative terms,

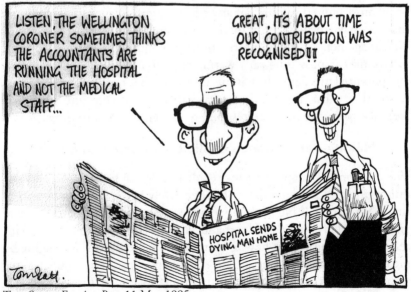

Tom Scott, *Evening Post*, 11 May 1995

the contributions of staff and managers from different divisions towards overall organisational goals. Tensions between planning and control functions can be seen clearly in MBO systems. Drucker originally saw MBO as a means for giving staff autonomy to perform, based on clarity about individual objectives and how they fitted into the big picture. In practice, MBO systems have more frequently been used to cascade senior management strategies throughout an organisation, putting the emphasis on control rather than empowerment.

The theories of New Institutional Economics (NIE), influential in the thinking of New Zealand reformers in the late 1980s and 1990s, treat clarity of roles and objectives as central principles of effective organisation. Agency theory raises concerns similar to those of scientific management, that is to ensure that agents do not pursue personal agendas, principals need to spell out their expectations. Transaction cost theory promotes analysis of organisational relationships in terms of formal and informal contracts between parties: effective formal contracts require clear objectives. Public choice theory emphasises monitoring as a way of guarding against 'rational utility maximisers' capturing the benefits of services for themselves: such monitoring requires clear objectives.

Clear objectives and performance measures can help provide a 'return on management' (Simons, 1995: 2000). Management time and attention is the most limited resource of any organisation. Diagnostic techniques that can make the best use of this scarce resource will improve the 'return on management'. Explicit information is the equivalent of the dashboard panels in a car, providing early warning signals about speed, petrol levels and potential problems. Just as this information is needed to travel safely at speed in a car, fast-moving organisations need constant diagnostic feedback to ensure they can respond to changing circumstances.

Making performance explicit – a history of doubt

The case for making performance explicit has been so successfully made during the past 20 years that it has effectively become a proposition of the TINA (There Is No Alternative) variety. Despite this assertion, there are indeed alternatives, as Hood and Jackson (1991) demonstrate with their 99 doctrines about how to manage public resources. Managing by measurable results or outputs is effectively a reaction against three alternative doctrines dominant in traditional public sector controls.

1. Control by inputs works by establishing limits on spending for categories of resources, including people. Input controls have the advantage of simplicity for recording and assessing. A focus on inputs lessens the possibility of political interference, with the most critical decision being made at the points of hiring and confirming tenure for staff.

2. Control by process provides a way of shaping activities and tasks that are the building blocks of outputs or results. While process controls have been criticised as degenerating into inflexible rulebooks, they can also be a way of improving performance before it becomes an issue for clients or customers. The extent to which quality management initiatives focus on process controls provides an argument against the theory that process inevitably means rule-bound bureaucratic inertia.

3. Profession-based controls, a form of input control, use training, peer pressure and standards to influence the complex mix of knowledge, skills and behaviour that lies behind the delivery of a professional service.

Where the focus is on making performance explicit, and monitoring results, the problem described by Merton (1957) as 'goal displacement' can be anticipated. Objectives which are intended to be means to an end, can become ends in themselves. Focusing attention on public records of performance can encourage practices designed merely to affect the measure of performance and not the performance itself (Blau, 1963: 50). Thus the 'goal' of employees shifts from doing a good job to achieving the pre-set goals. For instance, staff in a public sector employment agency studied by Blau (1963) responded to an emphasis on job placement numbers by focusing on the more easily employed at the expense of the more difficult to employ.

Goal setting should be seen as less important than norm setting, Vickers (1965: 31) argues. He believes that 'great confusion results from the common assumption that all course-holding can be reduced to the pursuit of an endless succession of goals'. Psychologists who have made 'goal-seeking' the paradigm of rational behaviour must take some of the blame, he argues, by having drawn conclusions from studies of how 'rats maintain their metabolic balance' and some humans 'maintain their solvency by periodic excursions after money'. Rather than focusing on goals, which can encourage 'action for its own sake', leaders are better advised to focus on norms, arising from maintaining relationships over time, as the most effective means for regulating results (ibid, 33).

Clearly defined results coupled with extrinsic rewards can crowd out intrinsic motivation and reduce creativity, Kohn (1993) claims. 'Do this and you'll get that' makes people focus on the 'that', not the 'this'. The recipient of the reward will calculate 'if they have to bribe me to do this, it must be something I wouldn't want to do', and the intrinsic motivation to think and work creatively will be undermined (Kohn, 1993: 76).

Too much focus on the measurable can lead to managers adopting a 'mechanistic approach to decision-making, obsessively managing by the numbers, oversimplifying and distancing themselves from the work' (Kravchuk and Schack, 1996: 356). These concerns, raised by Kravchuk and Schack about the effects of the United States' Government Performance and Results Act (GPRA) 1993, ironically can also be seen at work in the downfall of the centrally planned economy of the Soviet Union. Soviet planners started with a modest number of indicators but managers soon learned how to play the system, leading to stories about massive sheets of glass produced to meet weight targets, or hugely expensive canteen meals created to meet turnover targets. Such failures were met with even more detailed specifications, leading to such complexity that managers and planners could not properly understand the rules. Finally reformers would set in motion a process of simplification and decentralisation, and thus new opportunities for gaming (Pollitt, 1989: 51).

Using Soviet experience as an example, Pollitt (1989) theorises that clear measures can lead to either improved or decreased performance. Performance is likely to improve if initial anxieties about measurement are overcome and people focus on performance rather than the indicators. The cost of collecting data decreases as customised systems are developed and information is improved. It is also possible that performance measures diminish in value over time, either because of the volume of information or politicians' tendencies to want to move on to something new after establishing a system, or because gaming of the measures increases as people become more familiar with them (Pollitt, 1989: 51–3).

Clarity taken to an extreme can exaggerate the parts at the expense of the whole, as suggested by the following satire about the way the Treasury might analyse Schubert's Unfinished Symphony:

For long periods the oboe players did nothing. Numbers should be reduced and their work spread over the orchestra to eliminate inactivity peaks. All 12 violins played identical notes. Their numbers should be drastically cut and, if large volume was needed, could be produced with an electronic amplifier. Much effort was expended in playing demi-semi-quavers yet, if all notes were rounded up to the nearest semi-quaver, trainees and low-grade operators could be hired to play them. Repeating with horns the passage that had already been played by strings was also unnecessary. Removing all redundant passages cut concert time from two hours to 20 minutes. If Schubert had attended to these matters, he probably would have finished this Symphony.[40]

Making performance explicit in a public sector environment

The public sector environment creates particular challenges for the managerial principle of clarity. It is a principle that derives from the relatively secretive decision-making world of the private sector. Businesses, in common with many not-for-profit organisations, can claim that they affect only a 'voluntary' group of participants. They usually make decisions through small governing bodies that meet in private and stage-manage the public release of their intentions. Clarity takes on a different meaning in the political environment of democratically controlled organisations.

Performing in the middle of a goldfish bowl

Public sector organisations must make decisions in the equivalent of a goldfish bowl, open to scrutiny from all sides by a wide range of often-conflicting stakeholders. The glare of publicity is part of democratic control of the special and coercive powers that governments have to compel participation through legislation and taxation. In the spotlight of publicity, clear objectives can become magnets for controversy.

Public organisations operate in an arena in which conflict is institutionalised and kept constantly before the public. As Pollitt (1990: 119) points out, the democratic tradition of opposition parties has no real parallel in the private sector. Private sector directors are usually appointed, not elected, and when elections are held, results are invariably predetermined by the holders of large numbers of proxy votes. Directors

40 *The Press* 16 May 1994, quoted in Weir (1998).

do not (normally) campaign on the basis of a manifesto, or have to work under the glare of publicity created by a permanent alternative board (the equivalent of an opposition) seeking to discredit current efforts and put forward its own alternatives. Directors can usually assume that shareholders hold common interests, an assumption which cannot apply for an electorate. The role of director is largely a private one, not requiring consultation with a constituency.

The performance of politics, in contrast, is played out under the full glare of media publicity. A single public sector failure can draw more publicity than a dozen successes.

The survey group keenly felt the glare of public and media attention.

Media attention has created among public servants a nervousness to do anything that might be viewed by the press and public as a possible misuse of public money.

There is not a lot of incentive to be at the top as a chief executive in the public sector because of the problem of working in a goldfish bowl. You can feel exposed and powerless when sometimes you are strapped for resources and then blamed for not delivering.

For an MP with private sector experience, there were notable differences between behaviour in a private sector boardroom and Parliamentary select committees. In a board meeting, fewer people would be present, and those present could assume focused discussion and straight answers. At a select committee, MPs could expect that Cabinet Ministers and public servants would provide evasive answers. Portfolio Ministers would consider a meeting a success if they could emerge from the process with the press and MPs believing that they were sufficiently well informed about the department. As a result, the select committee was more like a theatre or a courtroom than a private sector decision-making forum, the MP thought.

Fuzzy goals

Clear and limited objectives, and stable and explicit priorities are seldom the reality for public service organisations (Pollitt, 1990: 120–1). Frequently legislators deliberately leave policies, priorities and legislation fuzzy to retain political support that might be alienated if intentions were too fully spelt out. Often results cannot be predicted ahead of time.

Governments seek to tackle multi-dimensional and multi-generational issues that are considerably more complex than the quest for bottom-line survival of the private sector. Broad goals can create the political illusions necessary to keep a coalition of interests together. As Pollitt (1990: 121) comments, tightly defined objectives are 'liable to reveal all too clearly which groups are likely to be satisfied and which are not – with the result that the latter desert the coalition or move from passive acceptance to raucous opposition'.

The reluctance of governments to be explicit about their intentions was noted by the Auditor-General (1999). Outcome descriptions have often been vague, with little indication given of how progress towards them might be determined. One of the realities of such reporting is that governments are reluctant to be more specific about desired outcomes in order to 'avoid complications that might arise if they failed to achieve them' (ibid, 50).

Goals may also be ambiguous because of the peculiar tensions that public sector organisations face through delivering services to clients who are also citizens (Lipsky, 1980: 41).

1. Client-centred goals can conflict with social engineering goals, a tension seen clearly in prisons that are expected to both punish and rehabilitate, and in town planning where planners are expected to provide prompt customer service for building applicants, while also upholding the citizenship rights of neighbours who might object.
2. Client-centred goals can conflict with organisation-centred goals of containing and reducing costs. Client demands in areas such as social services, health and education are potentially limitless, subject to rationing of public provision.
3. Goals may conflict as a result of differences in approach within a profession, eg vocational and academic approaches to teaching, or tensions between hospital and public health views about allocation of health resources.

Lack of clarity as a feature of many public sector tasks

One of the main reasons that many tasks are managed through public organisations is that the services provided do not fit well with the market model of buying and selling. Manufacturing and retail businesses deal with completed products, available for inspection before purchase, and

Figure 6.1: Observability of outputs and outcomes

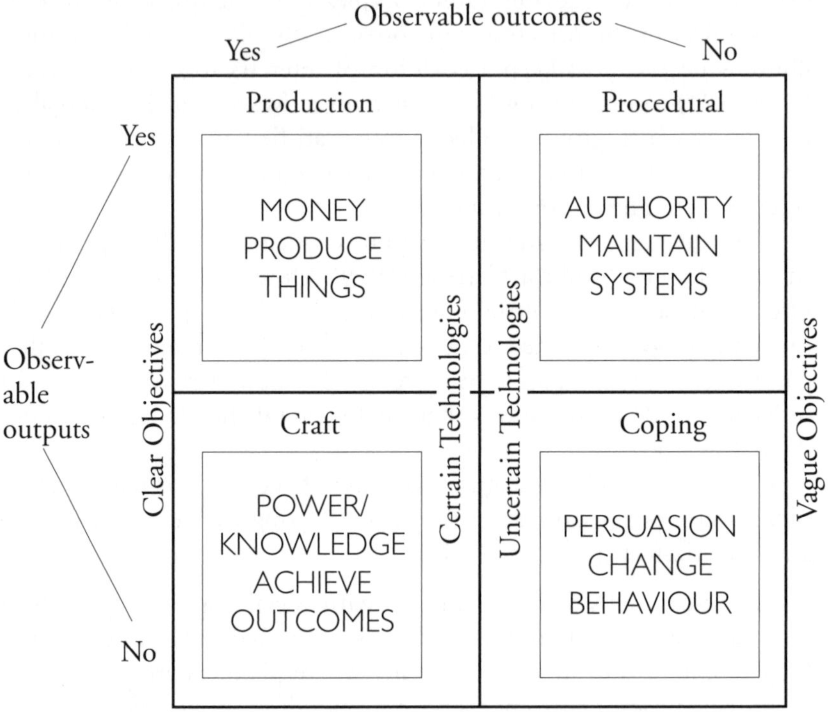

Observable outcomes

	Yes	No
	Production	Procedural
Yes	MONEY PRODUCE THINGS	AUTHORITY MAINTAIN SYSTEMS
	Craft	Coping
No	POWER/ KNOWLEDGE ACHIEVE OUTCOMES	PERSUASION CHANGE BEHAVIOUR

Observable outputs

Clear Objectives — Certain Technologies | Uncertain Technologies — Vague Objectives

Source: Gregory, 1995.

standardised in character. Private sector services have many possible purchasers and providers, and the benefits of the services are clearly private in nature. Public services exist because markets do not or cannot provide the service, or because of democratic support for a particular type of service, such as education, health or broadcasting. Many services are the modern equivalent of the commons of medieval times – providing an infrastructure and benefits advantageous to a total community that would be diminished in effectiveness if available to only a few. Privatisation of many state-owned enterprises during the late 1980s and early 1990s has reduced public sector provision in New Zealand largely to services that cannot easily be provided through markets. Those that remain in government ownership are mostly distinctively public in nature. As a corporate services manager put it, 'If the work was easy it would have been sold off a long time ago.'

One way of viewing the diversity of public services is contained in the typology proposed by Wilson (1989: 158–9), and developed into a diagram by Gregory (1995), reproduced as Figure 6.1. Far from sharing the optimism of advocates for clarity, Wilson classifies services in a matrix that highlights the difficulty of observing the outputs or outcomes of many services.

Production tasks, those in which both outputs and outcomes are clearly observable, are products and services that can most readily be specified. Production tasks are the dominant work of the private sector, particularly manufacturing and retailing, in which money is the prime resource, and the purpose is to produce or sell things. Public sector tasks with these characteristics include the collection of income tax or the assessment and payment of social welfare benefits.

Procedural tasks are those in which outputs are observable, but outcomes are not. The purpose of such tasks is to maintain systems. The authority of the state is a main resource, and the issue of citizen rights a major constraint. Care for patients who are mentally ill provides an example. Administrators can observe what the medical staff do but cannot easily observe the results of many kinds of treatment, 'either because there is no result, or because it will occur in the distant future' (Wilson, 1989: 163). Other procedural tasks include the work of the military in peacetime, occupational safety and health, and custodial care for young offenders.

Craft tasks are those in which outcomes are readily observable but the outputs involved in their delivery are not. Managers can evaluate and reward on the basis of the result, even if they do not know how the result is gained (ibid, 175). Managers do, however, have to consider the potential for improper or illegal action in gaining the result. The power that comes from the knowledge that operators use to achieve outcomes is a primary resource. Trained professionals have a large degree of autonomy to produce what Gregory terms 'crafted outcomes' such as criminal detection work by police, fire-fighting, the military in combat situations, wildlife conservation, scientific research and the provision of medical care.

Coping tasks involve neither observable outcomes nor outputs in their efforts to change the behaviour of others. A school administrator, for example, 'cannot watch teachers teach (except through visits that may change the teacher's behaviour) and cannot tell how much students have learned (except by standardised tests that do not clearly differentiate between what the teacher has imparted and what the student has acquired otherwise)' (ibid, 168). Police officers can neither be easily watched nor assessed on the level of order they maintain, which in any case could not be easily attributed solely to the efforts of an officer. Social work, probation work and aspects of diplomacy provide other examples of coping tasks. Faced with the impossibility of demonstrating external effects, managers are likely to focus on measurable, and therefore controllable processes.

Gregory (1995) calls for public managers to exercise 'conceptual discrimination' between the different types of tasks and avoid using one-size-fits-all models. He sees the production model inherent in the New Zealand outputs framework as being perhaps the 'purest statutory prescription for goal displacement existing in any of the so-called western democracies' (Gregory, 2000: 112).

New Zealand experience with clarity-creating techniques

Structural change

The creation of clarity was a primary justification for extensive reorganisation of the structures of the New Zealand public sector in the late 1980s and early 1990s. Structural separation of policy and delivery functions, and in some cases funding functions, was adopted to institutionalise pressures for performance.

Clarity is seen by Scott (1996: 16) as one of the major advantages that separated organisations have over integrated organisations. Trade-offs that would have been resolved internally become transparent to outsiders. Accountability for client service becomes clearer.

The science, transport and broadcasting sectors provide the most complete examples of structural separation. Science, research and technology have a ministry responsible for providing policy advice; a foundation that allocates funds on a contestable, transparent basis; and government owned Crown Research Institutes that compete for these funds and private sector work. Where there was previously a single government department, the Department of Scientific and Industrial Research, 11 organisations now deliver the services.

The current Ministry of Transport is a small policy ministry with 70 staff that contrasts sharply with the 5000-person integrated organisation that it was in 1986. The Ministry now provides policy advice, and funds and monitors eight separate agencies that deliver services such as road construction, land safety, maritime and air safety, and weather forecasting.[41]

By the end of the 1990s, enthusiasm for structural separation had given way to concerns about a proliferation of small entities, and the Labour-led governments since 1999 have moved to re-integrate policy, funding and delivery functions in health and social welfare and remerge service delivery functions in special education and early childhood education with the policy oriented Ministry of Education.

The emphasis placed on restructuring during the late 1980s and 1990s has also created a backlash. In 1997, for instance, 60 percent of the public service was undergoing some form of significant restructuring (Upton, 1999). For the survey group, weariness with restructuring was shown in the statement, '*I wish people would stop trying to solve problems by changing organisations or structures.*'

Risks of clarity are fragmentation and turf protection (Wilson, 1989: 179–95). Structural boundaries mean that formal methods of coordination are needed instead of informal, internal arrangements. While hierarchical clarity may be achieved, new barriers are created. As the survey group noted, '*trying to get programmes working horizontally, across organisation boundaries, is particularly difficult to achieve.*'

Such organisational fragmentation was experienced by one MP as leading to 'an atomised fortress state', in which organisations have set up moats and drawbridges to safeguard themselves against the outside world.

The issues of turf protection are seen most strongly in relationships between policy ministries and the delivery functions that they assess and critique. Wilson defines turf as autonomy, and sees it as frequently being a more important driver of organisational responses than growth in resources. Organisations that are high in autonomy have few or no organisational rivals and a minimum of political constraints (Wilson, 1989: 182).

Policy ministries are in effect a direct challenge to the turf or autonomy of their related organisations. The primary role of a policy ministry is to be an institutional source of clarity and a constant threat to the turf of

41 Information from Ministry of Transport website, http://www.transport.govt.nz/ html/02 about.shtml. Accessed 13 February 2002.

operational agencies. This has clear implications for the nature and quality of information that policy agencies can be expected to gather, as discussed in Chapter 7.

The survey group was not convinced about the effectiveness of policy ministries, agreeing that:

Contractual models that have separated policy and delivery have led to fragmentation, constant squabbles over who has the funding and to Wellington agencies speaking a language that the rest of the country doesn't understand.

The CE who had originally made this comment thought the model of separation had led to a fragmentation, particularly in health, with 'people forgetting they are using taxpayers' money to provide a service. What you get is a lot of pointy heads in Wellington monitoring things like mad which has bugger all to do with the people who want a decent health service.'

Seeking clarity through strategic planning

'Would you tell me, please, which way I ought to go from here?'
'That depends a good deal, on where you want to get to,' said the Cat.
'I don't much care where – ' said Alice.
—Lewis Carroll, Alice in Wonderland, *1865*[42]

Strategic planning is a clarity-seeking alternative to the situation described in the quote above. It is 'a disciplined effort to produce fundamental decisions and actions that shape and guide what an organisation is, what it does, and why it does' (Bryson, 1995: 4–5). Strategic planning can 'help facilitate communication and participation, accommodate divergent interests and values, foster wise and reasonably analytic decision making, and promote successful implementation' (ibid).

Planning is promoted as a way that organisations can actively shape their own futures, using resources to enhance strengths and minimise weaknesses to respond to external opportunities or threats. Planning helps

42 From *Alice's Adventures in Wonderland* and *Through the Looking Glass: and what Alice found there* by Lewis Carroll, Oxford University Press, London, 1971: 57.

clarify organisational vision, mission and broad goals, and translates these into objectives and indicators to track progress.

Difficulties emerge, however, if the terms strategy and planning are treated interchangeably, Mintzberg (1994) argues. While proponents of planning insist that strategy-making is simply a process of planning, the term strategic planning can be seen as an oxymoron. Planning is reductionist in nature, reducing states and processes to their component parts. Planning follows the logic of the machine and the assembly line. In contrast, strategy is about synthesis, making connections where none existed before.

Analysis may precede and support synthesis by defining the parts that can be combined as wholes. But synthesis is the essence of strategy and cannot be substituted by analysis. It is not possible, for instance, to forecast discontinuities through analysis, or to create novel strategies in isolation from operations (Mintzberg, 1994: 321).

The New Zealand model of planning has, until the introduction of the Statement of Intent process, emphasised the type of analysis that Mintzberg (1994) sees as a barrier to strategy as synthesis. The model emphasises reductionist planning, analysed into outcomes, outputs and indicators. It is a rationalistic process set in place through legislation, an example of how governments, ironically, may have become mesmerised by strategic planning just at the time business had become disenchanted with it (Behn, 1991: 143).

Strategic planning and politics

Scepticism about the ability of rational analysis to contribute to the political process is a strong theme of Public Administration literature, crystallised by Lindblom (1959) in a landmark article entitled 'The Science of Muddling Through'. The 'rational-comprehensive' approach is limited by human intellectual capacities and by the availability of information. Administrators must find ways to drastically simplify complex problems. They are more likely to use a method that Lindblom terms 'successive limited comparisons'. This involves 'continually building out from the current situation, step-by-step and by small degrees (ibid, 81). Successive limited comparisons is 'not a failure of method for which administrators ought to apologise' and superior to a 'futile attempt at superhuman comprehensiveness' (ibid, 87, 88).

Behn (1991: 133) proposes the metaphor of 'groping along' as an alternative to 'muddling'. In his view it more fully conveys the means by which strategy is converted into action, as analysed in a case study entitled *Leadership Counts*. The process by which strategy is implemented included a testing of ideas and the use of 'different combinations and permutations of the more productive ideas'. 'Rather than develop a detailed strategy to be followed unswervingly, a good manager establishes a specific direction – a very clear objective – and then gropes his way toward it. He knows where he is trying to go but is not sure how to get there. So he tries a lot of different things. Some work. Some do not. Some are partially productive and are modified to see if they can be improved. Finally, what works best begins to take hold.'

Formal plans which seek prespecified outputs seriously limit the potential for 'managing by groping along'.

Scepticism about formal planning is not limited to the public sector. Hayes and Abernathy (1980) argued that modern management principles might be a cause rather than a cure for sluggish performance in business. Planning can encourage a preference for 'analytic detachment rather than the insight that comes from hands on experience'. It promotes 'short-term cost reduction rather than long-term development of technological competitiveness' (Hayes and Abernathy, 1980: 67–77).

A notable theme in interviews was the distinction between the rational, analytical dictates of planning methods and 'just do it' attitudes of many politicians. Politicians are distinctly reluctant to engage in the clear thinking that planning frameworks advocate. Reactions of New Zealand public servants echoed those of politicians and public servants interviewed by Aberbach et al (1981). Many politicians have ideals and partisan passions to a degree which is quite alien to most civil servants. Prudence, practicality, moderation and avoidance of risk are the preferred traits of a civil servant (Aberbach et al, 1981: 12).

The statements below amount to a collective sigh by senior public servants about the unwillingness of politicians to engage with the rational planning that the public management model prescribes. Freed by confidentiality to critique their political masters, the survey group agreed with these statements:

I would like to have a structured debate about issues of strategic direction, capability and performance, so we can report to Parliament on our ability and performance. We need to be accountable but want to be accountable properly.

I would like the government to take a very clear line, make its expectations crystal clear, get people of good calibre, let them get on with it, talk about outcomes and not about money spent on inputs. But I suppose the nature of politicians acts against the possibility of this happening.

The reality was perhaps more that *'for ministers, to be seen to not be failing is just as important as to be seen to be succeeding'.*

Long-term strategic planning from politicians is very rare. This makes it even more important that the chief executives and departments have good long-term strategic vision and a focus on retaining capability for the longer term.

Strategy as priority setting was seen as particularly difficult in the policy arena, with the group agreeing:

As a small country we don't have the resources or talent to do everything we would like to do. We need to prioritise, but this is exactly what politicians most dislike doing.

Strategic planning as ritual

A well noted risk of formal strategic planning is the potential for the creation of paper-based rituals that have little practical impact on an organisation. Such plans too easily become SPOTS or Strategic Plans on Top Shelf (Ulrich, 1997: 57).

With a budget-based annual cycle, reinforced by annual account-abilities, the New Zealand system seeks clarity and regularity at the expense of spontaneity. Schick (1996: 58) warns about the risks of requiring all departments to issue plans on a fixed schedule. 'Genuine strategic planning is costly . . . Effective planning is opportunistic, undertaken willingly when conditions are favourable, not when the calendar dictates that another round of plans is due.'

Evidence of plans focusing on the ritual and trivial came through strongly in interviews, and particularly those about one case study output. A planning manager for this output described the planning process as a corporate office ritual of reworking the previous year's numbers, adjusting for knowledge of likely future trends, with minimal input from field staff. 'Basically that's an automatic process. So far as I know no one else would have looked at it. No one else cares – it's seen as a necessary evil.'

A middle manager for a different output noted that there is always 'the temptation to put down standards that won't embarrass one's chief executive'. A staff member in the same case study felt it was an 'intrinsically human thing to go for the lowest targets' to try to ensure as much achievement as possible. This staff member thought a vicious cycle had emerged as planning had become procedural and mechanical. More emphasis came to be placed on methodological routines than vision and purpose. The routines increasingly looked to the auditor – to be able to prove that objectives had been met. The result was conservative plans, that could be readily met, and a more risk averse climate. Twenty opinions might be called for when five were enough.

Outcomes as a means for developing clarity

Outcomes and outputs are the main devices used to clarify performance expectations in the New Zealand public management model. Outputs are goods and services such as policy advice, administration of regulations, administration of transfer payments, education or prison management. Outputs contribute towards outcomes, which are broader political and social purposes, such as lowered incidence of disease or crime. The distinction was made to establish accountabilities for a particular department or ministry. If performance were to be assessed on the basis of outcomes, the risk would be 'a readily available set of excuses for poor performance' (Boston et al 1996: 264). For instance in the case of Police, the causes of serious crime 'include factors largely outside the control of the police, such as high levels of unemployment, drug abuse, or changing social values. On the other hand, it is easier in theory to hold the police accountable for the quantity and quality of police patrolling.'[43]

Outcomes have in practice been the most vague part of the accountability model, leading to the introduction of the Statement of Intent form of planning in 2003 as a way of addressing the gap. A special report by the Auditor-General (1999) noted that the Public Finance Act 1989 implied but did not require that outcomes be measured and reported. As a result, the Audit Office concluded, links between outputs

43 In practice, an interviewee noted, the public and politicians care much more about levels of crime and resolution rates than the quantity and quality of Police patrols, so that Police are effectively held accountable for outcomes rather than outputs.

and outcomes have been interpreted narrowly, and usually limited to assertions rather than empirical research about how a class of outputs would contribute to an outcome.

Participants experienced the use of outcomes in this way, as voted by the survey group:

Specification of outcomes for which Ministers were to be accountable is the major unfinished part of the model of the late 1980s.

One central agency analyst thought outcomes had become something of a guessing game for public servants, a 'desperate rush to link outputs to outcomes as part of bidding for resources'. Another central agency analyst observed organisations trying to pick up signals from the Prime Minister or the manifestos of the governing parties. The analysis thought linkages between outcomes and departmental outputs were at best contrived and often accidental, presented basically as 'this is what we do and let's find a link to as many outcomes as we can find'.

Interviewees were well aware of the theoretical difficulties of using outcomes for accountability. It can be difficult to establish a baseline against which to evaluate outcomes, particularly if a policy is introduced quickly. Reliable and up-to-date data can be difficult to obtain. A range of factors other than government spending or the activities of a particular organisation can affect outcomes.

If Ministers tried to enforce outcome accountability on departments, some predictable responses would follow, a planning manager believed. Departments would monitor processes that they could control. For instance, they would emphasise tracking the number of calls not getting through to a call centre, an example of process information, rather than focus on outcomes that were difficult to pinpoint.

But while public servants were uncomfortable with being coerced into accountability for outcomes, they were also conscious that outcomes are the real purpose of their work. One policy manager in particular captured this dichotomy between the motivational pulling power of outcomes and coercive accountability based on outputs.

Outcomes were the real purpose of the work, the manager observed. They are 'what we are really doing, what our heart is in and we are responsible for'. The manager saw a disjuncture between committing 'psychologically' to produce outcomes, but limiting formal paper contracting to outputs. There needed to be a 'safe way' for writing down outcomes, but to avoid making this risky for chief executives' pay and continued employment.

A funding manager had tried to work around the duality of outputs and outcomes by focusing in negotiations with non-government organisations on the 'why'. 'Get common agreement on what is the point of the money and the measures that will tell. This requires you to build up a relationship contracting approach and then to have some very simple, effective and agreed measures. You are both then counting the same things and you can jointly believe the stories.'

Outputs as a means for gaining clarity

As the basis for appropriating funding through Parliament, and the unit of analysis used to plan and report on public service activity, outputs are the major means for establishing accountability in the New Zealand system. The hard edge of accountability based on outputs is reflected in a technique used by implementers of reform from the Treasury during the late 1980s (Norman, 1997a). Most departments then wanted to express their results in terms of outcomes, and a common difficulty was the tendency to associate outputs with existing departmental structures. The Treasury change team used an analogy from business relationships to challenge thinking:

> Imagine your department is not here any longer. It's gone. The government wants to buy those services in the private sector. What would they contract for? How would you write the contract?

The logic of this question highlights the extent to which outputs are an externally created device for accountability. Outputs were introduced to make it possible for central agencies to move away from detailed controls over inputs.

The size of output classes has been a continuing cause of debate. The Treasury implementation team held that outputs needed to be sufficiently small and discrete to give Ministers real decision-making power about the outputs they wished to purchase and the costs associated with them. Outputs that were too large would be little different from funding inputs or organisations. Departments, on the other hand, have been keen to keep output classes as broad as possible to give them maximum flexibility. The size of the output class is of great importance for a chief executive. Once appropriations are set through the budget process, only 5 percent of an output class can be transferred to another purpose, and then only with the written approval of the Minister. A larger output class allows both the chief executive and the Minister greater discretion to move money between outputs. At one extreme, 71 percent of the Child, Youth and Family departmental vote is contained in a single output.[44] At the other extreme are appropriations of less than $1 million dollars for the outputs of some small ministries.[45] For the larger outputs, the reality is institution-based funding within which managers have wide discretion. For small organisations with even smaller outputs, the freedom to move funds is by contrast extremely restricted.

The original formalisation of outputs was a major exercise in analysis and reductionism, an explosion in the naming of parts of the whole, carrying with it the drawbacks identified in the quotation at the beginning of the chapter. In the last year of the old financial system (1988/89), there were 56 separate annual appropriations. By 1992–93, the estimates contained 774 separate appropriations (Logan, 1991). The pressures towards consolidation show in the subsequent figures, 508 by 1996–7 and 488 for the year ended 30 June 2000.[46]

As outputs have become institutionalised, they have become a 'mandate, a direction given to work', to use the description of a Corporate Services manager. They are a funding mechanism that buys a capability such as the delivery of policy advice, and have stopped being strategic in focus because of the difficulties of changing them. The manager's department had learned an important lesson about outputs as a new form of 'turf battle' (Wilson, 1989). The department had once sought to change an output description, only to have the Treasury cease funding the old output and declare that a proposed new one did not match the Government's priorities.

Views about the impact of outputs varied from support, to resigned acceptance, to scepticism about their value. A typical response was an endorsement of outputs as superior to inputs as a basis for funding allocations, followed by a series of 'buts'. Typical of this type of response

44 In 2002–03, Child, Youth and Family was appropriated $211,395,000 for its 'care and protection services' output, out of a total departmental budget of $297,453,000.
45 For example, the Ministry of Youth Affairs, with a total budget for 2002–03 of $3,081,000, has three outputs, two of which are under $800,000 in value.
46 There were 475 in 2002–03.

was one from a consultant who described outputs as 'no panacea' but certainly better than focusing on overseas travel or cleaning costs. Outputs were still pretty broad grained, requiring Ministers to think clearly about their priorities. A CE of a department with production-like outputs provided one of the most positive endorsements of outputs. The chief executive felt there had been a considerable improvement in the creation of measures that were relevant and meaningful – those that were as close as possible to outcomes rather than being a surrogate for them. Pressure from the Audit Office over the years had helped to focus Ministers' minds on what they were actually buying so they now have a clearer understanding of, and input into, their purchases. It had also helped the department to define what it was producing. The use of outputs helped to benchmark against other organisations. This fostered good management in terms of understanding what would be produced, what resources used, and ensuring there was a cost benefit.

One recurring doubt was whether outputs had turned out to be anything more than a corporate overlay, doing little to change actual performance. The survey group agreed:

Much of output accounting goes no deeper into organisations than the corporate office.

Case study analysis supported this observation, with the exception of one organisation in which outputs were delivered through a largely self-contained division. Within the other three case studies, outputs were a reality for senior managers and corporate office staff, but little more than an arbitrary time sheet allocation for those working with the organisation's clients. Outputs are more likely to be grounded in reality if they work with the grain of organisation structure, not against it.

By functioning as both a unit of planning and a means for control, outputs create a constant pressure for specification of detail, an issue considered more fully in the section that follows about indicators. The paradox is, as one divisional manager put it, that the greater the level of detail, the less confidence anyone can have that the outputs actually contribute to stated outcomes. The lower down in the organisational hierarchy the measures are placed, the easier it is to quantify and control delivery. Yet it is only at the bigger picture level, higher up the hierarchy, that the link to outcomes becomes clearer, albeit with less control over delivery.

Indicators and measurement as a path to clarity

Measurable indicators are the means to specify the quality, quantity and timeliness of outputs. The creation of indicators is a critical step towards clarity and accountability, again creating paradoxes arising from seeking to use the same information for both planning and control.

As Waldersee (1999: 38) argues, formal measurement has its place in service leadership but so do other forms of assessment such as 'personal experience of the service, observation, frontline input, customer meetings and a raft of informal monitoring activities'. These provide other ways of knowing that can be as reliable, valid and manageable. More quantification does not necessarily improve results – instead leaders of services need to understand when to use the 'science of measurement and when to develop the art of management'.

Waldersee identifies four major potential problems with measurement:

1. Partial assessment
Faced with barriers to measuring services, managers frequently respond by measuring the parts that can be measured, diverting attention from hard to measure factors, while not identifying significant problems.

2. The problem of aggregation
Aggregation is necessary to avoid drowning in data, but it may hide small but significant issues or smooth over key areas of difference. Only 'other knowledge' held by managers can safeguard against 'erroneous actions' and is at least as important as the measures.

3. The problem of manager intuition
Intuitive decision-making may be more appropriate than reliance on measures. Frequently in service delivery there is 'high uncertainty, the variables are not predictable, the facts are limited, the facts do not point the way forward, time is limited and there are several plausible alternatives' (Waldersee, 1999). In such circumstances, intuition can be very effective as a basis for decision-making. Such intuition stems from sensitivity and openness to right-brained cues integrated with experience (Agor, 1989: 97).

4. Context dependent meaning
Lower level actions are more easily measured – but for issues at the bigger systems level, the precision of a measure is less important than the quality

of 'tacit understanding' about the relationships between the variables.

Waldersee (1999: 42) concludes that measurement at its best is a 'subset of needed information', and at its worst can 'provide misleading information for management decision making'.

A similar perspective on the role of measurement emerged from the survey group in these agreed statements:

Performance measures too easily get focused on form and lose sight of substance.

We have excessive contractualism that doesn't capture the reality of what we are doing and leads to blinkered narrow responses. It causes a focus on what's measurable and written down as opposed to what's really important.

Such responses provided support for the analysis of Merton (1957) and Blau (1963) that one of the major risks of specified objectives is that of 'goal displacement' in which pursuit of the specifications becomes the goal. Among the 91 interviewees, the most marked concern about the role of indicators came from those engaged in policy development. Indicators of a Minister's satisfaction are particularly problematic. Does ministerial satisfaction really indicate an effective job of providing policy advice, without fear or favour, or has the agency provided what the Minister wants to hear? The assessment of such indicators is 'all art and no science', according to a central agency analyst, a former scientist.

Such responses correspond with findings of Alford and Baird (1997), that the success of performance indicators depends strongly on the nature of the task they are used to assess. In a survey of Australia's Financial Management Improvement Programme, the authors found that two top performers, Social Security and Veterans Affairs, were reasonably successful in showing causal relationships between the ends and means of their activities, because they were involved in high volume processing work with single products. The two worst, Attorney General and Department of Primary Industries, faced difficulty with both ends and means, and with products that are less routine and predictable. The first two services can use measurement easily because they are most like production tasks as described by Wilson (1989) and Gregory (1995).

It is not only central agencies or the Audit Office that press for indicators. A middle manager in one of the case study organisations pointed to a large number of activity indicators that were limited in meaning. The indicators were in place mainly because of staff demand.

'The staff are very keen for everything they do to be counted . . . so they can be seen to be working their little butts off.'

Conclusion

Emphasis on clarity changes the nature of performance, particularly when planning techniques are used for control purposes. Effective performance is best understood as resulting from a mix of individual motivation and external pressure. Clear, ambitious goals can result in higher levels of performance as individuals and groups take up the challenge. But clear objectives equally can lead to decreased motivation and a series of defensive routines if the purpose of clarity is to provide a basis for blame or punishment.

The emphasis on clear objectives in the New Zealand public management model is a statement of faith in the ability of strategic planning to provide purposeful influence on organisational directions. By integrating the planning processes tightly with accountability, the system sets up a variety of defences that drive managers towards the easily measurable, auditable, and readily achievable.

Clarity has the paradoxical quality of being potentially both an agent for improved performance and a spur to self-defensive game playing. The public sector environment provides many reasons why clear objectives are likely to be difficult. The combination of this paradoxical nature of clarity and the difficult context of the public sector results in clear objectives being an issue of personal risk to chief executives and senior managers. The human response has been to play a game of planning and reporting in which formulaic responses have come to dominate.

CHAPTER 7

Creating quality information

Where is the Life we have lost in living?
Where is the wisdom we have lost in knowledge?
Where is the knowledge we have lost in information?
—T S Eliot, Choruses from 'The Rock', 1934[47]

Information can be likened to water: 'too little and you
die of thirst; too much and you can drown'.
(Cohen and Eimicke, 1995: 139)

The control systems of the NPM model set out to tackle the problem labelled in agency theory as 'information asymmetry' – where an 'agent' has more expert knowledge than a 'principal'. Elected representatives are seen to be at a disadvantage in relation to their own bureaucracy because of this asymmetry, or one-sided information flow (The Treasury, 1987: 44). Asymmetry 'creates the potential for opportunism or sub goal pursuit by the bureaucracy including shirking, budget maximisation and generally inefficient policies for society as a whole' (ibid).

In this context, decision-makers need quality information to maintain control. Managing for performance depends on this, but definitions of quality vary considerably depending on the provider or user. For officials from spending departments, for example, quality information may be data that tells a sufficiently compelling story to secure more resources for the future. For officials from a central agency, it may be information on which to base budget cuts. Government politicians may regard quality information as that which helps claim success for a politically initiated programme. For opposition politicians, the best quality information is that which most embarrasses the Government.

Information is under pressure in such an environment of conflicting expectations. As will become clear from interview comments in this

47 Published by Faber and Faber Ltd, London, 1934: 7.

chapter, the potential for information asymmetry does not diminish with the use of NPM devices for clarifying roles and increasing formal reporting – it merely changes location.

Specialist policy ministries, established as a means for safeguarding politicians against provider capture by operational departments, have brought a shift in the location at which information is power. In the view of the survey group[48] *'operational departments can easily pull the wool over the eyes of policy ministries because they have so much more information about delivery issues'*. The dynamic of this situation was well expressed by one policy analyst who observed that personal relationships matter most in overcoming this problem. Information is power, and the operational agency has the upper hand. It is very difficult to monitor how well things are going from outside and knowledge of the situation depends critically on relationships. Such relationships are hard to build up and easy to destroy.

Formal reporting routines may make available a great deal of information but this is not necessarily useful knowledge. Many interviewees commented on the extent to which they treated formal reports as self-serving, requiring reading between the lines, and the supplementation of information through communication with personal contacts such as those described by the policy analyst above.

Such a finding is consistent with research indicating that managers tend to gain most of their information through oral communication. As Mintzberg (1994: 259–60) summarises, 'hard information is often limited in scope, lacking richness and often failing to encompass important non-economic and non-quantitative factors. Formal information tends to provide the basis for description but not explanation, for example, revealing that sales were lost but not what drove the buyers away . . . much information important for strategy making never does become hard fact. The expression on a customer's face, the mood in the factory, the tone of voice of a government official, all of this can be information for the manager but not for the Management Information System.'

Formal reporting is necessarily limited to 'explicit knowledge', that can be expressed through formal language, using grammatical, mathematical and other devices. Such knowledge can be transmitted

48 The 41 people interviewed during 2000 who were surveyed to derive a group response to common themes.

between individuals formally and easily. In contrast, 'tacit knowledge' is hard to express through formal language. 'It is personal knowledge embedded in individual experience and involves intangible factors such as personal belief, perspective, and the value system' (Nonaka and Takeuchi, 1995: viii).

Management control systems that seek to make performance explicit have to contend with human fears about the use to which information will be put. The risk is that threatening issues can become 'undiscussable' (Argyris, 1980). Most individuals are socialised to respond automatically to threatening issues by 'easing in', 'appropriately covering', or by 'being civilised'. For humans, truth is a good idea 'when it is not threatening. When information is threatening, the normal tendency is to hide the fact that this is the case and to act as if you are not hiding the facts' (Argyris, 1980: 205–6). Embarrassment or threat will easily result in defensive routines that are anti-learning and overprotective (Argyris, 1990: 503–4).

Such defensive routines can be readily seen among comments from interviewees about the ways information can be presented to minimise threat. The difficulties of creating 'quality information' are evident throughout the New Zealand public sector reporting system.

The cycle of annual planning and reporting

Two major annual documents are central to the clarity-forcing reporting systems of the New Zealand model. All government organisations must produce an annual plan, since 2002 known as a Statement of Intent,[49] in time for the 1 July–30 June budget cycle. A year later organisations must compare results with intentions in their annual reports to Parliament. Alongside these public reports, Chief Executives must provide their Ministers with an 'output agreement' which spells out the work plan for the year, for subsequent monitoring by the Treasury and State Services Commission.[50]

Typical of interviewee responses to this cycle of reporting was a comment from a corporate services manager that it is 'an elaborate process

---

49 Previously known as Departmental Forecast Reports.
50 Prior to 2002, two documents were used, a purchase agreement monitored by the Treasury and a Chief Executive Performance Agreement, monitored by the State Services Commission.

that we all regard as a game that must be played', and a comment from a central agency manager that 'producing documents may have become more important than management and actually achieving results'. Corporate services officials in particular were conscious that it is their role to do as much as possible to remove 'the burden of reporting' from the rest of their organisation.

Considerably more effort goes into ex ante specifications than ex post review. A corporate services manager thought there was 'a lot more scope for the central agencies to really delve into the annual report and accounts', but no one seemed to really analyse these. A reason for this, according to an auditor, is that the monitoring of results is seen as spending on administration – and agencies are keen to cut back on an expense seen as bureaucratic. By paring back on administration budgets, they also remove the ability to know whether agreed targets have actually been delivered.

At their best, the formal reports are a starting point for verbal enquiries. Central agency staff noted that they use reports merely as a basis for probing further. Members of Parliament (MPs) considered their most useful information came from constituents or Audit Office questions or comments. The presentation of an effective annual report is a necessary and vital game – poor quality in this area invites unwelcome external scrutiny. But formal reports have essentially become public relations documents, falling well short of providing all the information necessary for effective decision-making or accountability.

The most trenchant criticism of the formal reporting cycle came from a planning manager who observed that the formal reports do not provide answers to questions that could really be used to influence performance. The reports failed, for instance, to make it possible to answer questions such as the following:

- Who gained the best value for IT investment?
- Who are the good employers?
- Who gets the best value from people?
- Who is really assiduous in dealing with ethical concerns?
- Who are the best coaches for people with potential?
- Who has really good performance management systems?
- Who really consults well with the public?

The 'highly stylised and encoded' formal reports provided no help with such issues, the manager argued.

A paradox is observable in reactions of interviewees to the information requirements of the control systems. The systems continue to ask for more information than can reasonably be used for decision-making, yet decision-makers are dissatisfied that they don't have sufficient information. Such a paradox was identified by Feldman and March (1981), who conclude that information is as much a signal and symbol, as a basis for decision-making. 'Conspicuous consumption of information' is a sensible strategy for decision makers when they seek legitimacy for decisions. Requests for information symbolise a commitment to rational choice decision-making, a social value that signals 'personal and organisational competence' (ibid).

Financial management information

As befits a system dominated by the financial control style (Goold and Campbell, 1987), financial information and measurable indicators are the primary means through which performance is reported. The New Zealand public sector has been a testing ground for two major innovations – the adoption of the private sector's accrual accounting standards and the use of contract budgeting based on outputs.

Accrual accounting was seen by interviewees to have provided a significant advance in the quality of reported financial information. Prior to 1989, New Zealand, like other countries, reported on the use of cash for purchasing inputs. There had been a brief experiment with the use of accrual accounting in the 1930s but this was stopped during the Second World War because of a shortage of accountants and paper. Cash accounting was cheaper to operate, requiring largely clerical reporting, but producing management reports of limited value because transactions are recorded only when cash is banked or paid out for expenses. Accrual accounting uses double-entry bookkeeping procedures known as accruals to match cash transactions to the periods in which activities occur. It provides a continuous recording of changes in the assets, liabilities and owner's equity – giving a reader the ability to assess at any time what an organisation owns and owes. (See Norman (1997a), for a full account of the introduction of financial management reform.)

Information about activities in a given period is provided in a Statement of Financial Performance (also known as the Operating Statement or the Profit and Loss Statement). What an organisation owns or owes is recorded through periodic snapshots in a Statement of Financial Position (also known as the Balance Sheet). Cash accounting provides a third set of insights into organisational performance, recording where cash has been raised from and where it has been applied.

The introduction of outputs and accruals through the Public Finance Act 1989 created new standards for reporting financial information. By 1992, New Zealand had become the first government to report its full government accounts on an accruals basis. The experiment has helped convince other governments to follow this path, with Australia and Britain adopting full accrual budgeting by 2002, and Canada, Korea, the Netherlands, Sweden and Switzerland planning to move the same way.[51]

With the introduction of accrual accounting, the New Zealand public sector gained a richer and more widely usable form of information about the state of public sector organisations and that of the Government as a whole. Coupled with the Fiscal Responsibility Act 1994 which requires forecasts of future commitments, financial reporting has become an accepted and trusted feature of the public reporting system. In an earlier study, undertaken by the researcher, accrual accounting was seen by a cross-section of managers as the single most successful result of public management reform (Stace and Norman, 1997). Interviews in the current study echoed that earlier conclusion, with the survey group agreeing that:

It is costing less to produce accrual accounting reports than it used to cost for cash accounting. The information is considerably more useful for analysis and planning and in a format which can be understood by people with commercial backgrounds.

A major benefit noted by the survey group, is that *contingent liabilities and deferred maintenance are explicit.* This means, in the words of an auditor, liabilities are recorded when they occur 'instead of bad news being saved up for the future'. Reliable financial information, forecast three years ahead, is a considerable advance over past practices in which Governments could defer cash payments in election years, providing a

51 Source: Accrual accounting and budgeting practices in members' countries: an overview for the International Accrual Accounting and Budgeting Symposium, Paris, 13–14 November 2000. (Document: PUMA/SBO(2000)11/REV3) Available through the website of the OECD, http://www.oecd.org/EN/home/0,,EN-home-0-nodirectorate-no-no-no-0,FF.html. Accessed 27 August 2002.

rosy one-year financial result, while saving up potential problems for a new Government.

While accrual accounting provides more rounded information, indeed a flood of information at times, it is strictly limited in its usefulness, as highlighted later in this chapter. The use of numbers in accounting reports gives them an appearance of certainty that belies the extent of interpretation they contain. As Herzlinger and Nitterhouse (1994) observe, the rigid mechanics of double-entry bookkeeping can mask what is essentially an interpretative discipline, based on social conventions rather than physical-science principles. These conventions are negotiated and invented more than they are discovered, and seldom provide a single, hard and fast right answer.

Outputs-based budgeting

While the budget process has been reshaped by accrual accounting, it remains more influenced by politics than the technical discipline. The survey group agreed that '*a lot of the reporting and accountability in the budget cycle has become a game. Departments and central agencies have become increasingly adept at playing the game.*'

The use of outputs has greatly increased the number of sub-categories for budget decision-making, but the complexity of comparing across unlike outputs seems to have defeated New Zealand decision-makers, with the possible exception of the first budget based on outputs, in 1991–92, when a Cabinet Committee went through billion dollar budgets at the level of $100,000 outputs, deciding which they would and would not accept. For a policy manager who had witnessed the process, this was the last time that scrutiny had been undertaken at this level. Public servants at the time had thought the process was ridiculous and 'right beyond the pale', the manager commented.

Since that period of zero-based budgeting, the outputs system has settled into a familiar pattern of incremental budgeting (Wildavsky, 1992: 82). Budgeting is incremental, with the largest determining factor of the current year's budget being that of the previous year. Most of each budget is a product of previous decisions, with by far the largest part lying below the surface like the bulk of the weight of an iceberg, 'outside the control of anyone' (ibid).

Capital charge

A distinctive and widely unloved feature of the financial information system is the 'capital charge'. This accounting device was introduced by the Treasury in 1991 to encourage or force organisations to consider how they used their capital; rewarding those that choose to rationalise with a reduced charge on the value of their assets. The intention of the charge is to ensure that the cost of outputs of public sector organisations can be fairly compared with those in the private sector, where a cost of capital is factored into prices. The method followed is to charge departments an interest rate equivalent to private sector cost of capital against the net assets of a department. For those organisations that are totally funded by the state, the charge is added to the funds provided for outputs, a book entry rather than real cash. For organisations that earn external revenue, the charge has to be recovered from clients. In such services, this information about the cost of capital has certainly had an impact. For instance, the meat industry during the 1990s decided to pay levies for meat inspection to the Ministry of Agriculture in advance rather than have levies recorded as debts or 'assets' and see the Ministry charged more than the industry's average cost of capital. At the Department for Courts, the charge on a large pool of overdue fines (a debt and therefore an asset) focused the department on ways of improving its collection rate. The charge has also provided an 'incentive' for the Ministry of Foreign Affairs and Trade to sell highly valuable properties internationally because the charge greatly exceeds the cost of current rents in these locations. The New Zealand Defence Force has also been 'incentivised' to sell large areas of land in major urban areas and rationalise the number of its bases.

While 'efficiency' gains like these have been made, the charge was largely seen by those interviewees that mentioned it as a minor irritant for the planners and finance managers of departments. For organisations with few assets, the charge is 'just a nuisance' and a 'money go round' to quote two corporate services managers.

The information base of 'output agreements'

Contract budgeting is put into action through the formal agreement between departments and ministers known, until 2002, as a purchase agreement and subsequently as an output agreement. For interviewees, the existence of two documents, one purchasing outputs, and the other for assessing the performance of chief executives had resulted in overlapping requests for information from central agencies, providing an example of the overuse of information observed by Feldman and March (1981: 182). This occurs where one part of an organisation can transfer the costs of gathering information to other parts, while retaining the potential benefits that come from the information.

Change since 2002 is intended to address the high levels of frustration expressed by interviewees about overlap and complexity. Whether it will address the fundamental purpose of such information is another issue. A striking theme to emerge from interviews was how few Cabinet Ministers over a period of 10 years have used these formal reports as a central feature of their relationship with the public service.

In theory Ministers have had the opportunity to engage advisers to negotiate agreements on their behalf, but few have taken up this option. With or without an adviser, the advantage is strongly with the provider rather than the purchasing Minister. Providers largely determine their own performance measurements, with minimal input from the Audit Office and varying input from policy ministries. A central agency manager observed that purchase agreements had been essentially requests for people to define their own work programmes. While in theory the relationship between a policy ministry and a Minister was like the purchase of consultancy advice, a lot of what Government was looking for was 'judgement', not normally sought in consultancy work, and it was in any case very hard to define precisely.

Consciously developed defensive routines ensure the risks of the contractual reporting are reduced. One CE described the art of reporting as being to provide as little information as possible. The challenge was to under promise and over deliver, and avoid the problems that emerged with the world changing. A distinction should be made between planning and accountability information. As an accountability document, the purchase agreement should contain only fixed results that really could be delivered.

As decision-makers, Cabinet Ministers' preferences for information are strongly orientated towards the verbal and face-to-face. The formal agreements are largely carried through for the sake of formality. The experience of the CE of a small organisation was representative. Towards the end of the year, the agreement would be tidied up for form's sake. More important than the formal document was a dialogue that took place about the preferences, desires and expectations of the Minister.

A flood of financial information

The rise of the importance of accounting is linked to the rise of large organisations from the late nineteenth century (Johnson and Kaplan, 1987). Before the early nineteenth century, business exchanges were almost all between an owner entrepreneur and external parties so that market-related measures of results were easily reported. With the growth of large organisations, many more transactions occurred within an organisation and needed allocation by accountants to different products. Until the 1920s, managers relied on information about underlying processes, transactions and events that produce financial numbers. By the 1960s and 1970s, they were commonly relying on financial numbers alone. The result was like using a rear view mirror to drive a car or a tennis player watching the scoreboard to play tennis (Johnson, 1992: 21).

Kaplan and Norton (1996, 2001) have subsequently developed the balanced scorecard as an alternative to narrowly focused financial information. Their solution is to also track additional information about *customer relationships*, *internal processes* and their efficiency, and ways in which the organisation is *learning* to prepare for growth, the source of future income.

The concept of a balanced scorecard is built into the New Zealand reporting system, with more emphasis on customer relationships and internal processes than measures related to learning. Following a format recommended by the Audit Office in the early 1990s, government organisations provide a range of quantity, quality and timeliness indicators. The balanced scorecard is no panacea, as later comments from interviewees confirm. The New Zealand experience is similar to issues identified by Pfeffer and Sutton (2000: 148). The balanced scorecard can become 'too complex, with too many measures', be highly subjective in implementation, and 'miss important elements of performance that are more difficult to quantify'.

A significant, yet easily overlooked limitation of accounting, is its focus on entity reporting. By creating responsibility centres for the management of budgets, accounting tends to fragment organisations and programmes. Entity-based reporting narrows statements about performance to those which can be pinned back to organisational structures. Interestingly, in interviews, it was accountants who emphasised the limitation of this aspect of accounting practice and the impact of periodic reporting. Performance is subdivided into time-based snapshots not necessarily reflective of the activity's natural flow.

As a result of the Public Finance Act 1989, qualified accountants have played a considerably larger role in the New Zealand public sector than they did previously. Representative of the tension created by this new profession-based control was an interviewee who objected to the extent an accounting manager questioned profession-based judgements about priorities for spending. 'I have no objection to going through the financial process but it is different when accountants can question the professional direction. It's the question of whether gynaecologists can practice dentistry.'

The credibility of financial information and the types of indicators that are needed to create a balanced scorecard of qualitative measures depends ultimately on the acquiescence or support of operators who actually deliver public services. All public sector information is subject to the problem encapsulated in the following quote from Downs and Larkey (1986: 59):

> The Government are very keen on amassing statistics – they collect them, add them, raise them to the nth power, take the cube root and prepare wonderful diagrams. But what you must never forget is that every one of those figures comes in the first instance from the village watchman, who just puts down what he damn pleases. —Sir Josiah Stamp.[52]

In the New Zealand context, the requirement that outputs be tracked through time costing systems provides an equivalent challenge to the reliability of information. Police staff have, for instance, been publicly critical of the time required to code activities against outputs. Police managers introduced a very precise system of activity management to make it possible to report to Government on the time spent in court, with interviewing, traffic safety, sports events etc. As one interviewee put it, this system is

---

52 *Some Economic Factors in Modern Life*, by Sir Josiah Stamp, P S King and Son Ltd, London, 1929: 258–9.

'universally hated' because staff cannot see the relationship between providing information and the end product. The interviewee described a common staff reaction as being: 'I didn't join this job to fill in bloody forms. I joined this job to catch bloody villains, thieves.'

Financial information focuses on the measurable and the objective. Financial management reform has resulted in a flood of information about physical assets and a useful matching of activities to the periods in which they occur. But this elaborate reporting system is strongly focused on the monetary and the measurable, and the drought occurs with information about people related issues.

A drought of information about people

Conventions defining the purpose of accounting information have strengths that are also weaknesses. First, accounting settles for 'certainty' based on monetary values. Money provides a common denominator, conveniently mathematical in its presentation. By definition financial reporting ignores major issues that cannot readily be converted into monetary values sufficiently robust to withstand the scrutiny of an

Tom Scott, *Evening Post*, 27 July 2001

auditor's questions. Secondly, accounting conventions of conservatism, and historic cost, seek reliability in financial information by setting high expectations for proof. Revenues are to be recorded only when they are legally verifiable; costs are to be recorded as soon as they become known, and valuations should be based on historic costs as far as possible.

These conventions serve an important purpose of safeguarding owners or stakeholders from unpleasant shocks that can come from over optimistic valuations of organisational worth.

Increasingly, however, traditional financial reporting fails to capture the reality of organisational capability. This is particularly the case for organisations that have few tangible, physical assets and create services that are totally dependent on the 'invisible' assets of the accumulated knowledge and skills of their people. These assets leave the organisation every night and weekend, and are almost totally overlooked in the financial statements, where they appear as expenses in the form of salaries and wages, or as liabilities for unpaid annual leave or entitlements to superannuation.

In adopting the outputs/accruals form of information provision, the New Zealand public sector model has made a distinction between the purchasing and the ownership dimensions of Government's interest in its organisations. Purchase decisions are based on a budget cycle in which the dominant information is financial, allocated within finite limits, and always in an atmosphere of contested funds. This is an allocation process in which the 'unshakeable facts' of finance and the coming year's demands will inevitably overpower the more subtle signals about longer-term capability and capacity that is the Government's ownership interest.

Limitations of information about ownership issues were seen this way by the survey group:

Treasury and other central agency analysts effectively only see the flagship and fire fighting activities of a department. They don't really see the routine of the research and development activities that is where future capability comes from. They make judgements only on the most visible of activities.

Debate about the extent to which intellectual capital is the generator of new wealth in business (Stewart, 1997; Sveiby, 1997; Roos et al, 1997) has highlighted this weakness of accrual accounting as a source of information about the performance of public sector agencies. Copious information is generated about what are frequently insignificant physical assets, while almost no information is provided about staff skills, experience and commitment at the heart of most public services. Ironically, finance-orientated reporting may provide fewer insights into the state of the public sector than that provided by the centralised personnel system before 1988. In annual reports of the State Services Commission prior to the break-up of the centralised bureaucracy, information was collated about the total number of staff working in different occupational classes, the number of new entrants, number of staff in different age groups – making it possible to see at a glance whether the service was retaining or building this capability.

The Statement of Intent format for planning certainly sets out to address the subject of capability, seeking more human resource information and more explanation than earlier reporting required.

The difficulties of obtaining useful information about 'human resource capability' were well identified in a report on the topic by the State Services Commission (SSC, 2001b: 2). This noted that the compliance costs of gaining information from agencies outside the core public service (those whose chief executives are appointed by SSC), could no longer be justified. Agencies have used their independence to resist providing detailed information. Such resistance was well encapsulated in a comment from one middle manager. The manager noted how reporting on Equal Employment Opportunities (EEO) and the Treaty of Waitangi[53] was required on an exception basis. The department was told it should inform the commission if it was moving outside guidelines. 'Exceptions hardly ever occur so we hardly ever report. Why would you own up? If you don't, who's going to know? The major exception would be if you end up in the employment court.'

Changes in reporting in New Zealand's museum sector (Thompson, 1999) illustrate the way in which the focus on financial and measurable information can crowd out more subtle information about organisational well-being.

Until the early 1970s, Thompson argues, museums were judged on their collections, their staff, adequacy and condition of their facilities, attendance and endowments. Subsequently, attention has shifted towards the use of collections and the impact of these on the community. This is

53 Treaty of Waitangi reporting refers to the requirement for government agencies to demonstrate how they are fulfilling the intent of New Zealand's founding constitutional document, a treaty between the British Government and Maori tribes.

partly a result of a shift towards popularisation within the museum community, but also stems from the introduction of NPM systems of budgeting and reporting.

In reporting on outputs, museums now tend to focus on maximising non-financial outputs, for a given level of financial inputs. Service measures fail to include 'cultural capital measures' about the productivity that stems from 'knowledge, expertise, ability, skill, and respect'. Different ways of describing performance could include focusing on educational qualifications, accreditation, professional ethics, evaluations of exhibitions and feedback from customers (Thompson, 1999: 518).

Indicators of ownership

In focusing separately on purchase and ownership interests, the New Zealand model makes a somewhat artificial distinction, resulting in what Schick (1996: 43) describes as a form of Gresham's Law: 'purchase drives out ownership'. A major reason for such an effect is the disparity between the hard financial numbers associated with budget and purchase considerations, and the soft, limited information associated with ownership issues – the most significant being the longer-term capability of staff.

Figure 7.1: Categories of staff contributions

Difficult to replace, low value added. (Use information technology to capture organisation-specific knowledge.)	**Difficult to replace, high value added.** (Human capital.)
Easy to replace, low value added. (Automate routine tasks so this becomes more difficult to replace.)	**Easy to replace, high value added.** (Differentiate the work.)

Source: Modified from Stewart, 1997: 91.

While large amounts of financial information are reported, even basic information about the turnover of staff is variable in quality. Turnover statistics are most likely to be presented as an aggregate for a ministry or department, potentially disguising major variations in occupational groups.

Aggregate staff turnover is a deceptive indicator of whether an organisation's capability is increasing or diminishing. The critical capability of an organisation is that which is difficult to replace and adds high value as shown in the table opposite from Stewart (1997: 91). The most difficult of managerial tasks is to find the right balance between rewarding and retaining its stars, while not alienating people in the other quadrants of performance, whose contribution is necessary, but not irreplaceable. Even moderate turnover among staff who are in the 'human capital' quadrant could be of major concern, whereas high turnover among staff in the 'easy to replace, low value added' quadrant could be of little consequence. Possible organisational strategies are given in brackets with each quadrant.

While there is copious information available in New Zealand public sector reports about the valuation of what are often trivial assets, there is almost no information about people whose contribution is in the quadrant that Stewart describes as 'human capital'. In effect such information, about the people-based issues of organisations, is limited to the anecdotal, the occasional leaks from dissatisfied staff and union initiated campaigns.

A problem with assessing ownership and capability levels is that described by one CE of a policy ministry. This CE saw central agencies being part of this running down process, following a general presumption that 'we can just squeeze a little bit more out. Hold the feet to the fire a little bit longer because we know there's fat still in the system.' The Government's approach had been like that of an owner of a group of factories who was 'never painting the roof or oiling the machinery'.

The CE found it frustrating to get acceptance of the lack of resources, but no commitment to fixing the problem, and wondered what a policy agency would have to do to get action without the emergence of a major scandal or disaster. 'We would literally have had to hit the wall.' The problem was that 'you can continue to disguise organisational failure in a policy ministry. What you end up with is a frustrated Government.'

Information for human resource management

Given the emphasis that the New Zealand system of decentralisation places on the managerial authority of chief executives, information about the performance of those chief executives is a critical and sensitive control. This has been managed through a formal performance agreement between the State Services Commission and each chief executive.[54] This document, not publicly available, sets out expectations for performance and what must be achieved if a chief executive is to receive a performance bonus of up to 15 percent of his or her total remuneration package. Information in this context has a direct relationship to incentives and, in a system of limited-term contracts, a direct bearing on the employment prospects of the chief executives. This information, when gathered together, illustrates the conflict inherent in human resources. Pressure to impose performance requirements coexists in conflict with the concept of self-management and development as the route to performance improvement (Rogers, 1999: 1–2).

Reputations and careers are at stake in this process of formal performance evaluation, with the use of fixed-term contracts for the appointment of chief executives being in sharp contrast to the tenure of 'permanent heads' in the pre-1988 public service. Terms of appointment were limited to five years by the State Sector Act 1988, and a Cabinet decision subsequently limited appointments to an initial five-year term followed by a renewal of up to three years.

Because of its strong link with personal reputation and career, the chief executive performance agreement is seen as a very influential document. Interviewees saw it as probably more powerful in its effect within organisations than any control other than the annual budget, despite it being an administrative device, without the legal authority of budget appropriations. Because it is more personal to chief executives than the annual budget it is seen to gain particular attention. In the experience of a consultant who has worked with many organisations, the performance agreement had more impact than other reports because senior staff knew that if they didn't perform, the CE would be 'beaten

---

54 Beginning in 2002, the performance agreement is being combined with the financially oriented 'purchase agreement' to form a single document, the 'output agreement'.

up' and lose his or her bonus. The consultant had heard staff say 'you can't do that because that would put the CE's job on the line'.

One of the consequences of the belief that the chief executive performance agreement effectively shapes performance has been an increase in expectations for this form of control. What started as a reasonably brief set of expectations has reached a situation described as follows by the survey group:

The CE performance agreement has become overloaded with issues that have been added on during the 1990s. It should be a high level agreement about expectations and behaviours.

A CE observed that tight specifications invited the problem of chief executives saying 'it's not in my job description' and having no one doing the work.

One CE described the game of managing the performance agreement as being to underpromise externally and then set targets internally that sought to over deliver. Once external targets were set, it was vital to guard against the possibility of underdelivery. A safeguard used by this manager was to delegate one individual, frequently a corporate relations manager, to manage the accountability relationships and follow through on the time-consuming processes involved.

One CE, who had applied his own performance agreement throughout the organisation, had concluded it took probably a year or two of consistent application of a performance management system before people made their own links between their performance, sanctions and rewards. He had decided to use an audit process to avoid reliance on self-report. A quality assurance team, including external involvement, had been established to report on management reports. The audit process meant there was a more objective view of reported results, which had sharpened up things considerably. The 'obsessively operational' nature of the department meant that such control was feasible, where it may not be with the nuances and shades of grey in a policy organisation. Such work might need to be tested in a different way, for instance through external peer review.

The CE had always taken performance agreements to heart because they were personal. They were also a major tool for managing internally. All the outputs in the agreement had to be allocated to different managers, except where they had to remain with the CE. The message was 'if I get kicked, you get kicked'. All the successes and failures of managers in the organisation went through the CE and became the CE's successes and failures.

Another CE used the performance agreement in a similar way. While arguing that documentation can get in the way of relationships with Ministers, the CE saw a document with the Minister's signature as 'a very useful mechanism for incentivising the staff and giving me some comfort they have a work programme that fits into the Government's stated priorities'.

The tenure of a chief executive has an impact on the nature of decision-making, a staff member observed. There were cycles of conservatism related to appointments of chief executives and senior managers as well as to the electoral cycle.

Impact of formal systems of reporting

In the reality of organisational life, one person's system is another's red tape (Waldo, 1946: 399). The 13-year experience of the reporting systems established by the State Sector Act 1988 and Public Finance Act 1989 has been one of fluctuating demand for information – increasing or decreasing depending on the focus of political debate. Overall, the history has been one of steady accretion of controls, to the extent that the increased red tape has provoked a pendulum swing away from complexity towards a search for simplicity. It is possible that interviewee comments date from a period of particular complexity, just before moves to simplify by amalgamating the purchase and Chief Executive performance agreements. The direction set in 2002 is to reduce information and accountability requirements by amalgamating purchase and performance agreements, and creating a 'Statement of Intent' that focuses more strongly on outcomes and capability issues. Such changes are intended to address concerns such as those of a corporate services manager who experienced a 'cylinder of continuous reporting'. The manager's department had decided to take a 'compliance rather than complaining' approach, but wanted a simpler system that just stated 'the minister's priorities'.

The effect of the diversity of information-based controls for interviewees had become that *'you are conscious there are an awful lot of people looking over your shoulder to make sure you are doing it right, whatever it is you are doing'.*

The corporate services manager who expressed this frustration did not underrate the importance of the controls or suggest that the public sector should be run like the private sector – appointing someone and letting them get on with it. 'I'm not naïve – I respect the differences, but I think we tend to go too far.' But this is a system which, with its quest for clarity of dividing lines and low trust approach, has fostered what another corporate services manager described as energy draining processes of 'senior bureaucrats arguing with each other'. It is a system that assumes a 'capacity to deal with a huge amount of information', something which one senior manager thought was probably not realistic.

The major value of the control system is to provide a basis for discussion about what really matters, a central agency manager believed. A major role of the formal systems was symbolic, providing a framework through which Parliament could appropriate money. For this, outputs were far better than inputs as a base. The major cost was the churn created by a 'compliance rather than performance industry' of people generally in corporate services roles producing the documents that 'report ex post against a world that has moved on'.

Conclusion

Information is central to effective control in a decentralised organisation. In the NPM model, transparent information has been used as an alternative to the provider capture thought to be a feature of hierarchical and procedure-based bureaucracies.

The realities of such information are more complex than NPM theory anticipated. These new systems produce both a flood and drought of information. While readings of temperature provide an external measure from which a thermostat can act, the thermostat controls of public management must deal with information infused with social implications. The emphasis on gathering information for accountability purposes has resulted in a flood of safe, measurable, financial information about assets that are frequently trivial contributors towards organisational performance. Concurrently there has been a drought of information about the difficult to assess and measure human capital issues underlying success in people-intensive service organisations. Formal information provides explicit, auditable clues about performance. It lacks, however, a richness and depth needed for decision-making. As interviews cited in this chapter demonstrate, participants in the system routinely treat the formal information as a starting point for seeking more informal, more person-based information.

The gathering of information is, as Feldman and March (1981) identify, a symbol of commitment to rational decision-making and a demonstration of personal and organisational competence. With their emphasis on visible and auditable information, most easily obtainable in the financial area, the NPM systems create a flood of one-dimensional information. Meanwhile they have provided too little assistance for decisions about strategy and staff capability, a weakness which current reporting changes are intended to address.

CHAPTER 8

The politics of accountability

'Accountability: a worthy constraint that everyone else in the organisation must demonstrate to a far greater extent than they do today. Not to be confused with authority, which is what I need more of.' (Shapiro, 1995: 45)

'What accountability means to the public is someone's going to swing from the gibbet.'
—Don Hunn, State Services Commissioner 1987–97[55]

Accountability for results is the counterpart of freedom to manage inputs. Accountability is not 'an after-thought or a by-product, but a central thread of the New Zealand model' (Schick, 2001a).

The systems for accountability reflect the determination of reformers to change what they saw as an unelected, permanent government, in which, to quote an interviewee, a former chief executive, department heads could do 'pretty well what they liked' with very little chance of being held to account unless a criminal offence was committed.

Accountability is 'the quality of being accountable; liability to give account of, and answer for, discharge of duties or conduct; responsibility, amenableness'.[56] It is the need to account for – to explain, justify, or tell a story about – one's actions to one's superiors in the hierarchical chain of command (Gregory, 1995: 19). In the democratic process, account-ability is a form of quality control (Lucas, 1976: 84).

The origins of accountability may be political, constitutional, statutory, hierarchical or contractual and usually consist of four components:
• assignment of responsibilities based on agreed goals
• an obligation to answer for those responsibilities

55 *Sunday Star-Times*, 23 February 1997
56 *Oxford English Dictionary*, Second Edition, Volume 1, Clarendon Press, Oxford, 1989.

- surveillance of performance to ensure compliance with directions
- possible sanctions and rewards (Thomas, 1998: 352).

The accountability systems of the New Zealand model have a clarity derived from the thermostat model of control, and the seemingly clear lines of authority prescribed by agency theory. The intention of the accountability systems is to create incentives and sanctions to 'modify the behaviour of managers' ensuring they act to meet established objectives rather than 'pursuing independent goals of their own'. Those on whose behalf they act 'must have the means to make that accountability stick' (The Treasury, 1987: 55–6).

Accountability involves answering questions such as the following (Scott, 2001: 20–1):

1. **Outputs** What are chief executives going to achieve and what have they achieved with the resources allocated to them?
2. **Ownership** What is the state of the department's human and organisational capital and will the department be better placed to meet the demands expected of it in the future than it is now?
3. **Strategic alignment and collective interests** Are the department's activities aligned effectively with the government's strategic goals and overall requirements?
4. **Contribution to outcomes** How well is the department doing in contributing to better outcomes from government activities?

Answering these questions and establishing links between the intentions of principals and the actions of agents is a considerably more convoluted and political process than envisaged in NPM theory. Experiences of interviewees in both the survey group and case study outputs reveal that at least three major paradoxes affect the process of accountability. First, formalised processes mean that the forms of accountability can readily become more important than the substance. Secondly, the more freedom that is given to managers to manage for results, the more politicians seek to hold them accountable for inputs. Thirdly, the more formal the processes become, the less they capture the personal dynamics and trust required for effective performance.

Accountability in the New Zealand model is managed at multiple levels; through Cabinet Ministers and appointed boards; select committees of Parliament, the central agencies of the Treasury and SSC and Parliament's watchdog, the Office of the Auditor-General. This chapter examines interviewees' experiences with accountability to elected representatives, while Chapter 9 focuses on 'bureaucratic' accountability.

Form or substance?

In an ideal world of thermostat-like feedback, accountability is based on clear objectives set at the beginning of a planning cycle. Quality information enables external monitors to assess how well plans were carried out. Chief executives sign up to responsibility for the cost, quality and timeliness of the delivery of outputs, and for the development of organisational capability.

The problem with this model, according to one CE, is that the environment in which outputs are delivered is more 'sophisticated and fluid' than contracting or agency theory suggests. 'What we expected to be doing yesterday is different from yesterday.' The model has created what one central agency manager described as 'a focus on what's measurable and written down as opposed to what's really important'. This did not 'capture the reality of what we are doing and can lead to blinkered, narrow responses'.

For the survey group, the verdict on the formal systems was that they *'don't drive behaviour. Often they are worked around. They only drive behaviour if Chief Executives choose to use them throughout their organisations'.*

One indicator of the emphasis on formality is a lack of follow through on plans to check what results have emerged. The survey group agreed that *'a lot more effort goes into the ex ante side of accountability, preparing budgets and performance indicators etc, than goes into monitoring of results'.*

A result of the formalities is, in the words of a central agency manager, an environment where 'producing documents is more important than management and actually achieving results' and accountability has become 'some god'. For one CE, the production of a huge amount of material resulted in a high degree of obfuscation, focusing on the 'unimportant, easy to measure and the routine'.

A consultant thought the formal reporting systems appear to favour chief executives with either Treasury or Foreign Affairs backgrounds. The consultant had observed that chief executives from these backgrounds were noticeably more proficient in having in place the monitoring and control mechanisms than those from other areas of work.

Despite a plethora of reporting requirements, interviewees were not convinced that the formal systems have a significant impact, agreeing that:

No visible consequences have been observed as a result of chief executives failing to deliver on performance agreements (in contrast to controversies focused on politically embarrassing actions).

A CE in an operational agency wondered why accountability was seen to have become so hard. Senior people need to 'understand that if they stuff up they have to admit they haven't done the job well enough and step down if bad enough'. It should be a clean process, handled closely, surely and appropriately, but instead had become entangled in a litigious environment of employment contracts.

Criticisms from interviewees mirrored those found in a review of the accountability systems by SSC (1999a). This found the number of reports required from each department had risen from approximately 20 in 1989, to 41 in 1994/95 and 50 in 1997/98. Such incremental controls had led to duplication of information, and poor alignment between internal and external reporting. Meanwhile there were still major gaps, in areas such as capability and non-financial indicators, as discussed in Chapter 7. The accountability system was found to demotivate chief executives, giving Ministers incentives to focus on short-term deliverables and leaving central agencies to rely on compliance reporting without using adequate judgement about the business of departments. Overemphasis on specification was seen to reward compliance rather than responsibility and responsiveness. Tight output specification, strict financial control, detailed specification of reporting, and the use of targets had been useful to create focus and enhance performance, but may be inhibiting performance, the report concluded (SSC, 1999a).

Amidst a profusion of external reporting requirements, the real processes of accountability rely on more complex and human processes such as the establishment of reputations and trust. An audit manager succinctly expressed the relative unimportance of formal reporting for effective management. The people he liked to have around were those who would get on with the job and not make a 'big breakfast' of it. 'I will only commit an instruction to writing and follow up and monitor its successful fulfilment if I think the matter is complex enough so that a clear instruction is required to protect both parties or I have reason to doubt that the person I'm talking to is going to get it first time and maybe needs a piece of paper to check against. Or they have some incentive not to do what I want to do. If constantly I'm dealing with people like that I'd rather not have them there.'

The survey group likewise saw formal reporting as playing at best a limited role in accountability, agreeing with this statement:

The real substance of accountability to the Minister does not come through the formal processes and documents, but through weekly meetings and informal exchanges. The formal system is only really relevant for when there are problems.

Formal, documented relationships, such as envisaged in the use of contracting methods, may actually undermine the process of account-ability. The survey group agreed with this statement:

Trust matters more than anything else in relationships between chief executives of policy ministries and Ministers. Documentation doesn't help build such trust and can get in the way of building this.

The emphasis on informality and trust was noticeably more important for policy managers and chief executives of policy organisations. While operational agencies might be able to report measurable activities, accountability for policy development was considerably more subjective. As a divisional manager with responsibility for both policy and operations put it, the essential test is to 'meet a need without pandering to a Minister'. Accountability comes from being able to give positive answers to subjective questions such as:

- Are you generating a good dialogue, getting a sense you are raising issues he or she appreciates, assisting informed decision-making?
- Do you feel satisfied if you have been able to make your point of view heard?
- Do you feel like you have made an overall favourable impression?

By contrast, quantitative measures of the production of policy advice could be quite misleading.

Responses of interviewees to the limitations of formal, external reporting highlighted an important distinction in performance manage-ment between extrinsic and intrinsic forces for behaviour change.

The New Zealand model has used the term accountability in a narrow sense, placing the emphasis on external controls and formal reporting.

Accountability can, however, be seen as contributing towards a broader definition of responsibility (Harmon, 1995). It can also be seen as professional responsibility, where by 'virtue of their professional expertise, experience, and standards of ethical conduct, public servants, as *makers*, play a legitimate role, not only in achieving public purposes, but also in formulating them' (Harmon 1995: 186). Whereas accountability is expressed to another party, responsibility implies some degree of 'prudence, good judgement or moral probity' (Gregory, 1995: 525).

Even in its more narrow definition, accountability in the New Zealand context has created a complex drama, well captured in a metaphor developed by Talbot (2000), who likens public sector reporting systems to the performance of a play. On stage are public service actors who must perform for the public, while concurrently receiving shouted instructions from backstage about the script from political directors and central agencies. Some of the backstage directors are seeking to rewrite the script as the performance progresses. In the audience are members of the public, the media and watchdogs such as the Audit Office. Each group is making its own assessment of the quality of the acting emerging from such interactions.

This chapter now considers the role played by the political scriptwriters.

A new distance in political accountability

The creation of performance-oriented public management creates a new distance between politicians and public servants. The NPM recipe of autonomous and accountable managers has been a challenge to a long established tradition of ministerial responsibility in countries using the British Westminster system of government. Ministerial responsibility required public servants to subordinate their personal views to those of their political masters. As a requirement of anonymity, public servants were expected to provide objective advice in private, 'carry out policies loyally and efficiently' and avoid actions that 'could undermine the confidence of future governments in their professional objectivity and capabilities' (Thomas, 1998: 364). The performance model of government has politicians acting in purchase mode, using contractual relationships to put pressure on public servants to deliver or face competition from the private or not-for-profit sectors.

In one sense the boundary line between politics and administration first formulated by Wilson (1887), has become sharper. As Peters (1998) points out in his discussion of the antiphons of reform, greater empowerment is sought for public employees at the same time as greater power is sought for political leaders.

The managerial freedoms established through NPM make political executives such as Cabinet Ministers hunger for more control over the bureaucracy, Maor (1999) argues. While the traditional language of public administration emphasised 'stability, rules and responsiveness to the law', the new vocabulary 'accentuates change, decentralisation, responsiveness to customers, performance and the need to earn rather than to spend'. A striking result of this process is that senior public servants, supposedly freer to act as managers, have become 'more insecure due to political executives' desire for control' (Maor, 1999: 5).

Fixed-term contracts for chief executives provide a strong example of politicians' new concern to keep public servants under closer control. Together with limited employment terms, has come a loss of anonymity as chief executives have been expected to defend their delivery of outputs to the media and select committees, a contrast to the previous system of ministerial accountability. The tensions of this new relationship are well captured by the story of the Cabinet Minister who told his department head that he would take responsibility for things that went well and the department head would take accountability for things that went wrong.[57]

Political and managerial perspectives on accountability

Politicians and managers operate in different organisational systems and face different pressures and incentives. Early reformers such as Woodrow Wilson,[58] writing in the 1880s, drew a sharp distinction between politics and administration, proposing that politicians make policy while civil servants administer. As Aberbach et al (1981) demonstrate in a study of relationships between politicians and public servants in a sample of democracies, the people carrying out the two roles differ considerably.

57 An anecdote used by Jonathan Boston, professor of public policy at Victoria University, to explain the differences between accountability and responsibility at a conference of the Commonwealth Association of Public Administration and Management, Wellington, November 1996.
58 Subsequently President of the United States between 1913 and 1921.

In temperament, politicians have passions, ideals and political antennae sensitive to diffuse public discontent and 'discrepancies between social realities and political ideals'. They are more likely than bureaucrats to agree with the view that 'only when a person devotes himself to an ideal or cause does life become meaningful'.

Politicians bring general direction, but rarely a concern for detail. By contrast, 'bureaucrats are integrators, preferring tranquillity, predictability, manageability, and tidiness' who must persuade politicians to 'confront vague goals with intractable facts'. Politicians in return 'sometimes must stretch the incrementalist instincts of bureaucrats' (Aberbach et al, 1981: 93).

For politicians, who depend on success at the ballot box for the rewards of status, power and income, the perceptions held by electors are a fundamental reality of accountability. In contrast, public servants can be expected to place more reliance on the 'objective' and measurable.

This clash of perspectives between politicians and public servants can be seen in the following statement, agreed by the survey group. The public servants supporting the statement draw a distinction between rational analysis and political decision-making.

The model assumes that rational purchasers will make rational choices and any scrutiny will be similarly rational. There has always been a difference between this view and the realities of the political process. This difference has become more pronounced with MMP in which relatively small groups set out to create a niche profile with issues that are not necessarily rational.

What may appear to be not 'rational' for a 'prudent, centrist, practical, pragmatic public servant' (Aberbach et al, 1981: 9), may appear highly rational to a partisan and passionate politician seeking ballot box support.

Frustration with political behaviour was a notable feature of interviews with chief executives and policy managers who have most frequent contact with politicians. A representative sample of their comments follows.

According to a former CE, very few politicians are seen as being 'trained or equipped for the role of running what are essentially large corporates'. They are highly motivated by politics and political point scoring.

Politicians are seen as having most interest in 'sound bites that make the front page' according to a service deliverer in one of the case studies. They are interested in the new and the visible, favouring what an audit manager described as the 'air force' approach to policy making. Through the creation of pilot projects, carefully spread geographically, it becomes possible to gain almost as much benefit at a fraction of the cost as a full introduction of a new service.

Managerial and political perspectives clash over the applicability of the managerial technique, the 'Pareto Effect', that theorises that in any situation 20 percent of effort, or clients, is likely to produce 80 percent of results (Koch, 1997). This 'rule of thumb', also known as the 80/20 rule, can be used to simplify the role of management by focusing on the all-important 20 percent. In politics, however, as a consultant and former central agency manager pointed out, the focus is frequently on the full 100 percent – given that any issue can be blown up to be important. This inherent tension between the managerial and political was captured in the following statement, agreed by the survey group:

You seldom ever have a minister tell you that you have done a good job. They are more likely to come down on you if something goes slightly wrong. That is one of the big disincentives. Even if you do 99 percent of your job well, that 1 percent wrong can get you in real trouble and may be the only thing noted from your minister because it might have had political ramifications.

What Ministers did, observed an audit manager, was to undertake a 'fairly clever calculus' in balancing competing priorities.

A new distance between public servants and cabinet ministers

The use of private sector-style contracts to establish accountability relationships between chief executives and ministers has been a major part of establishing more formal distance between the political and administrative arenas.

Since 2002 the 'output agreement' has replaced the purchase and performance agreements used during the 1990s. These agreements have used the language of private sector contracts and, as explicit, signed documents, appear to have the properties of classical contracts. However, they are not legally binding and are more accurately regarded as mutual undertakings or pseudo-contracts. They are an attempt to make more explicit reciprocal expectations of the parties involved and are relational rather than classical contracts (Boston 1997: 187).

In the NPM model, Ministers are expected to be discerning purchasers of public services on behalf of electors who seek to keep costs down, while maintaining the capability of the organisations that deliver services. The use of the purchase concept and the formalising of relationships through contracts has encouraged Cabinet Ministers to place a greater distance between themselves and the public service than previously. Chief executives interviewed were well aware that if attacked they could not necessarily expect Ministers to defend them.

For one CE the greater distance between chief executives and Cabinet Ministers meant that 'instructions come down from on high' in a command rather than management framework. 'One reads the decision and tries to work out what was behind it. If they are not clear, things get muddled.'

The role expected of Ministers by the Public Finance Act 1989 appears to be one of detached, strategic thinkers who can set expectations for outcomes, be clear about the 'what' of results expected, and leave managers to focus on the 'how' questions of delivery. The survey group's responses indicate that the role of Ministers has been anything but strategic, highlighting differences between the groups similar to those observed by Aberbach et al (1981).

The survey group agreed:

Ministers I have worked with have paid little attention to the performance agreement with the CE. They were more concerned that when they ask for something they get it.

The involvement of Ministers in CE accountability documents has generally been minuscule.

The unclear boundaries created by a change from the former doctrine of ministerial accountability also creates a frustration about the boundary lines between the two roles. The group, seeking accountability for Ministers, agreed that '*Ministers who repeatedly cross the line to interfere in managerial decisions should expect to suffer consequences*'.

In the experience of one CE, it was difficult to get a busy Minister or Government to step back and look at more conceptual issues. From the point of view of an audit manager, the limited attention Ministers could be expected to give any portfolio was a result of either inexperience or turnover among Ministers, or more capable Ministers getting more portfolios so their expertise was spread thinly.

Ministers find prioritising difficult, a consultant observed, not because they are lazy or inept but because this is inherently difficult to do. The system of accountability asks Ministers to determine and articulate their priorities, but Ministers vary widely in their levels of enthusiasm for strategic planning. For some, the work was carried out by instinct or through tactical responses to issues as they arose. While it was desirable that Ministers focused on the big picture, this was more difficult to achieve than in the business sector where good or bad performance could be observed through the bottom line.

Political imperatives make it hard to get any government to have a coherent and published view of the world, a CE argued. 'No Minister wants to make this commitment. They want the ability to make decisions at the last possible moment, and make decisions different to what they would have made six months ago.'

The formalities of the reporting systems appear to be carried over to the management of interpersonal relationships. The experience of one chief executive appeared to be representative. This CE could recall only a few 'gentleman' Ministers who had given praise for work well done, and speculated about others that 'perhaps they think they lose their power and authority if they do that'.

In such an environment, the primary requirement for chief executives is to not have a 'massive ego' a CE thought. The role of the chief executive is to 'reflect as much achievement and glory as you can on the Minister'. With a new Minister, the role is to interpret how the professional expertise within a public sector organisation could be harnessed 'without completely bending the organisation so that it is broken over the wheel of a new government'.

Ministers vary widely in the relationships they establish with chief executives. One CE recalled two contrasting approaches. One Minister with business experience had been willing to sign anything, accompanied by the message that trust would be withdrawn if found not to be warranted. An opposite experience was that of a Minister who tended to take a day to rewrite any piece of advice.

An extreme example of distance in the relationship was a Minister of a minority party, who never met the CE of an agency that was part of his portfolio. 'We arranged 23 meetings with him but they were all cancelled,' the CE commented.

The level of ministerial involvement depends to a considerable degree on the amount of controversy associated with the portfolio. As a planning manager put it, 'out of sight is out of mind', with politicians tending to care only if an issue gets out of hand.

While the theory of NPM holds that politicians are in charge of strategy, and public servants in charge of outputs, the reality is considerably more complex. The development of practical solutions to policy problems is a complicated interaction between the political and administrative arenas. The reality of the NPM model is, however, that public servants are more restrained in the type and breadth of advice, and tend to offer up outputs, while politicians are invariably seeking outcomes. As seen in Chapter 6, clear objectives and links between outputs and outcomes can be elusive. Only one Minister appears to have used the purchase framework to the full extent envisaged in the theory of the late 1980s. This Minister had avid supporters and strong detractors among interviewees who had directly experienced this style of ministerial management. The Minister, Simon Upton,[59] was one of the few to engage a purchase adviser, and work through purchase decisions for his portfolios in depth.

For one manager who had experienced the rigour of an Upton purchase agreement, the dialogue leading up to the signing of the contract had been positive. It provided a springboard through which the Minister could really work out what he was getting. However, ex post scrutiny of outputs proved to be a 'sterile discussion' about variations in costs created when the Government decided to commit, on a big scale, to a legislation review. The value of hands-on ministerial management had been in strategic debate; the costs came with in-depth ministerial involvement in compliance reporting after the event. For a policy manager, the contracting involved in the Upton approach was valuable for establishing expectations so 'Ministers can't come back and say we were expecting you to deliver this'. Clear agreement about what could be delivered within the budget available made it possible to reprioritise and avoid blame for non-delivery.

---

59 As a Minister in National Party led governments between 1990 and 1999, Simon Upton was Minsiter for the Environment, Science & Technology, and also for periods Minister for Biosecurity, Health and State Services. He is currently the full time chairperson of the Paris-based OECD Committee on Sustainable Development.

However, a manager in a third organisation had experienced detailed specification as a major waste of staff time. The exercise had required explaining where the 'last buck went', in a large report, subsequently hardly used by a succeeding Minister.

One advantage for chief executives of the formal systems for reporting, is the opportunity to reduce the risks of blame being pinned on them by Ministers. The response of one CE was representative. This CE began using documentation as a safeguard against being held to account by politicians if something went wrong. The CE anticipated that he might get a fair and proper hearing from SSC as the employer, but wanted a detailed paper trail for responding to politicians.

While some ministerial contracts were carefully negotiated, either because of ministerial interest or chief executive attention to risk, a more representative experience was that of the policy manager who had made a number of attempts to engage the attention of a new Minister in managing a controversial portfolio. After a number of attempts to draw up an agreement, the department had been told by the Minister's adviser to 'just do up an agreement and the Minister will sign it'.

A CE thought that the formal process through which feedback about CE performance is gathered is not taken very seriously. Ministers had no training in providing feedback through the questionnaires they received and varied widely in their responses. In the experience of one manager, Ministers were erratic in their responses, with some refusing on principle to give top scores and others taking time about completion of questionnaires. A planning manager had experienced one such occasion when a Minister thought he was giving the department a 'fantastic' score by giving a series of seven out of 10 ratings. The problem was that the department's CE had set an aspirational target of eight out of 10.

Accountability to Parliament

While ministerial accountability has many of the features of private sector-style boardroom secrecy, accountability to Parliament through select committees involves the glare of the spotlight. Whether the process is viewed as swinging from the gibbet,[60] or the equivalent of 'boiling in oil' (Lane 1999: 190), select committees provide a significant check on organisational and chief executive performance.

60 Don Hunn, State Services Commissioner, *Sunday Star-Times*, 23 February 1997.

Parliamentary accountability brings with it the goldfish bowl environment that is a distinctive feature of public management. Accountability to cabinet ministers takes place largely in private, through one-to-one relationships. Equally private processes are used by the SSC to assess the performance of chief executives. With select committees and Parliament, the presence of a permanent, paid Opposition means accountability differs considerably from that in the private or not-for-profit sectors.

The result of this goldfish bowl environment is a form of accountability that the survey group saw as both useful and unsettling. On the one hand:

Select committees are very useful because comments from members reflect what they are learning in their electorates.

But:

Select committees are a harsh and sometimes illogical environment.

Select committees have gained significantly in importance as a result of proportional representation. They provide a forum in which opposition parties can scrutinise government performance in more depth than is possible in the formal proceedings of Parliament. Proportional voting has increased the power of Parliament by allocating seats on the basis of votes cast for different parties, increasing the likelihood that the major party will need to work in coalition with at least one other party. In the three elections since its introduction at the 1996 election, the Mixed Member Proportional (MMP) system has certainly provided a check on the ability of cabinet government to operate as an 'elective dictatorship' (Mulgan, 1992).

With majority governments elected by the First-Fast-the-Post (FPP) system, select committees played a subservient role to that of the cabinet executive. Each committee was chaired by a member of the governing party, invariably an MP with aspirations to serve in cabinet, and would have more than half of its members drawn from the governing party. A Prime Minister or Cabinet Minister could minimise the effect of a select committee through a quiet word to the chairperson. Under MMP, the majority political party does not necessarily chair each committee or have a majority of members on the committee.

MMP has led to a significant increase in the number of parties represented in Parliament, and increased the diversity of views held by representatives. Whereas previously, under the FPP system, majority support from a single electorate was required to gain each individual seat in Parliament, under MMP, support from more than 5 percent of voters nationwide is usually sufficient to provide a party with seven seats.[61] Between 1999 and 2002, political perspectives represented in Parliament included right-wing advocacy by the ACT party for reduced government and taxes, traditional left-wing politics from the Alliance, environmental politics from the Greens, and opposition to foreign ownership and immigration by New Zealand First. Select committees have provided members of each of these minority parties a means for distinguishing their policies from those of other parties, and appealing to voters in their political niche.

Given new independence from the political executive, and information from the Audit Office, a number of select committees have become dogged in their pursuit of accountability for the delivery of public services. In many cases they have initiated enquiries that have subsequently forced executive action. Among examples of such issues are:

- cost overruns and quality problems with the Police computer system INCIS
- management of the Fire Service
- use of a chartered aircraft by the Department of Work and Income to transport managers to a departmental conference at a tourist resort
- excessive employment of consultants
- overzealous pursuit of taxpayers by the Inland Revenue Department
- payments of bonuses to managers and golden handshakes to board members.

Select committees can formally review each public organisation twice a year, once for a 'financial review' of the previous year's performance and once for an estimates examination. The first review compares expectations with results and the second assesses priorities in the estimates for the coming year. With uncontroversial organisations, reviews may be less frequent.

---

61 For example, the Green Party at the 1999 election gained 5.2 percent of the party vote and received seven seats in Parliament, a level of representation it increased to 7 percent and nine seats in 2002.

Useful accountability

Openness of information is the distinctive feature of select committee scrutiny. As an audit manager commented, committees are the one part of the accountability system to have a vested interest in open information. MPs, or more particularly opposition MPs, have an incentive to find out what is going on, whereas for Ministers and public servants a more comfortable option is to 'hide behind a veil of a lack of information'.

Frequently, information must be prised out from departmental representatives. An MP from a private sector background found the contrast with private sector governance to be striking. Whereas a private sector board would not expect evasive answers from its management, at a select committee, public servants tended to respond only to questions put to them. There were agendas other than simply providing free and frank information. The select committee environment, the MP observed, was similar to that of a courtroom. Departments would put up their best committee room performers, not necessarily their experts, just as barristers would present in court the work of backroom lawyers. The best expert witness in a court was the advocate who could effectively conceal the advocacy and present information that appeared technically neutral.

The role of a select committee, as described by a committee chair, is to act as a representative for ordinary people who do not have the time, energy or inclination to question government spending. It is the role of committees to ask questions – including dumb questions – on behalf of their constituents the chairperson believed. Sometimes questions are related to broader trends in a sector rather than the specific agency, creating something of a guessing game for public servants presenting. Questioning varies considerably in relation to the experience or interest of MPs, an audit manager commented. For new MPs, a major risk of asking a question is getting an answer they don't understand. It tended to take two years for new MPs to begin to understand the departments they were assessing. Until then new MPs were 'better to sit there, nodding your head wisely and saying nothing'.

With organisations usually receiving only an average of an hour at a meeting, for each review, coverage is limited in depth, and strongly reliant on the research and recommendations of the Audit Office. Probably the most eagerly sought advice from the Audit Office is where the management of a particular organisation is rated on a scale from excellent to unsatisfactory. On the other hand, questions proposed by the Audit Office often tend to be overlooked in favour of Opposition efforts to embarrass the Minister or to get officials to say things that might embarrass the Minister. Indeed, select committees are used as a way of holding Ministers to account for a greater length of time than is possible on the floor of Parliament. As an opposition committee member noted, a Minister who might be able to deflect questions in Parliament or counter written questions with use of the Official Information Act 1982, could not hide so easily when being questioned by a committee.

For public servants, appearance at a select committee is both a source of fear and a motivator, with the more negative experiences described in the next section. At one level, a select committee appearance is a process 'to be endured' and got through with the 'least fuss the better'. But it is also, as a divisional manager described, a form of accountability that has a greater impact in driving performance than internal performance reviews. Public reputation is at stake with a select committee appearance, providing either an opportunity for recognition or the possibility of a 'caning'. Knowing the press is present, and information is likely to be published and used on Parliament's floor, managers learn to respond to a particular type of discipline. It is a tough discipline, described by one CE as a forum in which 'successes and failings of the organisation are all manifest in the person of the poor old chief executive'. Such experiences certainly motivated this CE to have internal systems in place to spread this sense of accountability widely among managers and staff.

Public servants use select committees for insights into issues raised through electorates, caucus and Parliament. They watch for questions that can help show expectations of the type of performance sought. For those in policy roles, engaged in programmes of legislation, developing a reputation and good relationship is important for the passage of legislation.

Questioning by MPs, through select committees, the House, or the Official Information Act 1982, has effectively resulted in organisations keeping two sets of financial information to be able to answer enquiries about inputs. While the intent of the Public Finance Act 1989 had been to free up controls over inputs, the drive from select committee members has effectively ensured that inputs are closely scrutinised. Predictable requests for information are about confidential payments made for personal grievances, terms and conditions of hiring consultants, and travel costs. The volume of questioning has increased markedly with the presence of smaller parties as a result of MMP. For instance, during the first six months of Parliament in 2000, 12,518 parliamentary questions were asked, more than the total for the previous year. One ACT Party MP, Muriel Newman, asked nearly 3000 questions, almost five times as many as the 29 backbench MPs of the Labour Party. Two other ACT MPs asked more than 2300 questions between them.[62]

'A harsh and illogical environment'

A central agency manager summed up the harsher aspect of political accountability through select committees. The parliamentary process fundamentally isn't about holding managers accountable for results. 'They are digging for dirt.'

The following criticisms from public servants of select committees' performance illustrate the different and conflicting incentives of public servants and opposition MPs. In the view of a corporate services manager, select committees have a 'lack of objectivity' and are unable to ask focused questions. For one CE, they focus on input controls or local issues at the expense of long-term strategic thinking For a policy manager the experience has been that committees are a place for political point scoring to 'slag off the government back in the house'.

In the words of one CE, the interests and motivations of the politicians are 'miles away from the accountability sought by central agencies' – effectively a hotbed of politics compared with the cooler objectivity of the central agencies.

For another CE, who had been in a controversial role, select committees had been a 'bloody shambles', like question time in Parliament with no rules. Officials would be cross-examined at length, with the agenda run by opposition MPs, while television cameras caught the action.

One MP conceded that the worst thing that can happen to a chief executive is for an issue to blow up in his or her department close to a scheduled appearance. Where this happens, the committee's entire focus

---

62 *Dominion*, 24 October 2000, in an article headed 'Burton questions "pointless" queries'. Labour Party MP Mark Burton was at this time the deputy leader of the House. For Dr Newman the fruits of such questioning came with the ability to reveal that, since 1994, government agencies had secretly paid off at least 332 employees.

would be on that incident, with the meeting time doubled 'in the pursuit of a 30-second spot on television'.

Select committee scrutiny is at its most difficult when political views about a policy are deeply divided and government performance with its chosen policy option is not going well. As the same MP observed, the only workable approach for a chief executive is to 'play a straight bat and give truthful answers'. Nothing prompts a committee more to continue investigation than a suspicion that questions are being evaded. The MP, aware of public service discomfort about select committee appearances, was surprised at how few chief executives use their appearances to showcase their work and take an active role in demonstrating the value of their organisation.

A climate of fear?

The tension between accountability as a spur to performance, and accountability as a control to create compliance, could be seen frequently in interviewee responses. Public criticism of public sector performance had made interviewees uneasy that they might have become similarly exposed as a result of bad luck or bad management. The survey group agreed with the following statements:

All chief executives tend to get penalised when one steps out of line, because politicians and central agencies tend to take a structural solution to the type of issue that occurred with spending at Work and Income on chartered aircraft.

At the moment public sector staff have hard hats on. This doesn't provide a climate in which improvement can occur. The government won't get the results it wants by telling the public sector to do it or else.

Accountability had effectively become associated with public embarrassment – of 'enquiries crawling all over you' a central agency manager commented. The use of enquiries leading to public servants preparing briefs of evidence, sent a message to people that compliance was more important than management. A result of public controversies has been the inconsistent message from politicians that 'we don't trust you but we want to build public service capability'. They were sending a message that 'we want you to learn from mistakes and we want you to be innovative but don't make mistakes and don't take risks'.

The survey group agreed that:

Political scrutiny leads to a risk averse approach. Innovation and creativity have been discouraged to some extent. Settling on safe measures at lower levels in the hierarchy of results is a way of avoiding criticism.

Avoiding mistakes has become more important than achieving positive things.

The creation of a distance between politicians and public servants can be seen to have an impact on the ability to provide in-depth advice. This problem was most strongly identified by a former CE who had a Minister who continuously gave the impression that the whole organisation was on probation. In the experience of the CE, such a relationship made it impossible to develop a policy advice role in which specialist knowledge and experience could be used to tease out what the Minister really wanted. The ability to develop advice was impeded when 'politicians are so sparing with any words of thanks or praise for work done that if you are praised you are highly suspicious'.

Conclusion

Accountability in the public sector differs considerably from that in the private sector. Far from being a simple process of telling a story about progress compared with predetermined standards, accountability involves interaction within a political context where opposition politicians enhance their reputations by finding fault with public service performance. Private sector techniques of purchasing, arms-length relationships, contracts and choice among providers operate uneasily in this framework.

These techniques seek to replicate a marketplace where good performance is rewarded, poor performance penalised and failing organisations turned around through the introduction of new people and new energy. The private sector's single-minded focus on efficiency is not well matched with the multiple values that are involved in political accountability (Caiden, 1998: 271).

In the experience of interviewees, the public sector model's aspiration of arms-length, market-like accountability is more rhetoric than reality. However, the model does create a greater distance than under the pre-NPM model in the relationships between politicians and public servants. This reinforces differences already created by the tendency of the different types of work to attract people with different personality preferences and aspirations. The risk of the increased division, as pointed out by Schick (1996: 43), is that a minister can be 'like a general without an army, free to set out on any course but not likely to get very far'.

Processes of accountability have a game-like quality, complete with rules of engagement and expectations about how the different players will interact. The systems established by NPM doctrines have been designed to impose a market rationality over political interactions, resulting in an artificial playing field well described in an occasional paper of the SSC (1998: 10). The market model presumes buyers and sellers 'haggling over price against a backdrop of competitive supply, discriminating demand, efficient price, symmetrical information and minimal transactions costs'. None of these conditions are present in the public sector even in a weak form. Rather, 'the market for the New Zealand public service outputs' is 'characterised by monopoly supply, compliant demand, arbitrary price, asymmetry of information and time horizon, and significant transaction costs many of which arise well after the transaction' (ibid).

The concept that public service accountability can be equated to the thermostat-like information flows of a marketplace is seriously at odds with the experience of those who work with these systems. A result of such mismatch between theory and reality is an ambiguous and confusing set of role relationships that have oscillated between the two antiphons identified by Peters (1998). For public servants there is the frustration of trying to work with new systems that supposedly empower managerial action, but have increasingly become politicised. For politicians, there is the frustration of assuming they have greater power to direct strategy, but finding this comes with major restrictions arising from rituals associated with planning, contracting and formalised interactions with public servants.

The NPM formula for accountability involved a strong shift towards formality, relational distance between public servants and politicians, and governance by contract. Such methods have created a complex and adversarial environment, currently subject to a swing of the pendulum away from formal contracts and detailed specifications. The likely implications of this swing for political accountability are discussed in Chapter 10.

CHAPTER 9

At the centre or in control?

'Probably less is known about the characteristic
behaviour of civil servants and their political masters
than about fertility cults of ancient tribes. We certainly
know less about the customs and mores of finance officers
and Treasury principals than about witch doctors and
faith healers, though each shares a bit of the others'
function.' (Heclo and Wildavksy, 1981: lxvi)

Decentralisation of managerial authority has meant major changes for control agencies – the Government's main agents of accountability for financial and human resource management. Yet, the renamed 'central agencies' are in some respects more in control in an output-focused system than when they acted as gatekeepers for most decisions about inputs. This paradoxical result stems from the Treasury's intention, noted in Chapter 5, to give away 'control of small numbers in exchange for control of large numbers' (Scott, 1996: 89).

The hierarchical structure of democratic governance means central agencies, interacting frequently with politicians, are in a powerful position as overseers of other public services. As Hart (1998: 303–5) observes, decentralisation can actually strengthen the need for central coordination, because of the fragmentation that inevitably results from 'genuine devolution of authority and empowerment of line officials'. The power of central agencies can also increase as political leaders seek 'responsive' rather than 'neutral competence' and turn to central agencies to drive political strategies (ibid).

In contrast to some countries (Hart, 1998), New Zealand has reduced the size and scope of work carried out at the centre as a result of reform, although the relatively small Department of the Prime Minister and Cabinet did increase in size for a period during the early 1990s.[63] The

63 The growth occurred during the early 1990s when the department was given the task of managing structural change in the health sector. The department's staff numbers grew from 55 in 1985 to 141 in 1994, and then reduced to 109 by 2001.

State Services Commission has seen the most significant reduction in size, largely because property and information technology services were converted into state-owned enterprises and subsequently sold. From 800 staff in 1985, SSC had reduced to 142 by 2001. The Treasury has also reduced in staff numbers, from 489 to 300, as a result of delegating clerical financial roles to departments and devolving the management of superannuation for central and local government officials to independent entities.

These three departments are the major central agencies, with much of the work of the Treasury and SSC focusing on holding decentralised managers to account, while the Department of Prime Minister and Cabinet coordinates government-wide strategies and plays a trouble-shooting role. Te Puni Kokiri, the Ministry of Maori Development, also performs a central agency function in its monitoring of how effectively other government agencies deliver services for Maori.

Central agencies are part of the 'regulatory' functions of government (Hood et al, 1998) and have been given new prominence by NPM concerns about 'provider capture' of services. This concern, as expressed by the Treasury (1987: 75) is that an agency 'whose existence is inextricably linked to the continuation of existing policy is likely to be biased in favour of existing policy'. With devolution of operational detail as part of the process of letting managers manage, central agencies have become more distant from the agencies they assess. Heclo and Wildavsky (1981) interpreted the management of relationships between the British Treasury and spending departments, as a 'system of reputations' which were measured and traded through 'units of esteem' based on intellect, influence and especially trust (ibid, 14). The emphasis on greater transparency of information, and separation of structures, in the NPM doctrines adopted in New Zealand, has resulted in more formality and greater distance in relationships but 'units of esteem' remains as an effective description of the dynamics of the relationships.

The experience of interviewees suggests that the quest for transparency has at times resulted in an unproductive distance, based on distrust and reliance on formal, paper-based relationships.

Battles for turf

Confusion about the authority and importance of central agencies was the most dominant theme to emerge from interviews. The Treasury and SSC can be seen to have engaged in a classic battle for turf (Wilson, 1989: 177). Wilson theorises that agencies will seek to increase their autonomy by minimising the number of their rivals and the constraints they face. Organisations are like fish in a coral reef – they need to find a supportive ecological niche in order to survive.

Amidst the reorganisation of the public sector in the late 1980s, the former control agencies needed to develop new niches. The Treasury, as the major initiator of change, supported by political leaders of the period, was considerably more secure than SSC. SSC survived primarily to provide a mechanism through which employment conditions for chief executives could be managed at arms-length from the political process.[64]

Confusion about the roles of SSC and the Treasury created what one consultant described as an 'ugly organisational jealousy', particularly prevalent during the early 1990s. Which agency dominated at a particular time depended on the strength of the thinking capacity or political support it could muster. Slight changes in the relationships between these 'very ambitious' agencies would result in one or the other agency attempting to increase its assertiveness about compliance issues, a CE commented.

The turf battle was a concern for the survey group, which agreed with the following view:

We have too many control agencies competing for influence. We should have a strengthened Department of Prime Minister that has real power and authority, with chief executive appointments left to an independent State Services Commissioner and with the Treasury operating as a Ministry of Finance. There should be one clear authority so we can avoid the power plays that happen at present between the Treasury, SSC, the Department of Prime Minister and Cabinet, and now Te Puni Kokiri.

Central agencies have had a difficult time trying to find the right balance between exercising leadership and fostering decentralised

---

64 Prior to 1988, the SSC had full responsibility for making appointments of Permanent Heads of departments. Under the State Sector Act 1988, its role is to recommend appointees for Cabinet approval.

management. On the one hand, as a consultant noted, if a central agency provides strong advice about a devolved service, and the advice is accepted by ministers, the question of who is accountable for results becomes blurred. On the other hand, according to a policy manager, if a central agency holds back from giving clear instructions, delivery organisations must play a 'guessing game' about how strongly the 'guidance' should be followed.

A clear order of agencies' importance emerged from interviews. The single most feared and respected agency is the Audit Office, an agency of Parliament, not an arm of executive government. Its power derives primarily from its ability to publicise its findings. Despite this lack of executive power, it looms large in the minds of managers. One CE summed up a widespread view about the accountability power of the Audit Office in stating that 'if you get a tagged audit, you are in deep schtuck'.

The Treasury is the next most powerful agent of accountability because of its constant contact with departments through monthly financial reports. Also it has the ability to use this and other financial information to contest departmental budget proposals, particularly when departments seek new funds. However, the Treasury's ability to influence strategic priorities within departments is perceived as being less significant than that of chief executive performance agreements, managed by the third most important agency, the SSC. Comments about the Department of the Prime Minister and Cabinet rarely emerged in interviews, because its focus on one-off, politically sensitive issues means that for most managers the contact is infrequent. Least mentioned by interviewees was the agency with the newest monitoring role, Te Puni Kokiri, the Ministry of Maori Development, whose work as a monitoring agency was being extended during the period of interviewing and had not become a major influence.

Managers and staff in operational agencies are deeply ambivalent about the work of their colleagues in central agencies. For one CE, central agencies have not found 'the right questions to ask'. Assessments from central agencies were felt by a corporate services manager to be 'superficial or sometimes plain wrong'. Another CE summed up the approach taken by many interviewees in commenting that central agencies were a 'risk to be managed away' by putting someone in charge of getting an accountability plan created. The plan may not add any value, but would take care of the risk.

Alongside this distrust was a realistic respect for the role and capabilities of central agencies, as shown in the support from the survey group for this statement:

The value of central agency relationships is enormous. I never think of the central agencies as control agencies but as colleagues and collaborators. The Treasury staff are your very best peer reviewers — if you can't convince them it's probably not in a fit state to convince Ministers.

Accountability to the Treasury

Budgeting is the lifeblood of government, the medium through which flows 'the essential life-support systems of public policy' (Wildavsky, 1992: xvii). The Treasury's role as the coordinator of the Government's budget gives it a powerful position as an agent for accountability. As the largest single employer of policy analysts, it has the intellectual capacity to be a powerful 'guardian', a counterbalance to proposals from spending agencies.

The role of treasuries internationally is to 'rationalise the negative', and to always remember that they are 'the taxpayer's last stand'.[65] Guardian agencies of this type perform a necessary role of restricting resources, although spenders are equally necessary for the delivery of politically popular real services (Wanna et al, 2000: 41–2).

The tensions of the institutionalised conflict between a guardian agency and spenders were highlighted in the following comment agreed by the survey group:

The Treasury second-guesses departments and through imposing budget cuts can place a department in the difficult situation of failing to deliver and taking flack for this. Meanwhile the Treasury escapes accountability for its role in setting the budget.

The predictable conflict between guardians and spenders was a recurring theme in interviews.

65 The essence of the role of treasuries world wide, as summarised by a senior official from the Treasury of the Republic of Ireland at a conference about 'Partnership in the Modern Public Service', organised by the Public Service Association, Wellington, 26–7 June 2001.

The Treasury's standard message to spending departments was characterised by a Treasury analyst as being 'don't spend any money. Absorb, absorb, absorb. Fund within baselines, reprioritise, stop doing something.' The view of spending agencies was illustrated by an MP who described the response of the Treasury to a request for additional funding for a Parliamentary agency as 'quite sterile'. 'I think they are a good watchdog. We know what their role is. That was a classic example where we disagreed. We won, they lost.'

The tensions of the accountability relationship were expressed in this statement, which received moderate agreement from the survey group:

Vote analysts from the Treasury have been young, arrogant, lacking in their willingness to understand departmental issues and positional in their negotiating tactics. They have not served the Treasury well.

Some interviewees subsequently suggested that the statement fell short because *older* vote analysts share the same characteristics.

The above statements capture the essence of relationships conducted in an arena of institutionalised conflict. As Heclo and Wildavsky (1981: 42, 45, 64) observed, the Treasury staff pride themselves on being able to see 'the whole picture' and compare the quality of different programmes. They play an expenditure game that involves never saying 'yes', without thorough questioning, as a means to overcome the limited information they have available. Comparisons with previous years or other organisations are the key means for controlling expenditure. An ever-present dream of the Treasury is to 'foster competition and have departments scrambling for the ball while the Treasury remains on the sidelines' (ibid, 95).

That dream has been played out in the New Zealand model, with the creation of 'contract budgeting' (Robinson, 2000) seeking to establish market-like relationships between public sector providers and Ministers. As discussed in previous chapters, Ministers 'purchase' outputs from government agencies. In theory, a budget system with 475 output classes[66] gives the Treasury the potential to compare value for money across the range of public services. In practice, the market analogy has proved to be of limited application. In the simple market model there would be losses for the producer if it was not competing successfully. With internal

---

66 A reduction from 772 in the initial design of the system, in 1992.

contracting, however, both parties are ultimately part of the same entity. As Robinson (2000) notes, reducing the budget of an unsuccessful provider might merely guarantee a larger failure.

Accountability for outputs or old-fashioned budget cuts?

Given the centrality of outputs as a means for focusing managers on the delivery of results, a surprise from interviews was the extent to which outputs have become a formality rather than a central feature of accountability. The survey group, for instance, described the budget process this way:

Budgets for outputs are still run in 'jam jars' called ministerial portfolios. There is no real comparison of the value of shifting resources from one output to another.

The group also thought that fiscal restraint effectively meant that *'funding is still based on input costs rather than output prices'.*

Politicians have been unwilling to choose between outputs and to transfer money to where it might provide the greatest value – resulting in a system described by one CE as involving 'quite arbitrary constraints on the capabilities of individual organisations'. A new form of incremental budgeting has been institutionalised, this time based on appropriations for outputs. The only serious analysis by Ministers is focused on a small pool of funding available for allocation on top of the baseline system of expenditure control. This small pool of funding is like a 'sandpit' that public servants are quite happy to let Ministers play in as long as the central baseline is not touched, according to a policy manager.

The outputs and contract budgeting framework is based on the assumption that a rational and orderly process for Ministers deciding between priorities is feasible. The reality is far more fluid and political, as indicated in this statement, agreed by the survey group:

Ministers aren't interested in purchase agreements. They focus on responsiveness and capability. The purchase concept assumes a rationality at this level of the system that just isn't there. But given alternatives between rational technocratic judgements and political judgements, who is to say which is correct?

The control of the budget cycle continues as described by Wildavsky in *The New Politics of the Budgetary Process*. Rather than try for the best of all possible worlds, officials try to get by and avoid trouble (Wildavsky, 1992: 83–4). Budgeting continues to be a process of 'satisficing', a combination of the words satisfy + suffice (Simon, 1957). Attempts by the Treasury or politicians to play the role of 'demanding customer' have become 'indistinguishable in practice from old-fashioned arbitrary budget cuts' (Robinson, 2000: 88).

Indeed the major method of budget control, far from being a comparison across outputs, has been the holding of 'baseline' budgets at 1992 levels, with no compensation for inflation during a period of inflation rates of between 1 and 3 percent per year. One result of this control measure has been a decline in the number of public servants in the core public service from nearly 33,000 in 1996 to 29,000 in 2001 (SSC, 2001b).[67] The extent to which this decline in staff numbers represents a productivity gain or a loss of capability is a hotly contested issue.

The major benefit of closely controlled budgeting has been an effective restraint on spending. Whereas unplanned blowouts of budgets were a motivator for change in the public sector in the 1980s, they are now extremely rare. A combination of fixed output budgets and fixed-term contracts for chief executives has achieved a result likened to the creation of an enormous electric fence around spending limits.[68] Much of the Treasury's role involves enforcing the boundaries of that fence, guarding against overspending and ensuring spending is within the terms of the Public Finance Act 1989. As a guardianship device, contract and outputs budgeting has been a major factor in enabling the New Zealand Government to move from deficits during the 1980s to surpluses since 1994. These surpluses, coupled with proceeds from the sale of state assets have enabled a paying back of government debt, that as noted in Chapter 4, had reached a peak of $37.67 billion in 1992. By 2002, foreign debt had been repaid, leaving $19.2 billion remaining in New Zealand based-debt.[69]

---

67 Staff numbers are based on Full Time Equivalent measures. During the first full year of the Labour Government, staff numbers increased by 1300, of which a quarter was a result of bringing staff in a crown agency back within the core public service.

68 A comment by the Associate Minister of Finance, Maurice McTigue, *The Press*, 6 June 1992.

69 Source: website of the Debt Management Office of the Treasury: http:// www.nzdmo.govt.nz/govtdebt/historytable.asp Accessed 9 June 2003.

However, in contrast to its impact on debt reduction, the outputs and contract budgeting system has not delivered on expectations that it would enable more effective prioritising of budgets. After initially being used by the Government to assist with budget cuts in the early 1990s, the budget process has settled into a new game, described by one central agency manager as an 'overpowering inertia'. The manager commented that 'the incentives should be there to stop doing things that are not paying off and to seek to do things that might pay off . . . We are not encouraging change in other than a very superficial way. We talk about a demand for new things but don't make it easy for people to disengage.'

The reality is an annual budget game that fosters short-term perspectives. In the experience of a corporate services manager, 'one lurches from year to year through this donnybrook with the Treasury and then the Treasury Ministers'. The manager believed that the considerable time and effort spent this way could better be spent taking a longer-term and more strategic view of the issues and resources needed.

The budget process results in 'discontent shared around more or less equally but weighted for the seniority of those involved' according to an audit manager. Decisions made by Ministers are focused on the calculus of how much political damage might be created, leading to a focus on seeking savings among people who typically wouldn't vote for the party in government.

The tight control on budget allocations applies even more strongly with capital injections. Accrual accounting makes allowance for the replacement of capital items through depreciation, having the effect of enabling organisations to set aside cash reserves for replacement purchases. Outside this source of capital funding, the steps involved in gaining a capital allocation are so difficult that it is not worth bothering to try, in the experience of a policy manager. Restrictions on capital spending have become a 'suffocating mechanism' in which it is not worth trying to get investment funding, however well it might pay off in the future. Making the case for spending up front is so hard, that it is easier to take the approach of 'I'll just take it slowly over a number of years'.

Accountability for routine financial management

The decentralising of management authority creates a particular need by central agencies for reliable information from departments to which managerial authority has been devolved. The collation of regular and timely financial information about departments has become an uncontroversial feature of the New Zealand system, something taken for granted by interviewees. One reason for this has been the introduction of straightforward templates for reporting in the mid-1990s. In the view of a corporate services manager this resulted in a dramatic improvement in the flow and quality of information, and a reduction in tensions in relationships between the Treasury and departments. Treasury staff are 'justifiably pious' about organisations reporting on time according to one CE, but the requirements are not onerous.

This regular reporting is strongly focused on financial data, not directly linked to information about quality or delivery. As a consultant observed, departments are paid when they incur their costs not when they deliver outputs, effectively creating an incentive to keep up input costs. The survey group agreed:

Financial controls are more closely monitored than indicators of service level quality. Missing these quality targets is not a hanging offence.

While contracted to produce outputs through a purchase agreement, departments are still paid whether or not they meet performance specifications. A Treasury analyst gave an example of a large department that achieved only 25 percent of its measures in one year. The following year, the department succeeded in changing its performance expectations to just above the 25 percent level it had attained.

The power of the Treasury is in fact largely limited to holding agencies to account for what are now rare examples of overspending or poor performance with financial routines. A number of Treasury staff viewed SSC as being more powerful because of its ability to link the achievement of strategic results to performance bonuses for chief executives.

Relationships in an adversarial environment

Amongst the institutionalised conflict of relationships between the guardians at the Treasury and spenders elsewhere in the public service, one theme proved to create particular passion. This was the phenomenon of the 'whippersnapper' – a term which describes the attitude of senior executives in spending departments to young Treasury analysts. For one CE, a major frustration of the role was having to deal with 'a little wet behind the ears two years-out-of-university person who thinks they can lord it over you'. Such a monitoring role requires extraordinary sensitivity and avoidance of threats such as 'you must do this or we will tell our Minister', the CE commented. While tensions with inexperienced analysts could normally be resolved by talking to the Treasury secretary or a branch head, they were illustrative of a cultural problem at the Treasury. For a different CE, a major problem was that initiatives by the Treasury to manage relationships with agencies start with a 'bang' and quite quickly become a 'whimper' and die. Reasons for this were a combination of staff turnover, changing perceptions among Treasury managers, and workload pressures.

One Treasury analyst thought the culture of the Treasury seemed to expect that departments should be treated 'like children' who did not know what they were doing or were asking for more money than they needed. The skill of managing relationships with departments was 'to come across as if you trust the department, knowing that you don't really trust them and that they know you don't really trust them'. The job was easier if undertaken with an approach of 'prove it to me or I'm not going to OK this'.

Both the Treasury and spending departments play games of avoiding consulting with each other, the analyst thought. The Treasury frequently did not consult departments before providing advice to the Minister of Finance, and departments frequently did not let the Treasury know what was coming up until a paper was drafted. 'Some people say we don't get consulted on purpose.'

A planning manager of a spending department thought that Treasury staff had an 'institutional predisposition to always hold a card up their sleeves'. A case for additional capital the manager had pursued, was stopped at the last minute when Treasury officials said they weren't persuaded by data on 'a relatively trivial issue'. The experience had raised the question of whether Treasury staff had really taken part in the process of development or had merely been a 'cynical external observer'.

Interestingly, former Treasury officials, now in spending departments, tended to be particularly critical of relationships with the Treasury. One divisional manager, undoubtedly reflecting prejudices created within the Treasury culture, had found 'the level of professionalism and commitment of people' in the organisation he had joined to be a major surprise. People were trying hard, yet there was something about the mechanisms and processes of reporting which did not capture that.

An insight into the adversarial nature of relationships with the Treasury lies in the small number of departments which have chosen to undertake an 'output price review'. This involves a fundamental review of the department's efficiency, with central agencies generally using specialist external consultants. The terms of reference for such reviews are written to create the risk of a reduction in funding as well as a rise, making it likely that only departments confident of a positive result will seek a review (Petrie and Webber, 1999: 8).[70]

Incentives and sanctions

'Incentives matter', the Treasury (1987: 2) commented in making the case for major change in public management systems. The incentives contained in the financial management system fall far short of the promise of reform. The systems have settled into a new status quo where incentives are distinctively oriented towards financial control. Barely distinguishable from old-fashioned budget cuts, they have been made more palatable to managers through the discretion involved in deciding how to cut.

The incentives of the system were well described by one consultant. Pressure is on managers to deliver and not exceed their budgets, with the result that financial control dominates at the expense of other results, particularly capability and risk management. The rational message of the budgeting system is to look after the short run.

Another incentive is to spend up to a budget allocation, no less and definitely no more. The use of accrual accounting has changed the practices of cash accounting, that previously included opportunities to pay cash in advance of service delivery, or to hold back bills for a new budget year. New practices have emerged for what one manager described as 'cargo cult' time. At the end of a budget year, the pressure is on to ensure the completion of sufficient work so the cost can be accrued for the current year. An auditor commented that given the risk to a department that an unspent budget might be a signal for a subsequent cut, such spending is understandable. Managers store up nice-to-have

70 The only departments to have undergone output price reviews have been Statistics, the Ministry of Foreign Affairs and Trade, and Police, while the baseline funding for the Education Review Office (ERO) was also reviewed. In only two of these, Foreign Affairs and ERO, was clear underpricing established.

items for their workplaces, such as attendance at training courses, and if the money is available in June, spend on these. At one stage auditors would have frowned on an end-of-year spend, but now there was more understanding that this practice was a way to keep up morale and reward staff effectively.

Some relaxation of the one-year routine is seen in the introduction for the first time in 2001–2002, of pilot projects for three-year funding, for example one providing the National Library with the ability to spread purchases for major works over three years instead of managing them annually.

One of the major concepts of the contract budgeting system is that Ministers purchase outputs. What happens in practice is that a budget is set and public servants are exhorted to deliver as much as possible for the sum available. Reductions in funding work in the following way, according to the survey group:

In reducing funding, Ministers normally say – just rearrange your priorities. It takes a bold CE to say I can't deliver with the resources. Rather than a loss of capability occurring, there has been in some agencies a mismatch between the outputs sought and resources provided.

One result, in the view of a policy manager, has been that the Government has effectively 'appropriated' 10–20 hours a week of unpaid time from public servants.

While significant achievements have been made by the public sector in containing costs, the results of the financial management systems fall frustratingly short of the theoretical promise. This is perhaps inevitable, however, during a period of fiscal constraint. With the exception of externally contracted, contestable funds, it is indeed questionable whether financial management accountability in New Zealand can accurately be described as an output system. For core government services, outputs are more an artificial constraint, a level of control below that of an organisation, and one which is frequently accompanied by focus on the cost of inputs rather than a comparison of prices. The contracts budgeting approach has shown itself to be an effective lever for fiscal control and a means for creating pressures for efficiency. Whether it delivers more effective outcomes is more debatable.

Accountability to the State Services Commission

While money is the basis for the authority exercised by the Treasury, the authority of the State Services Commission (SSC) stems from its ability to sign employment contracts with chief executives. As the employer of the chief executives of 39 core public service ministries and departments, SSC is a powerful agent of accountability, responsible for recommending appointments of chief executives and for reviewing their performance. The Commission was retained as a means for maintaining a politically neutral process for appointing public servants, a major concern at the time of reform in 1988. Of more than 80 recommendations for appointments and reappointments of chief executives made since 1988, only one has been rejected, in 1990 (Boston, 2001: 202).[71] Since that rejection, SSC has followed a policy that Ministers should expect recommendations for people who not only meet the requirements for the job, but also are people in whom the Government can have confidence (Wintringham, 2001a: 6).

Decentralisation of management authority has affected the SSC more dramatically than either the Treasury or Audit Office. During the 1990s, the SSC has undergone near continuous restructuring and refocusing as it has sought to create a new role in a decentralised system of management. As the pendulum has swung since 2000 away from laissez-faire decentralisation towards concern about the effects of fragmentation of service delivery, a new role as a leader for coordination has begun to emerge.

As the Government's human resources adviser, SSC has experienced a period of transition similar to that of human resources units in large and diversified corporations that have delegated authority to line managers. Such units face multiple and potentially conflicting roles (Ulrich, 1997: 24). They must find an appropriate balance between day-to-day operational issues and a strategic focus on the future, and find a balance between emphasis on processes and focus on people.

71 The Labour Government rejected a recommendation for the appointment of Gerald Hensley as Head of the Ministry of Defence in 1990. Mr Hensley, a former head of the Department of Prime Minister and Cabinet, was not favoured because of his foreign policy views. A second recommendation was put forward and accepted. A year later, the Defence position again became available and a new National Government accepted a recommendation that Gerald Hensley be appointed.

In its pre-1988 form, SSC was involved in day-to-day operational issues, administering job classification and appeal systems for the internal labour market of a lifetime career system. Reformers saw such systems as bureaucratic obstacles that impeded organisational performance.

The State Sector Act 1988 initiated a radical devolution of authority for the employment of staff to chief executives, leaving SSC as the employer of chief executives. Such devolution has had the effect of shifting SSC away from an operational focus to an almost exclusive focus on processes and strategy. During the early 1990s, under budget pressure, SSC stopped direct involvement in the delivery of training services, and finished publishing a magazine that sought to give a human face to the new look public service. With the removal of these functions, SSC became totally focused on the employment of chief executives and policy development, and was increasingly distanced from day-to-day operational details. Ulrich (1997) comments that the concept of making a transition from operational to strategic focus is too simplistic. 'In reality Human Resources professionals must fulfil both operational and strategic roles; they must be both police and partners; and they must take responsibility for both qualitative and quantitative goals over the short and long term' (Ulrich, 1997: 24). A risk of working on strategic issues in isolation is that effective strategy frequently emerges from operational details, and successful implementation depends on understanding such details.

SSC has also had to grapple with problems that arise from the nature of the human resources function. Human resources units have advisory roles, and are dependent for success on their ability to influence the actions of operational managers. Such units can accumulate a range of tasks declared too hard by other units, and become a home for unresolvable issues. They suffer from a problem named in a classic article as 'Big Hat, No Cattle' (Skinner, 1981), a Texan phrase used to describe a function with big responsibilities and many theories, but problems in proving achievement. SSC has indeed been given large responsibilities, such as the promotion of equal employment opportunities, public service ethics, introduction of a coordinated strategy for electronic government, investigation into varying standards of governance for Crown Agencies and reducing fragmentation in the delivery of public services by 'strengthening the centre'. In common with the human resources function in other large organisations, expectations of performance are considerable and diverse in nature. Its influence is often indirect, and results are difficult to measure and frequently long-term. The complications arising from such constraints were strongly evident in responses from interviewees.

Leader, partner or police officer? Problems of role definition

Interviewees were more critical about SSC than the Treasury or Audit Office, reflecting problems the Commission had during the 1990s creating its 'ecological niche' in the new NPM environment. Perceptions of the Commission's work are dominated by its hierarchical control of employment contracts and performance reviews of chief executives. This part of the SSC is clear but not necessarily welcomed, as indicated by a former CE, who commented that 'the only reason I gave Hunn (CE of SSC between 1987 and 1997) air time was that once a year he assessed my performance, otherwise there was nothing coming out of SSC that added any value'.

A statement agreed to by the survey group reflects age-old tensions between head office and operational functions:

SSC has failed to exercise leadership. Like other central agencies, it has people who don't know what it is like to be running a business so they ask inappropriate questions and basically clutter up the process of getting on with making a difference in the world.

More specifically, the survey group felt that *SSC has not been seen visibly to deal with good and poor performance in a fair but effective way.*

The tensions involved in finding an appropriate balance between control and empowerment, were strongly evident in interviewee responses. On the one hand, many interviewees sought stronger leadership, but on the other hand they resented 'interference' with their decentralised autonomy. This view was summarised by a corporate services manager, who thought departments and ministries were looking for central leadership and were frustrated about a lack of this. The manager saw SSC as a central agency in search of a role, lacking an overall vision, perhaps because of the need for the commissioner to focus on the appointment of chief executives to the detriment of everything else.

One CE thought SSC staff were insecure in their role. The CE experienced the agency as wanting to see everything and not trust work. 'We would run into trouble if we weren't constantly in touch.' For another CE, SSC was an 'experimental organisation', very fad dictated, always looking for a role, which meant it was potentially more intrusive than the Treasury.

Such criticisms would not have been news to the State Services Commissioner, Michael Wintringham, who identified a range of concerns after his appointment in 1997 (Wintringham, 2001a: 45–7, 49). These included:

- Reviews that used scarce resources to discover what happened after an event rather than add value for the future.
- Constant revisiting of the role and objectives of the Commission.
- Steadily increasing busyness, while still being surprised by real or perceived performance failures in public sector organisations.
- Multiple and often unconnected relationships between the Commission and departments, creating transaction costs which frustrated all involved.
- A balance sheet that precluded any comprehensive reinvestment in capital assets (an issue addressed in 1999).
- An unmanageable span of control for the Commissioner, which included direct relationships with 36 chief executives as well as eight reports internally, making for a job that was not able to be done.

The multiple roles expected of the Commission are evident in Mr Wintringham's description of the demands typically placed on it by stakeholders. It is a 'tripartite relationship' requiring a balancing of two requirements – being fair and honest with a chief executive and acting as an adviser to a minister who is having difficulty in a working relationship with that executive (Wintringham, 2001a: 5).

The tensions faced by SSC stem from expectations from Government and public servants that it be a leader, from public service organisations that it be a partner, and from politicians that it be a police officer. Such tensions guarantee a degree of unpopularity and an ambiguity of role. As summed up by one consultant, SSC has had a problem of knowing whether it exists to act as an advocate, as the 'head of the club', or to drive chief executives to achieve good performance. In the end the Commission has not wanted to upset relationships with chief executives, an understandable rationale, given the difficulty of finding good chief executives. The balancing act, according to a CE, is that the Commission provides real and effective protection for chief executives because political interference can not happen except at high risk to the interferer, a 'hugely comforting' feature of the system.

Holding chief executives accountable

Far from being 'permanent heads', chief executives under the new system have had strictly limited terms. For the core public service, tenure in the chief executive role has been limited to an initial contract of five years followed by renewal for a further three years. New Zealand is the only country in the Westminster tradition to place senior executives on fixed-term contracts (Halligan, 2001: 164). This system has been adhered to so closely that of 36 chief executives holding office at 1 April 1994, only two remained nine years later, in April 2003, with both serving as chief executives in other departments.[72] This result could either be interpreted as healthy turnover or a loss of institutional knowledge.

A system of results-oriented contracting, supposedly modelled on private sector practice, has taken on a life of its own, analogous to the development of Trobriand cricket (Hood, 1998b).[73] Hood suggests that contractualisation in New Zealand has been a reaction to the previous situation in which it was almost impossible to remove permanent heads. The creation of contracts, he suggests, may in practice make it harder to sack high profile public servants or move them to another role in the case of bad chemistry with a Cabinet Minister. By contrast, governments in Britain have long had the prerogative of removing departmental heads and, after an initial period, fixed-term contracts for heads of Next Step agencies[74] have been replaced by continuous contracts. A risk of fixed contracts, identified by Schick (1996), is that they can place a great deal of pressure on the State Services Commissioner to leave alone 'middling performers who may have done well enough for a full term but do not merit reappointment'.

---

72 The two chief executives were Chris Blake, Department of Internal Affairs (formerly CE of the National Library and before that the Ministry of Cultural Affairs) and Dr Russ Ballard, Land Information New Zealand (formerly CE of the Ministry of Agriculture and Fisheries) who retired in mid 2003.
73 The analogy refers to the introduction of cricket to the Trobriand Islands by Methodist missionaries in the early part of the twentieth century. The existing culture reshaped cricket, allowing it to be played by rival teams of any size. The umpire is the war magician of the side batting and he aims to put the evil eye on the bowlers. Teams come on with songs and war dances intended to intimidate the other side.
74 Next Steps agencies were established in Britain in 1988 to provide freedoms and accountabilities for managers in operational services.

In fact, no departmental head has had a contract terminated before expiry because of poor performance, but the contract of a chief executive of the Ministry of Youth Affairs was not renewed, and in at least three cases uneasy working relationships with Ministers were a contributing factor in early resignations. A high profile example was the resignation of the chief executive of the Department of Internal Affairs, in 1994, over a conflict with his Minister about a senior appointment of a former high-ranking air force member who had left the air force because of controversy about spending (Boston, 2001).

The only legally tested chief executive employment contract has been the much-publicised case taken by the chief executive of the Department of Work and Income, Christine Rankin, in 2001 and discussed in Chapter 5. The net result of the case was confirmation of the difficulties involved in removing a chief executive during a term, but also confirmation that limited term fixed contracts can be enforced.

Chief executives in the core public service are employed by the State Services Commissioner, but work for Ministers, an unusual employment relationship in that 'employed by' and 'works for' are not synonymous (Wintringham, 2001a: 5). As the employer, SSC has two major levers of control. The first is the use of the limited-term contracts. The second is annual feedback in the form of at-risk pay, amounting to up to 15 percent of total remuneration for a chief executive. Both are informed by annual performance reviews, in which a thermostat-like cycle of clarity, planning and feedback is brought together.

The hiring and firing power of the State Services Commission was either feared, resented or seen as a non-event by interviewees. One clear trend from interviews was the increased importance of the chief executive performance agreement since variable performance pay was increased to 15 percent in 1997. The effect of this pay for performance system has been, according to one CE, that 'you feel if you do a good job you will be rewarded', and in the words of another, it makes 'someone pass a judgement and determine how well you have performed. I like that sort of incentive.'

The main impact of the performance agreement appears to be on the completion of milestone tasks listed at the beginning of the year. There is some indication that this leads to goal displacement (Blau, 1963). Pre-specification of tasks provides a spur to their completion within the period covered by the performance agreement, if necessary at the expense of long hours put in by staff. But it also fosters a game of setting those targets and milestones at levels that cannot fail to be met, as indicated by the survey group's agreement with this statement:

The CE's performance bonus is an incentive to ensure that activities placed in the performance agreement will be achievable during the coming year.

The effect of such contractual milestones is that what is measured gets done, a planning manager observed. 'It's very clear to all of us what will be looked for at the end of the year. There is a focus on making sure you hit these spots.'

The role of SSC staff as judges of performance carries with it concerns about their skills, typified by a comment from a planning manager that too few have had sufficient experience of 'managing large and unruly organisations'. One corporate services manager decided to 'inundate' SSC with information because requirements were unclear. The following year, the manager commented, 'they told us a bit sheepishly' they weren't interested in so much information and would prefer a 'strategic conversation'.

The unmanageable size of the Commissioner's span of control, addressed in 2001 with the creation of Deputy Commissioner roles, was highlighted in this statement agreed by the survey group:

For chief executives, the State Services Commissioner is effectively an absentee employer, failing to get to know staff sufficiently to know their capabilities, strengths, deficiencies, weaknesses and problems.

Chief executive appointments as symbols

Choices made by SSC about whom to recommend as public service chief executives provide insights into the importance placed on applicants' system-wide managerial experience, as opposed to institution or profession-based expertise. Until the late 1980s, more than two thirds of departmental secretaries were internal appointments. In the 1990s, the percentage fell to under 40 percent (Boston, 2001). Between 1994 and mid-1998, only 3 of 27 appointments were made from within the department where the vacancy was occurring (SSC, 1998). Between 1994 and 1999, of chief executives surveyed by Boston, 37.5 percent had economics qualifications and a third had central agency experience. In early 1999, no fewer than nine departmental heads had served for significant periods in the Treasury, including the heads of important ministries such as the Department of Prime Minister and Cabinet, Ministry of Economic Development, Ministry of Education and the Department of Labour (Boston, 2001: 197).

Senior appointments provide a very visible form of control – providing staff of organisations with highly personalised messages about valued expertise and style. Since the 1990s, the distinct message of the control system embodied in chief executive appointments has been a favouring of outsiders with economics training and central agency experience. The economics-based, thermostat-like system of controls at the centre of the New Zealand model of management has created its own dynamic. The emphasis placed on formal reporting and contracting increases the value and importance of managerial leaders who have the skill and experience to respond to such demands. The reforms sought to avoid 'provider capture' by service delivery professions such as engineering, teaching or medicine. The techniques used have turned out to favour capture of important roles by people with training in economics, the discipline that has most strongly influenced design of the new system.

Changing the focus of SSC

Criticisms raised in interviews about the performance of SSC paralleled criticism the organisation itself has drawn on to prompt a process of change since late 2000.

The change sought is described in Wintringham (2001a) as an effort to shift focus from the characteristics in the left-hand column to those on the right:

FROM	TO
Backward looking	Forward looking
Process driven	Outcome driven
Performance review	Performance management
Compliance	Adding value
Capability	Performance
Departmental	System-wide
One size	Tailored

The Commission was restructured in late 2001 to create four Deputy Commissioner posts, with each supported by teams of about nine staff, focused on organisation portfolios. The new structure has been accompanied by a shift towards use of shorter and simplified accountability documents, bringing together purchase and performance agreements. It has also seen a change of focus for strategic plans, with the use of the term 'statement of intent' intended to put the emphasis on looking forward. These changes provide a comprehensive response to criticisms of the agency made by interviewees. The extent to which this new system can achieve a balance of the multiple roles expected of this central human resources unit merits follow-up research.

The accountability role of the Audit Office

The rise in the importance of Parliament as a result of MMP (discussed in Chapter 8) has led to an increase in the influence of the Office of the Auditor-General,[75] by far the largest and most powerful agency of Parliament.[76]

Alone among the accountability agencies reviewed in detail, in this research, the Audit Office emerged from interviews with considerably more praise than criticism. Whether interviewees were chief executives, divisional managers, corporate services managers or Members of Parliament, a similar picture emerged of a necessary, professional service, which seeks to assist as well as check. The most significant criticisms came interestingly from self-critical Audit staff, who were concerned about the meaningfulness of some of the information they were scrutinising. In similar vein, one CE thought that audit staff 'frequently get bogged down and can't see the wood for the trees'.

More typical comments from managers were:

'A healthy relationship that has helped us develop our controls' (corporate services manager).

'Our interaction with the auditor has always been constructive' (CE).

'We rely on them to give us a close going over. They have been very good in willingness to provide advice and support on internal audit systems' (CE).

---

75 Formerly known as the Controller and Auditor-General, the title was abbreviated to Auditor-General with the passing of the Public Audit Act 2001.
76 The other two agencies are the Office of the Ombudsman and the Parliamentary Commissioner for the Environment.

'A very good relationship actively managed, a professional, capable and pretty slick operation' (CE).

'Audit's role is a useful one – it always has been' (divisional manager).

Without exception, MPs placed considerable store on Audit advice as background for select committee reviews of estimates and performance reports, even if such advice was cast aside during the committee hearings in the pursuit of headline-creating political debate.

The acceptance given to the audit role results in an irony noted by a planning manager. Audit staff have become the only people who have a comprehensive picture of the entire government system – and they are 'working for the other side' – reporting to Parliament rather than executive Government. The Audit Office relies on information and publicity rather than executive power for its effectiveness. As the central agencies of executive Government have wrestled with the creation of effective new roles in a system of decentralised management, the Audit Office has gained in status and power. The audit function in the New Zealand public sector has achieved this accountability without creating the 'audit explosion' observed in Britain (Power, 1994; 1997). In Britain, the costs of regulating government have so increased in formality, complexity, intensity and specialisation that these activities are probably as large as the government regulation of the private sector (Hood et al, 1998). The dominance of central government, and minimal transfer of funds to local government in New Zealand, as well as the small scale of the country, has meant the experience of audit has been very different. Management strategies adopted by the Audit Office can also be seen to have played a major part in creating a system of audit which has achieved an unusually high level of acceptance compared with other elements of decentralised management.

Audit as effective accountability

The role of audit is well summarised in the following quote. 'Without audit, no accountability; without accountability, no control; and if there is no control, where is the seat of power?' (Mackenzie, 1966: vii).

Audit benefits from having a clear and widely accepted role as the public's watchdog. The outcome goal for the Audit Office is that 'Parliament and the public will be confident that public entities are

HONESTLY, YOU WOULDN'T READ ABOUT IT!... I SAID "ROVER, IT'S YOUR JOB TO SIT IN THERE AND GUARD THE FILLET STEAK!"

Garrick Tremain, *Otago Daily Times,* 23 November 1994

delivering what they have been asked to; have operated lawfully and honestly, and have not been wasteful; and have fairly reported their performance'.[77]

Decentralisation of managerial authority has enhanced the importance of this set of outcomes, just as it has meant ambiguity and conflicting aims for the central agencies of executive Government. In developing its role, the Audit Office has built on these natural advantages.

One major cause of the high standing of the audit role stems ironically from a 'learned vulnerability' (Wilson, 1989), which initially seemed like a disaster for the Audit Office and the public service in general. The resignation in 1994 and imprisonment in March 1997 of Jeff Chapman, the Controller and Auditor-General, placed a spotlight on the Audit Office.[78] The process of rebuilding took place under the management of

77 Website, Office of the Auditor-General, www.oag.govt.nz, accessed January 2002.
78 Mr Chapman was found guilty of 10 fraud charges totalling $54, 594 and sentenced to 18 months in prison.

an outsider to the public service, David Macdonald, who came from a background as a partner with a major international accounting firm, and held the office between 1994 and 2002.

In an informative critique, a 'peer review' by the Australasian Council of Auditors (Auditors-General, 2001) provides the Audit Office with an accountability document of its own.[79] The Auditor-General was found in this review to be highly regarded by MPs, with his 'integrity, credibility and authority' being without question. Central agencies also described the credibility as high, but expressed concern about questions and advice provided to select committees. Local government agencies were reported to value a positive approach aimed at bringing about improvement through communication and persuasion rather than 'clobbering' an authority. 'Audit does not kick you unless you are recalcitrant', was one reported comment.

Audit Office staff have played an active role in shaping and critiquing the New Zealand public management model. A 1978 report (Auditor-General, 1978) laid the groundwork for the financial management reforms of a decade later. Audit staff were involved in the development, by the New Zealand Society of Accountants, of standards for public sector reporting. More recently, the Audit Office has taken a lead in critiquing aspects of the New Zealand model. A report on the *Accountability of Executive Government to Parliament* (Auditor-General, 1999) concluded that non-financial performance information could be significantly improved, and that Parliament should receive much better information about the Government's desired outcomes and the extent to which these are being achieved. The Treasury-originated distinction between purchase and ownership was seen to create distortions, failing to make clear the likely impact of expenditure on issues such as capability. The report proposed as an alternative, the creation of an explicit statement of reasons for the Crown's ownership of an organisation and categorisation of Government spending under the headings of current and capability expenditure. Current spending would be for day-to-day business and capability expenditure for that needed to establish or extend an agency's ability to produce outputs.

79 The review was carried out during a period of three weeks by senior representatives from Audit Offices in state government and the federal government in Australia as part of a professional quality assurance programme.

One of the reasons the Audit Office has enjoyed an uncontroversial role is that it has kept to a 'narrow product line' (Barzelay, 1996: 33), compared with other countries, putting its accountability focus strongly on the auditing of information – both financial and performance indicators.

This emphasis came from a strategic decision in 1993, to move away from 'Value for Money' auditing (Pallot, 1999). Experience in New Zealand and elsewhere had shown the difficulties faced by a legislative auditor in commenting on value for money. The auditor would tread a fine line between commenting on the standard of implementation of policy and on the quality of politically developed policy itself. Audits would be used for point scoring and limited budgets made it difficult to cover more than a half dozen audits per year. The Audit Office decided to step back from an evaluative role to the less controversial role of information assurance although it has continued to undertake special investigations and in 2003 is expanding its emphasis on evaluation.

The narrow focus enabled the Audit Office to concentrate its efforts, but it has also meant a sometimes formulaic approach to indicators about quantity, quality, timeliness and cost, which has encouraged or forced reporting entities to develop information about the easily measurable rather than necessarily capturing what is most important. Repeatedly, interviewees remarked that what gets reported is that which can be easily justified to an auditor, not necessarily what is most important. Audit staff interviewed were very aware of the limitations of such information and have been active in pushing for more outcome-related information.

The limitations of checking indicators were well described by one auditor who stated, 'we don't audit the performance per se. We audit the information presented by the department'. Auditing consists of sampling the output of the systems and checking that systems are in place to provide the accuracy claimed.

Perhaps the most powerful single form of accountability the Audit Office provides is a subjective rating about the quality of management. Select committee MPs and chief executives view this assessment very seriously. Averages for organisations are provided in the Office's reports, and ratings can potentially be discovered through Official Information Act 1982 enquiries. The pressure for organisations is to avoid a rating of 'unsatisfactory' – a warning signal that guarantees close scrutiny from a select committee. The problem, one auditor observed, is a reluctance by the Office to use the 'unsatisfactory' column and to tolerate mediocre performance as 'satisfactory'. The ratings are also biased against larger organisations where things can go wrong more easily than in small ministries. The bigger and more diverse a department, the harder it is to achieve a 'very satisfactory' rating.

Managed competition

An additional reason for positive perceptions of Audit Office performance is undoubtedly the use of managed competition to guard against the tensions inevitable in monopoly relationships such as those operated by the Treasury and SSC. Since 1992, the audit role has been structurally divided into a small policy office, the Office of the Auditor-General and a larger operational audit department, Audit New Zealand. The Office of the Auditor-General, with a staff of 50, manages the letting of contracts for auditing 3800 publicly owned bodies, including 2600 schools, and local government. Audit Office staff who advise select committees have been specially chosen for experience in a range of public service roles, and come from a range of occupational disciplines.

In contrast, Audit New Zealand, with 220 staff at 10 locations, is dominated by the accounting discipline. The effects of the contestability process are evident in the staffing of Audit New Zealand, down about 80, or nearly a quarter, since the introduction of the tender process. Assessed on hours worked, Audit New Zealand carries out about 60 percent of the total audits of publicly owned bodies, with the private sector carrying out most school audits. So far 35 percent of the non-school entities have been tendered on the open market, and with this work Audit New Zealand has been successful in 46 percent of cases (Auditors-General, 2001: 29–32).

The first four tender rounds, between 1992 and 1994, were found to have resulted in a lowering of audit fees of between 12 and 25 percent, with clients being almost uniformly positive in their responses, and commenting in particular on the improvement of Audit New Zealand's performance (McDonald and Anderson, 1997).

The organisational split has made it possible for the Auditor-General to work with the contrasting and potentially conflicting demands of audit clients and select committees. Public sector entities pay for audits from their budgets, and the advent of managed competition has enabled them to keep costs down, while also having leverage to gain client service. Major government departments that have opted to move to private sector auditors include the Ministry of Education, Land Information, and Police. Those who have stayed with Audit New Zealand report a relationship changed for the better as a result of competition. For instance, a corporate services manager found that the prospect of competition had contributed to a lower audit fee. The service provided was professional, and backed by knowledge of the practical and important accounting issues of the public sector.

Through keeping an internal capability to deliver audit services, the Audit Office has a continued capability as a smart buyer, able to define what it wants to buy, to know how to get it, and to be able to recognise and judge what it has bought (Kettl, 1993: viii), something it might lose if all work was contracted.

Legislative change and enlarged role

The Public Audit Act that came into effect on 1 July 2001, established the Auditor-General and Deputy Auditor-General as officers of Parliament, appointed on the recommendation of the House of Representatives and accountable directly to the House, not the Crown as had been the case. The right of the Auditor-General to carry out 'effectiveness and efficiency' audits was extended to cover all public entities, including research institutes and health boards, previously omitted. The authority to undertake inquiries was formalised and strengthened, with the emphasis on systemic issues rather than complaints about administrative decisions that are handled by the Ombudsman (Buchanan and Simpkins, 2001).

Conclusion

Money, chief executive contracts and provable information are the different power bases for the three major central accountability agencies. The role of the Audit Office is unquestionably the most straightforward, particularly given the Office's decision to minimise its involvement in the politically charged arena of evaluating value for money. The Audit Office provides a check on the quality of information, but in so doing limits the flow of self-reported information to that which is most easily measured and proved. The Treasury has been able to fall back on fiscal restraint as an easily identified and policed symbol of achievement. SSC has had the most difficult of the three roles as the manager of chief executive employment contracts, and as an agency with a wide-ranging and often nebulous brief. It also has considerably fewer resources than the other two agencies once payments to CEs are removed from the total.[80]

Common to all three is the limitation that self-reported information is the primary basis for accountability. The Audit Office's use of peer review suggests a possible alternative. Such in-depth analysis, with its focus on practical suggestions for future performance, provides an illuminating contrast to what interviewees' comments portray as a rather arid game of accountability, and control, based on annual, formula-driven reporting.

Central agencies are at the centre of a vast range of reported information, but outside the relatively narrow confines of financial management and chief executive contracts, they are relatively limited in what they can do to control the decentralised system. The accountability systems have a narrow focus, based on transparent, auditable information, generated through planning and budget cycles. These control techniques, supplemented by the relational distance favoured by the NPM concern about provider capture, have diminished the extent to which government has been able to operate as a collective entity.

The system of public management created in the late 1980s placed particular store on achieving results through focused public sector organisations, prompted to act by the threat or reality of competitive pressures. In a swing of the pendulum, the coordination problems that arise predictably from such focus and independent action have led to new interest in a stronger centre, without returning to a unified, bureaucratic structure.

A report examining the role of the centre (Advisory Group, 2001) is discussed in more detail in Chapter 10. This report has foreshadowed a move towards a different form of central agency control. After more than a decade of arms-length control based largely on finances and

---

80 Estimated expenditure for 2003–04 was: Treasury: $71million (including $14 million for non-departmental purposes), Audit: $44.5 million, State Services Commission: $44.3 million (including $11.3 million for salaries of public service chief executives).

measures, a new value is being placed on the more intangible, but potentially powerful, cultural controls of expectations, standards and relationship building.

For the Audit Office, this change in emphasis is likely to have little impact. But for the other central agencies, it means rethinking the identities established during an era of arms-length contracting. For both the Treasury and SSC, this is an era for redefining relationships and learning new games of control.

CHAPTER 10

Efficiency and effectiveness –
the Holy Grail of public management

'The Second Law [of thermodynamics] is one piece of technical bad news from science that has established itself firmly in the non-scientific culture. Everything tends towards disorder . . . Perfect efficiency is impossible. The universe is a one-way street.' (Gleick, 1987: 307–8)

Freedom to manage, clarity of objectives, quality information and proper accountability provide the means. The end purpose is effective services, specified in preset targets. The management role is to assemble efficiently the resources needed to deliver effectiveness.

Efficiency and effectiveness are elusive and constantly shifting ideals of public management, abstractions that drive a modern equivalent of the quest for the Holy Grail.[81] Management efficiency is the measure of the ratio of inputs to outputs (Downs and Larkey, 1986: 6). Efficiency is said to increase if more outputs can be delivered for the same level of inputs, or fewer inputs are needed to deliver the same level of outputs. But efficiency is an instrumental value that always requires a follow up question of 'efficiency for what' (Goodin and Wilenski, 1984). The 'what' is an effectiveness question, which is equally problematic given that different constituencies can be expected to have different criteria for effectiveness (Kanter and Summers, 1987: 228). Ultimately, power affects the definition of effectiveness (Perrow, 1977: 101).

Democratic governance means that definitions of effectiveness are periodically re-examined. Rather than an end state, effectiveness is better

---

81 The Holy Grail was the object of the legendary quest of King Arthur's knights. The grail was a wide-mouthed vessel, which in different versions of the legend was either the cup used by Christ at the Last Supper, or used to catch blood from Christ's wounds as he hung on the Cross. (Source: *The New Encyclopaedia Britannica*, fifteenth edition, 1988, Vol. 5, University of Chicago Press.)

viewed as the progress of a pendulum that emphasises different values at different periods. As the pendulum swings, different doctrines of administration move in and out of favour (Hood and Jackson, 1991).

New Public Management (NPM) doctrines examined in this thesis place a premium on efficiency and economy, seeking to emulate the self-regulating, thermostat-like properties of the marketplace. They focus strongly on means – using market analogies to emphasise increased delivery of outputs for the same costs, and customer or client satisfaction as indicators of effectiveness. A single-minded focus on efficiency has simplified the managerial task, but has sat uneasily alongside a fundamental challenge of work in the 'public domain', which is to accommodate and reconcile the 'necessary diversity of interests within society' (Ranson and Stewart, 1994: 5).

Managerial efficiency and political effectiveness do not necessarily coincide, as the survey group noted in this statement:

Departments are still not rewarded for being efficient. For example, Police and Health are still rewarded for political clout rather than proven efficiency or effectiveness.

Public sector focus on efficiency issues has created a number of benefits, but also costs, in the experience of interviewees. This chapter summarises interviewees' perceptions about these benefits and costs and explores the ingredients of a pendulum swing that is emerging as a result of political change and public service frustration with the solutions of the late 1980s.

Benefits of reform

Freedom to manage and fiscal control are the two major achievements of the New Zealand public management model. Understandably, the public service interviewees in this study valued the freedom to employ staff and to vary the mix of resources more than they valued fiscal constraint. Those in the survey group compared themselves with counterparts in other countries in this way:

The benefits of the reforms of the late 1980s have been enormous, compared with the bureaucratic and unresponsive systems still commonplace in other governments.

Tom Scott, *Evening Post,* 20 August 1997

The public service is now a 'magnificent machine' compared with that of 15 years ago, one CE argued. New Zealand public managers are much more focused on management issues and sources of funding than counterparts in larger, more specialised and bureaucratised organisations elsewhere in the world, a policy manager thought. The emphasis on efficiency has not been at the expense of equity, one consultant, formerly a central agency official, argued. Emphasis was now placed on where money was allocated, with an increasing use of targeting, rather than a universal approach.

The use of accrual accounting, the language of business, has made it easier for MPs to create what one manager described as a 'very real heat of accountability'. As one MP explained, having the same accounting language for private and public sectors, makes it much easier for MPs to understand and use government financial information. As a consultant pointed out, the system forces managers to think about their assets, where money is tied up and what liabilities they have responsibility for. This is a substantial change from the prereform situation, described by an audit manager as one where the typical public manager 'simply didn't understand money at all'. The reforms had confronted managers with the need to manage finances and now the financial skills of public managers are at least as good as those of private sector counterparts.

Accrual accounting may even be costing less than the old systems for cash accounting, if the experience of a finance manager is a guide. A decade previously the manager's unit had about 250 people devoted largely to 'a lot of processing and producing low quality information'. Now with 37 people, the unit was producing better, cheaper information, presented in the same format as private sector accounting and useful for business support, analysis and advisory work. This is an area in which reform has been assisted by the pace of computerisation over the same period.

Of the three E's of the public sector quest for efficiency, effectiveness and economy, efficiency and effectiveness are constantly debated, but there is no doubting the model's performance in terms of economy. The pressing issue of the 1980s had been persistent budget deficits that steadily increased government indebtedness. The 'electric fence' created by contract budgeting, coupled with employment consequences for chief executives in the event of overspending, has put a limit on state spending, and enabled repayment of debt during the 1990s. Budget surpluses have been achieved in every year since 1993–94. Government spending as a proportion of Gross Domestic Product has fallen from 36 percent in 1995–96 to an estimated actual for 2001–02 of 32.5 percent.[82] An economy drive of this magnitude has inevitable costs, as described in the next section.

Costs of reform

The major costs of NPM reforms are effectively the opposites of the major benefits. Managerial freedoms have led to concerns about fragmentation of service delivery, while fiscal control has created concerns about the future capability of public service organisations.

The effects of fiscal control were uppermost in the minds of those in the survey group, who agreed with the following statements.

Public organisations have been run down during the past decade – with only disasters creating the climate in which resources are reviewed.

82 Source: Pre-election Economic and Fiscal Outlook updates for 1996 and 2002, the Treasury website http://www.treasury.govt.nz/forecasts/archive.asp, accessed 24 July 2002.

There are now few people without grey hair who will proudly say that their occupation is that of 'public servant'. The significance and status given to the role has been eroded during the 1990s.

Chief executives had merely responded to the incentives they faced during the past 10 years, a consultant suggested. Ministers had wanted more output for the same budgets, and pressures for financial performance from the Treasury had not been counterbalanced because the State Service Commission's monitoring system had been 'weak' in comparison. As a result, chief executives found it easiest to cut back on areas of discretion, such as research and development, staff training, and computer upgrades rather than mandatory outputs.

As Schick (1996) observed, the concept that Ministers have separate purchase and ownership interests has encouraged Cabinet Ministers to focus on outputs rather than institutional health, resulting in a relative disinterest in long-term capability described by one policy manager:

'Where are the Ministers that ask how much are you putting into staff development; how many have had what sort of training and development opportunities over the last 12 months, do you have a career development programme, a programme for identifying the managers of tomorrow? What are you doing to ensure your organisation is in touch with best practice? What investments are you making in organisational redesign or review. What sort of investment are you making into strategic research?'

An overriding impression from interviewees during 2000 and 2001 was that of a system based on an intellectual agenda that had run its course. As one auditor put it, the New Zealand revolution came to a 'grinding halt' in the mid-1990s, after reformers at the Treasury left. It had run out of steam and was 'running up and down on the same spot'. The auditor observed the irony of a decentralised system is that it requires a central agency to show leadership and pick up the model 'by the scruff of the neck and provide direction'.

NPM ideas have followed a path from revolutionary status to that of a new orthodoxy, creating a series of frustrations that have contributed towards pressure for a pendulum swing of ideas, described later in this chapter. Dissatisfaction expressed by interviewees is summarised under the following headings, focusing on issues of compliance, fragmentation and distrust.

A compliance industry?

Many interviewees expressed concern that control routines merely foster minimum compliance, not efficiency or effectiveness. For some, the reporting systems were a burden, distracting from what they considered to be 'real work'. For others they were a relative non-event, largely deflected by corporate office staff. Compliance costs may indeed be no greater than those expected in the head office or regional office of a private sector organisation, a central agency analyst thought. The one exception was in the auditing of qualitative indicators. Private sector organisations were more likely to use fundamental indicators such as customers walking away.

The system has been captured by accountants, according to an auditor. As a result, reports focus on what accountants could count and measure while 'softer' issues get lost in the numbers. As one divisional manager commented, formal reports contained items 'you have real confidence about being able to measure' but may not reflect the softer issues which the organisation most needs to worry about. The result of such reporting is what one MP described as 'pretty cold and lifeless' documents.

For another MP, the real disadvantage of an accounting-dominated system was the measuring of activities in short blocks rather than a focus on bigger questions. Chief executives had become much more focused on immediacy than the long-term viability of their organisations. They were thinking about performance within a timeline, something to achieve quickly to be able to move on to the next rung of the ladder to success.

Corporate services and planning managers were particularly aware of their roles as go-betweens. They had to satisfy external requirements while avoiding aggravating staff of their own organisations with too many requests for information. As one manager put it, the internal job was partly to convince other managers that 'we haven't dreamt all this up' and partly to assist field staff by tidying up their reports.

Such activity did have value in providing public servants with cover for political scrutiny, a central agency manager suggested. The reporting provided cover in the event of scrutiny by select committees, and a paper trail in readiness for a 'tick the box' approach from the Audit Office. Because 'politics is about scoring points, not about achieving results' governments and public servants needed formal systems that provided them with such cover.

The overriding impression from interviewees was of a set of control routines that have become highly mechanistic as opposed to organic (Burns and Stalker, 1961). They emphasise mechanistic features such as structures, accountability, and depersonalised, quantitative information. 'Organic' features such as processes, responsibility, and the use of qualitative and personalised information are underemphasised.

Fragmentation of services

The principles of clarity and accountability have their counterpart in the consequence of fragmentation. By sharpening the focus of individual managers, the control systems have also narrowed the nature of the work, creating focus at the expense of coordination.

Interviewees varied considerably in their views about whether functional units of the public sectors had become 'silos' which resulted in fragmented services and a lack of communication between organisations. Within a small public service in a small capital city, the barriers to cooperation are reduced by many informal links. The survey group was more concerned about political than administrative silos, as shown in this agreed statement:

The extent to which a silo mentality exists among departments has little or nothing to do with the management framework. It stems mostly from the degree of cooperation that Ministers want.

The issue of collaboration was linked directly to what politicians wanted, a CE thought. The 1984–90 Labour Government had not wanted cooperation. The National Government (1990–96) and National–New Zealand First Government (1996–99) had wanted cooperation and some relearning was needed. Chief executives had taken advantage of a ministerial team approach adopted in the late 1990s. The lesson was that if the boss wanted cooperation, it would happen.

Significant change was on the horizon, according to the survey group in this agreed statement:

Electronic developments mean that old silo departmental structures will be irrelevant within 10 years. We need to move to a much more organic structure which will operate almost like a consulting firm, in which policy advisers with different competencies work on different projects. There is a need for a matrix approach similar to that in research organisations.

As a corporate services manager observed, trends in information technology are pushing government organisations towards a central-ised direction on issues such as technology and purchasing. To make the most of the size and purchasing power of the sector, agreements on security and common standards were needed. High profile mistakes with systems in individual organisations accentuate the cost to Government as a whole of insufficient knowledge about technology issues. The estab-lishment of an 'E-Government' unit of the State Services Commission since 2000 has provided a major push in the direction of common approaches.

Despite technological change in the direction of cooperation, the logic of the structures and routines of the control systems works 'insidiously against collaboration', according to a planning manager. Institutional boundaries invariably do not line up with longer-term problems for governments, and the default position for Ministers and officials is to retreat to original boundaries, to be accountable solely for what is in performance agreements. 'There are always good reasons for doing nothing,' the manager argued. For one MP, the result of managers pursuing their individual goals was an 'awful lot of hanging on to your own territory' rather than operating in a problem-solving way, seeking to integrate services.

It is almost a disincentive to tie oneself into another department's work programme, a corporate services manager thought. While there were big areas where departments should be working collaboratively, there wasn't much evidence of this occurring. 'Maybe it's just a capacity thing that no one has the time to talk to other organisations any more.' Unless a cabinet committee was established and seen to be driving cooperation, things didn't change.

The use of competition as a method for spurring on performance has been a major factor in the creation of silos, a middle manager commented. The result of competition had been organisations in similar lines of work competing for budget allocations and putting their hands firmly around what they obtained. While technology sharing could make real sense in terms of the wider public sector interest it was in practice very difficult to organise.

One area of successful cross-boundary work had been programmes for biodiversity and the oceans, but this was seen as rare, a central agency analyst commented. Generally there was no feedback from one territory to another. Innovation was discouraged because invariably it involved someone else's business.

A policy manager thought the tendency to create silos has created a perception among the public and politicians of an uncoordinated and unresponsive public service. One of the causes was the number of organisations involved, with the transport area providing a striking example. The large number of small agencies in this sector led to 'small groups of policy people who weren't thinking broadly enough'.

The Public Finance Act 1989 should be loosened to allow multi-agency arrangements, a CE advocated. Such funding could probably provide a glue to counter the fragmenting of services, the CE commented.

As a system for reflection and the creation of learning, the New Zealand model was something of a 'dumb system', a planning manager believed. There was no sense of systematic learning in the way that a multi-national enterprise of similar or greater size might go about this. There were plenty of multi-national companies able to share learning between their global branches, yet the public service, all based in the one town, wasn't able to. For example a planners' network had failed for lack of anyone being prepared to put time into basic administration. Such learning was 'low hanging fruit' for performance improvement, but was not being tackled effectively the planning manager said.

For a minority of interviewees, silos were a myth. For one CE, they had been a feature of the early years following the decentralisation of public service organisations, which probably peaked in the early 1990s. It still occurred to some extent when new chief executives sought to ride their boundaries to establish their turf and independence. It did not take long for them to realise that to achieve what they wanted to achieve and to make themselves look good they often had to rely quite strongly on working in with other agencies in building good cooperative relationships.

A more significant problem with the creation of silos probably lay at the level of middle managers who could feel threatened if their upward mobility was coming to an end, and worry that their territory might be dispersed and given to others as a result of collaboration and project teams across organisations.

Another CE thought interagency cooperation was of much greater quality than in the previous system and comments about silos were clichés. There were fewer 'stupid bureaucratic games'.

A low trust environment?

Trust has been a significant casualty of systems designed to counter 'provider capture' by using competition as a method of control, and creating distance between principals and agents. The issue of trust emerged strongly in interviews, particularly in relation to the quality of information that flows between organisations, as described in Chapter 7. This issue emerged most explicitly in an interview with a planning manager whose comments are quoted below.

'In a public service where you have deliberately set out to fragment and distribute we shouldn't be surprised we have lost some of the trust and sense of mutual endeavour which is essential if you are to deliver on large issues which require joined up organisational effort.'

'The system at present is like having some muscles which are too well developed. . . . Strategically you won't get people taking risks unless there's greater trust and give and take.'

'It was little surprise that a system predicated on low trust had produced this type of performance. Fairly high trust was required if people were to commit themselves to risky targets and be honest about achievements. The environment from the late 1980s and 1990s was quite low trust. As a result there was particular emphasis on instruments of specification and measurement. But inevitably a lot of what government does is ambiguous, complex and hard to establish causal relationships for. Almost by definition the things you are going to commit to in monitoring are relatively trivial or accidental rather than essential.'

'We have a lot of the artefacts and instruments but we don't really have that soul. We haven't exploited anything like the potential. That requires leadership. . . . An awful lot has been achieved on the fiscal picture, but we don't have a high performing system.'

Incentives and sanctions

In NPM thinking, incentives and sanctions are a major means for directing managers towards the pursuit of efficiency and effectiveness. Incentives matter, the Treasury (1987: 2) states early in its prescriptions for redesign of the state sector. 'People will pursue their own ends, and their own interests.' While 'many people act altruistically for much of the time, . . . if even only a relative few act opportunistically all the time,

and most act so occasionally, then the problem [of self-interest] remains'
The Treasury, 1987:2).

This economics-based view of human nature emphasises external or
extrinsic motivators, while social scientists (eg Maslow, 1954; Herzberg,
Mausner, and Snyderman, 1959; McGregor, 1960; Amabile, 1983) place
more emphasis on internal or intrinsic motivators. Economists tend to
see incentives as a solution, while social scientists see external incentives
as a potential source of problems (Kohn, 1993).

For interviewees, the extrinsic incentives of the New Zealand public
management model appear to be limited to bonuses of up to 15 percent
of total remuneration for chief executives. For some this was an important
form of recognition, and in one of the case studies in particular,
achievement of results linked to the chief executive's bonus were
particularly strong drivers for the completion of tasks.

Otherwise, in financial terms, the system points only in the direction
of fiscal control. As described by one CE: 'if you overspend, it's a hanging
offence; if you deliver outputs at less cost, tough luck – the funds will be
taken away'. The incentive is to spend up to the appropriation limit,
using end of year adjustments to achieve a perfect match of actual
spending with the budget. As a central agency manager commented, in
the public sector it is rare to be able to spell out expectations and provide
private sector style rewards or promotion for making money. Linear
relationships between causes and effects were hard to identify. This
manager concluded, in the light of experience, that thinking from the
late 1980s about the design of incentives was 'very naïve'.

The real incentives lie in the work itself, encapsulated in this statement
from the survey group:

*The most appealing features of public sector work are challenging jobs with
the ability to paint on a broad scale, make things happen and have a big
impact on New Zealand.*

People want to know that their job is 'actually valuable', in creating,
enhancing, protecting or preserving value in public sector organisations,
a central agency manager commented. The freedom to achieve is an
important motivator. One CE spoke for many managers in commenting
that the extent to which Ministers were willing not to intervene provided
a motivator for achieving high quality work.

The issue of whether public management involves a special form of motivation has been much debated (eg Perry and Wise, 1990; DiLulio, 1994; Le Grand, 1997; Wright, 2001). A survey of senior public servants in New Zealand by Norman and McMillan (1997) concluded that for this group, 'variety and challenge' is a primary incentive. Goodman (1999), in surveying New Zealand chief executives, concluded that this group places a primary value on 'the ability to get things done'. Denhardt (1992) provides a useful way of thinking about the major driving force for public service work, in using the phrase 'pursuit of significance' to summarise the motivation of well-respected public managers who were the subjects for his study.

The maintenance of such motivation in the public sector environment requires considerable personal determination. The fear of losing reputation is undoubtedly a driving force for achievement. As one CE commented, the fear of damaging personal credibility or failing to meet expectations runs alongside a strong interest in the subject and pride in the work. 'I'm not someone who is ever motivated by having an agreement that has 15 tasks in it with deadlines associated.'

The harshness of the environment emerged in a comment from an experienced CE, who noted that only three of 11 Ministers the chief executive had worked with had provided positive feedback. They were more likely to 'come down on you' if something went slightly wrong. 'It would be nice occasionally to be told that you have done something well.'

Perceptions about the harshness of the environment had the following effect, the survey group concluded:

Senior managers observe the pressures placed on chief executives – particularly the pressures to report and conform at the risk of getting 'beaten up' by central agencies or the media. They have increasingly decided the chief executive role is not one to aspire to.

A new orthodoxy under challenge

In retrospect, the 2000–01 period, during which the 91 interviews for this study were conducted, might be seen as a high-water mark for the tide of reform unleashed in the late 1980s. This was a period of considerable unease among senior public servants about their working relationship with a new government, the first in 15 years to move clearly away from a 'new right' agenda summarised by Lane (1997b: 1) as 'deregulation, privatisation and marketisation'. The early result was, as James (2001) observed, that more work was done in Ministers' offices, and senior public servants were listened to less. Venter (2000) observed that the Treasury had a 'formal and ritualistic' relationship with the Minister of Finance, Michael Cullen, as a price for 'not recognising that Labour is serious about changing direction and for continuing to ply Ministers with advice based on the policy settings of the last government'.

The incoming Minister of State Services, Trevor Mallard (Mallard, 2000), spoke of a public perception of a 'culture of waste and extravagance' and argued that public agencies needed to be 'more transparent and accountable than those in the private sector' because it was using the public's money. 'Yet public administration has become dominated by a fragmentation into stand-alone administrative units and a contractualist output model for determining what those units do and how they get paid for what they do' (Mallard, 2000).

The difficulties of the new political/public service relationship were reflected in the keen interest that interviewees took in the issue of control. Alongside the change in political dynamics, there was also a considerable questioning similar to that of the auditor earlier in this chapter, who considered the systems of the late 1980s had 'run out of steam'. During the second half of the 1990s, views about the systems from public servants and academics had become increasingly critical. Problems of the accretion of controls and the ritualised formality of planning processes were identified by SSC in a series of working papers (eg SSC, 1998, 1999a, 1999b, 1999c). The State Services Commissioner, Michael Wintringham, expressed his frustration with the effects of reform in this way:

'I find it extraordinary that we have, for so long, clung to a belief that a decentralised system, with wide autonomy, different standards and approaches applying across 38 departments, with minimum rewards and sanctions, with a focus on annual delivery at the expense of long run investment generally, will deliver people with strong, shared values, with a keen sense of belonging to the Public Service and with the skills and attributes needed to lead the Public Service for another decade. I don't think it makes sense' (Wintringham, 2001b).

In his annual report for 2000–01 (Wintringham, 2001a), Mr Wintringham questioned the results of two central features of the NPM reforms. First, the separation of policy and delivery roles appeared to have 'an initial beneficial impact on both the policy function and on service delivery. But over time the separation may well create a situation where a reversal of the separation seems desirable' (Wintringham 2001a: 16). The emphasis on policy appeared to have created a degree of intellectual snobbery whereby 'policy' is viewed as more worthy than 'operations' (ibid, 20). An indicator lay in the overwhelming number of more highly paid managers who worked in Wellington rather than in the regions. Of 789 public servant managers earning over $80,000, 86 percent were in the capital, in predominately head office roles.

The development of a pendulum swing in thinking about NPM doctrines can be traced to debate initiated by a review commissioned in the mid-1990s by the Treasury and SSC and completed by Professor Allen Schick, a budgeting specialist from the University of Maryland.

In this review, Schick (1996) balanced praise with critique. He applauded achievements of the reporting system, but warned that transforming public management would entail much more than changing organisational forms and appropriation formats. Giving managers the freedom to manage would not mean that all would seize the opportunity and boldly revamp operations. The all-important factor in public sector reform is the behaviour of those in charge of government programmes and resources.

Schick was particularly critical of the distinction made between purchase and ownership. The concept that Ministers were purchasers in a marketplace ran the risk of establishing strong boundaries between Ministers and the public service. It also created the risk that, separated from departmental resources, most Ministers would become weak policy makers, despite their nominal control of appropriated funds and their contracting powers. It misinterpreted the extent to which Ministers could and should be interested in institution building as well as purchasing services.

Schick (1998) later extended his criticism about the contracting base of the New Zealand model, advising that developing countries should first strengthen rule-based government and pave the way for robust markets before creating market-like public service structures. A problem with contracts between public entities is that a government has weak redress when its own organisations fail to perform, and it might be subject to as much capture in negotiating and enforcing its contracts as it was under pre-reform management.

By 2001, Schick had concluded that New Zealand was an outlier in public sector reform, which had attracted more 'fascination than emulation'. Other developed countries had not adopted the 'magnificent conceptual architecture' in which outputs played a central role. Ministers had become frustrated by a system that focused on operations, while they wanted a dialogue that dealt with allocation. 'While managers focus on the minutiae of internal operations, ministers are interested in how to use their authority and resources to shape New Zealand's future' (Schick, 2001a: 5).

The NPM model had also been the subject of critique by New Zealand academics. For Gregory (1995) a central shortcoming of the model has been its 'production' orientation, which distorts information about not easily measured tasks. In Stace and Norman (1997) a group of managers identified financial reforms as a success but were highly critical of the human costs involved. Goldfinch (1998) questioned whether the benefits of reform had been oversold.

There has been a distinct change in literature in the late 1990s, with its critical focus based on experience, compared with the high expectations raised by advocates of reform in the late 1980s and early 1990s.

By the late 1990s, experience with reporting systems and reactions from parliamentary select committees had prompted the Audit Office (Auditor-General, 1999) to call for change to the ownership/purchase model. This model assumed a simple relationship between the purchase interest and output prices, and between the ownership interest and the value of balance sheet assets that did not exist in reality. It meant that issues that were less easy to measure in monetary terms, such as capability, were being neglected (ibid, 37). The Audit Office proposed that appropriations be classified differently, with funds provided for current and capability expenditure. Current spending would include outputs, transfer payments and debt servicing, while capability expenditure would focus on establishing or extending an agency's ability to produce outputs.

A review of evaluations about the reforms (Petrie and Webber, 1999) concluded that strengths of the model included more efficient production of outputs; a more responsive and innovative public sector delivering

model creates a distance between politicians and public servants which makes for a formalised interaction between the two groups. It presumes that Ministers can and will specify their requirements for public servants and other contractors. The reality, as Chapter 8 demonstrated, is that Cabinet Ministers are usually little interested in being purchasers of outputs, but want the capability to achieve political agendas. At the extreme, the contracting method reduces interaction to a formal, legally mediated exchange rather than an opportunity for learning from experience.

Having been redefined as purchasers, rather than carrying responsibility for their departments, Ministers have adopted more distant relationships with officials. Depending on one's viewpoint, the result is either a beneficial reduction of capture of politicians by advisers, or a barrier to interaction and flexible responses to changing circumstances.

The opportunity to use interactive controls for reshaping strategy is also restricted by the separation of policy and delivery roles. Structural separation reduces the opportunity for interaction between those who create policy and those who directly deliver service. The status and rewards for capital city policy and management roles appear to have grown substantially as discussed in Chapter 10 (Wintringham, 2001a: 20), but it is service delivery staff who retain the rounded insights that come from tacit knowledge about their work. Separating policy and operations places considerable store on rational goal setting and analysis as a contrast to the 'science of muddling through' (Lindblom, 1959). But this separation removes opportunities for learning from action, a process described by Behn (1991: 127–50) as 'management by groping along'. Groping along involves developing policy and strategy through constant interaction with clients and the environment, and building over time through the achievement of a succession of small wins. Strategy emerges from a 'bias for action' (Peters and Waterman, 1982) in which managers learn from action through the sequence of 'ready, fire, aim'. The aim gradually improves as a result of interaction with the environment. By contrast, policy analysis distanced from action runs the risk of following a sequence of 'ready, aim, aim', in which policy is sheltered from reality checks.

The rational goal assumptions of NPM, with particular emphasis on strategic planning and prespecification of results, make it difficult to either muddle or grope along and learn from the process of interaction.

Effective learning comes from being able to reflect and retry – to keep edging forward and modify responses through trial and error. The structural separation of policy and delivery forces both parties to rely on the more static processes of formal documents which use contractual language to spell out relationships. It narrows learning to a single-loop of pre-specified results checked through thermostat controls.

Balancing the paradoxes of control

Simons' four-sided model of control (Simons, 1995: 2000) provides a visual statement of the importance of balancing opposing forces when implementing strategy. The dark 'yin' of control coexists with the light 'yang' of empowerment to form a coherent whole. Diagnostics and boundary systems provide fact or rule-based limits as a counter to initiatives driven by the more person-based dynamics of beliefs or interaction. Controls are means that gain full meaning only when accompanied by a focus on ends that flow from beliefs or interaction.

The New Zealand public sector model of control has been unbalanced in its emphasis on diagnostics. To a large extent, this reflects the emphasis given to financial information and cost cutting in the development of the controls. This emphasis also stems from a one-dimensional focus on the economics-based understanding of organisational dynamics that dominated the development of the model in the late 1980s.

The Simons model of control systems provides a way of appreciating how formal information and human interactions combine to confirm or alter organisational direction. The model visually emphasises balance, a major shortcoming of the New Zealand model until the recent swing of the pendulum towards initiatives that seek to address this imbalance.

One-dimensional thinking about motivation

Whether beliefs and interaction can play a major role in shaping behaviour in an organisation depends to a significant degree on assumptions of those in top management roles. Diagnostic systems and boundaries can be imposed through the power of hierarchical position. Beliefs and interaction are effective as a means of control only if staff members volunteer discretionary effort. The real test of effective control and leadership 'is not what people do in your presence but what they do in your absence' (Patterson et al, 1996: 23). As Lipsky (1980) noted, many 'street level bureaucrats' have wide areas of discretion. They work in situations 'too complex to reduce to programmatic formats' (ibid, 15). Their actions effectively create policy and collectively create the behaviour of their agency.

Yet the New Institutional Economics theories, which have had a major effect on NPM thinking in New Zealand, dominantly view workers as effort-averse. This literature is concerned about provider capture, incentives, contracts and methods for ensuring agents are accountable to principals. Principal-agent theory, transaction cost theory and public choice theory are all strongly based on the concept of homo economicus, a representation of man as a 'rational, economic maximizer who will behave in a rational manner and make choices which maximize the results of his or her labour' (Gratton, 2000: 75)

The emphasis on external motivation in this model has led Baron (1988) to observe that:
'the imagery of the worker in these models is somewhat akin to Newton's first law of motion: employees remain in a state of rest unless compelled to change that state by a stronger force impressed upon them – namely, an optimal labour contract.'

The problem with this model, as Gratton (2000) argues, is that it fails to capture the complexity of individuals, by assuming everyone is the same, and by overestimating rational behaviour and underestimating the part played by our will and emotions. Such criticism could equally well be directed at the control model which emerged from NPM thinking.

Perhaps more damaging than a one-dimensional perspective on human behaviour is process by which theory can become a self-fulfilling prophecy, the phenomenon termed the Pygmalion effect.[88] People get from others the behaviour that they expect. Pfeffer and Sutton (2000: 191–2) provides a useful summary of this significant area of literature.

The homo economicus model is compelling because individuals can and do act on the basis of self-interest and seek to maximise personal benefits. For some individuals, at differing times of their lives, these may

---

88 This phenomenon is named after a Greek legend, a modern version of which was told by George Bernard Shaw in his play Pygmalion, subsequently adapted to create the musical 'My Fair Lady'. Legend has it that Pygmalion, a King of Cyprus, sculpted an ivory statue of a maiden named Galatea. Pygmalion fell in love with the statue and, at his prayer, Aphrodite, the goddess of love and beauty, gave it life. Pygmalion's fondest wish, his expectation, came true.

be driving motivators. But individuals can also be inspired by altruism and purpose and by expectations of the culture in which they live. According to Titmuss (1971: 243) people have a sociological and biological need to help, and to deny this is to deny them 'the freedom to enter into gift relationships'. For public sector employees whose opportunities to maximise self-interest are considerably more constrained than in private sector roles, a more useful theory is that advanced by Denhardt (1992) who suggests that 'pursuit of significance' is a driving motivator for effective public management.

Control systems based on the homo economicus model will inevitably be limited to a one-dimensional preoccupation with hierarchical control, rather than considering how commitment, based on beliefs and the opportunity to participate, can contribute. For this to occur, a different set of Pygamalion-like beliefs is necessary. A 'more holistic and rounded view of human nature' is presented in this summary of principles proposed by Simons (2000: 13):

1. People in organisations *want to contribute* to an organisation of which they can be proud.
2. People employed by business organisations know the difference between right and wrong and generally *choose to do right.*
3. People *strive to achieve.* In many instances, people work to capture extrinsic rewards such as money, promotion, and praise, but they also have an innate drive to feel a sense of satisfaction from personal achievement.
4. People *like to innovate.* The basic urge to experiment is a powerful human instinct that has allowed continual improvements of living standards.
5. People *want to do competent work.* Many, if not most, individuals take pride in their abilities. A job well done allows people to exercise skills and receive satisfaction from their competence. People would rather do something right than have to go back later to fix it.

A one-dimensional approach to thinking about motivation leads in the direction of financial incentives and the need to contract carefully to safeguard against opportunism. It leads to an increased focus on hierarchical control in which checking based on formally reported information raises risks of goal displacement or defensive routines. It leads towards increases in the cost of management. A more balanced understanding of motivation provides a way of incorporating the powerful forces of belief and interaction into the equation.

One-dimensional thinking about organisations

Management for results, the recipe at the heart of NPM theory, has a compelling appeal. It stands in contrast to managing through procedure, and the rulebooks of bureaucracy. But the economics-based thinking used for institutional design provides a one-dimensional perspective, viewing organisations as 'black boxes' that take in inputs and use processes to create outputs that contribute towards outcomes. With its focus on the visible and economic, management by results underestimates the role that organisations play in defining and shaping outputs. As compilers of organisational writings such as Pugh and Hickson (1996) demonstrate, organisations have a range of dimensions that can best be understood in a multi-discipline way, through disciplines such as sociology, psychology, anthropology, law and strategy. Organisations are as much human systems (Vickers, 1983) as machines for production, and theory that underestimates this human element is of limited explanatory power. As Handy (1981: 11) writes, the people factor makes predictions about organisational performance extremely difficult. Handy estimates that more than 60 variables are present in any organisational situation, making it impossible to predict the precise outcome of the interrelationships. In addition, human beings seem to have an inherent ability to override many of the influences on their behaviour (Handy, 1981). The contrasting views of organisations as production machines versus social organisms is well summarised in a metaphor used by Mant (1997) who poses the question of what is the difference between a bicycle and a frog. His answer is that the bicycle is a machine which, given sufficient expertise can be taken apart and can be put back together. A frog, in contrast, is a living system which, if taken apart, cannot be put back together.

Economics-based theories view organisations as bicycle-like phenomena. Analysis focuses in a one-dimensional way on issues such as principal-agent relationships and transaction costs and the role of structures and incentives. Meanwhile, lessons from physics, originally a discipline modelled on the logic of the machine, indicate that reality is more effectively represented as a web of energy flows and relationships rather than static structures (eg Zohar, 1997; Wheatley, 1999).

Management theory essentially alternates between focusing on 'tasks' and 'processes'. The economics perspectives that have dominated in the design and delivery of the New Zealand control systems have emphasised 'task' and underemphasised the importance of social processes, such as capability building, as a part of longer-term performance. As the recommendations of the 'Review of the Centre' discussed in Chapter 10 indicate, there is now a swing of the pendulum towards greater emphasis on social processes, such as the integration of service delivery, the culture of the public service and the development of future chief executives.

Reconciling the paradoxes of organisational control

Theory played a strong role in the creation of the thermostat model of public sector control in New Zealand. This theory is a product of a period of optimism about the effectiveness of markets, and the ability of information technology to enable large organisations to devolve authority yet also track new amounts of detail about performance. It is a product of a period of enthusiasm for breaking up large organisations and operating with a universe of subcontractors. It is a search for simplicity that comes from the creation of contract relationships between focused organisations. As Lane (1997b: 13) observes, the prescriptions of NPM for deregulation, privatisation and marketisation seem attractive in contrast to theories of public administration that emphasise complexity (McKevitt and Lawton, 1994).

This book captures the particular experiences of MPs, managers and staff working within a system that has been designed with a supposedly simple set of principles. As each chapter has discussed, the reality of management is a constant balancing of responses to paradoxes, a test of intelligence as described in the quote from F Scott Fitzgerald at the beginning of this chapter. The art of managing in such circumstances is well captured by Vickers (1965: 111–12) in his writing about 'the art of judgement'. Management requires the skill of balancing, involving 'constant evaluation and appraisal of risks, limitations, opportunities, and resources'. It requires integrating into one solution 'aims which first seem incompatible' and a 'rare measure of mental discipline' to determine priorities for the present, while also dreaming about future possibilities.

The rational approach to paradox is to choose between opposites. An alternative is to recognise, as Vickers recommends, the critical importance of the skill of balancing. The model developed by Simons (1995) illustrates the balancing act involved with control systems. Essentially the NPM prescription has sought simplicity through what Collins and Porras (1994: 43–5) describe as the 'tyranny of the or', emphasising diagnostic controls. Through their study of 18 long-lasting 'visionary' companies, Collins and Porras(1994) identified the creative potential of taking a 'both and' approach to managerial paradoxes.[89] Visionary companies sought to do very well in the short term and in the long term. They sought to be highly idealistic and highly profitable. They sought to preserve a core ideology, while also stimulating vigorous change. Like Simons, Collins and Porras use the yin and yang symbol to illustrate the management achievement. 'A highly visionary company doesn't want to blend yin and yang into a gray, indistinguishable circle that is neither highly yin nor highly yang; it aims to be distinctly yin and distinctly yang – both at the same time, all the time' (ibid, 45).

Figure 11.1: Yin and Yang symbol

A swing of the pendulum

As the pendulum of public, political and public service opinion has swung away from the NPM prescriptions of the late 1980s, there is a risk of a swing towards a different yet equally one-dimensional set of theories. Rather than interpret the NPM model as flawed advice, to be discarded in favour of a new approach, it is most usefully seen as an element of what Quinn (1988) terms management 'mastery'.

---

89 In this study, Collins and Porras compared strategies adopted by 18 long-lasting 'visionary' companies with comparison companies in similar fields.

The thermostat model described in this book is usefully seen as a prescription for a novice system. The doctrines adopted to bring it about provided a sharp break from bureaucratic traditions, and the introduction of an ideological commitment to a new best way. In a cycle of learning, the novice is limited by 'reliance on deductive rules, fear of failure, and hesitancy to engage risk and uncertainty'. In contrast, the master has a complex, holistic understanding that is frequently termed intuition, but is in fact 'very much dependent on rules, discipline, and structure' (Quinn, 1988: 25–6).

Prior to 1988, public service organisations were extremely limited in their capacity to manage human resources or finance. The bureaucracy-busting techniques of NPM created a series of dualisms, seeking to handle competing values by making choices. The challenge evident now, in the variety of responses to the 'Review of the Centre' described in Chapter 10, is to move 'beyond rational management' (Quinn, 1988) to a more creative balancing of opposites.

Performance systems need periodic change if they are to retain relevance. Baron and Kreps (1999: 210–11) point to this dynamic in a discussion about why two large and similar companies were adopting performance appraisal systems that each other had just dropped. The authors suggest the explanation lies in the adage that 'familiarity breeds contempt'. Performance evaluation is a difficult and uncomfortable task for 'both the evaluator and the person being evaluated' and 'those being evaluated quickly recognize and focus on the bad aspects of whatever system they are living with'. Improvements arise 'not so much from the changes themselves as from the *process of change*, which serves to refocus attention on performance, what it means, what the organisation values, and how to achieve it' (ibid, 211).

Conclusion

The New Zealand public sector control system was established during a period of rapid reform, driven by a like-minded elite group. This group defined expectations for performance that differed sharply from those of the previous bureaucratic era. In 2003, a different and less dramatic process of change is underway to address a growing unease about the unbalanced results of the earlier tide of reform.

NPM-inspired public sector reforms firmly changed the nature of debate about definitions of public sector performance, creating the pressure of real or potential competition for the delivery of outputs, reining in budget spending, and using financial and human resources strategies to press for efficiencies in the use of public resources. One significant lesson from experience in New Zealand (and Australia) is that major reform is possible, a contrast to previous conventional wisdom which centred on the difficulty of achieving reform (Halligan, 1997). Single-minded focus on the achievement of goals has brought significant achievements. As the pendulum swings towards concern about issues such as fragmentation, flexibility and staff commitment, the challenge will be to balance the competing values, rather than opt for the seeming simplicity of a new set of one-dimensional choices.

Complexity, ambiguity and intellectual stretch are key features of public sector roles – attributes that provide public sector staff with variety and challenge that are major motivational factors. Undervaluing such complexity by seeking to remove it through a narrowing of public sector tasks into tightly defined accountabilities shows a lack of understanding major motivators. Indeed, some of the ambiguities traditionally part of government roles are now featuring in the private sector through techniques such as triple bottom line reporting (eg Auditor-General 2001: 50), which considers staff and environmental well-being as well as returns for shareholders.

Single focus, results-oriented management is an unrealistic pursuit in the public sector context. Public managers face multiple constituents, including future generations whose voting preferences are not yet stated. They must lead through influence and persuasion rather than command, acting as backstage directors, enabling elected representatives to employ their skills and experiences as arbiters of what is politically acceptable and feasible.

Conclusions based on an understanding of paradox may lack the apparent simplicity and clarity of rational and analytical New Public Management rhetoric. They may lack the appeal of 'one best way' sound bites. They do, however, more closely capture the realities faced by those whose challenge it is to make such systems work.

Aspects of public sector control systems

Chapter 2 noted the tendency of different cycles of public sector reform to contradict each other.

Light (1997) uses the analogy of tides to describe this process.

The first tide was '**scientific management**', which used principles of specialisation and coordination, with efficiency as its primary aim. Specialisation is necessary because 'the range of knowledge and skill is so great that a man cannot within his lifespan know more than a small fraction of it' (Gulick and Urwick, 1937: 3) and hierarchies are required for coordination because 'the mind and will of man can span but a limited number of immediate managerial contacts' (ibid, 7). Such principles have brought about a 'thickening' of hierarchy as narrow spans of control have created multiple layers of management that have confused rather than tightened accountability.

The '**war on waste**' approach seeks to achieve economy in government spending, starting from a distrust that bureaucracies will control costs and spend effectively. Counter-bureaucracies are favoured techniques for such reform. Cutting costs and campaigning against fraud, waste or abuses are common themes. The potential drawback of such methods is that they create fear among government employees who may then do everything by the book, to the point of needless waste and inefficiency.

The '**watchful eye**' tide involves shedding light on the operation of bureaucracies, working on the assumption that publicity or legal action will be more effective than counter-bureaucracies. Protection for whistle-blowers is an example of the strategies proposed. The external scrutiny is a sign of distrust in the ability of bureaucracies to be fair and safeguard the rights of citizens. Safeguards are provided to enable whistle-blowing about undesirable practices.

'**Liberation management**' is the only one of the four tides to operate on a basis of trust, with its emphasis on cutting red tape, putting customers first, empowering employees to get results and cutting back to basics in the delivery of government programmes. Higher performance is sought through the setting of service standards and measurable goals. As with the other tides, other agendas can be incorporated. The Reinventing Government programme in the United States, for instance, included a promise of cost cutting alongside the empowerment of staff.

Light (1997) uses the metaphor of tides to emphasise the extent to which reforms overlap in their impact. As each tide comes in, it does so over the residue of a previous tide, that will have left a legacy of systems or organisational cultures.

As the most recent tide of reform, NPM has provided a mix of potentially contradictory measures that draw from each of the other tides described. It seeks to let managers manage ('liberation management'), while also holding them accountable for results, using methods derived from 'scientific management'. NPM prescriptions emphasise the 'watchful eye' of regular, transparent information and external auditing of results. The pursuit of efficiency is a new example of a 'war on waste'. NPM ideas draw extensively from the literature of New Institutional Economics and managerialism.

Such an eclectic adoption of ideas makes NPM particularly difficult to assess because 'there is no clear or agreed definition of what the new public management actually is and not only is there controversy about what [it] is, or what [it] is in the process of becoming, but also what [it] ought to be' (Ferlie et al, 1996: 10).

Different and sometimes conflicting techniques for management improvement have been used at different times or even concurrently under the guise of NPM. For example, four patterns of change could be observed in Britain during the 1980s and first half of the 1990s (Ferlie et al, 1996: 10–15):

Model 1: The efficiency drive, the earliest model to emerge, was dominant throughout the early and mid-1980s. It focused on efforts to make the public sector more business-like. The public sector was seen as a cause of economic problems and a target for cutbacks. Critics saw the efficiency drive as using inappropriate models that took no account of the public sector's distinctive context.

Model 2: Downsizing and decentralisation, of increasing importance in the 1990s, stemmed from awareness that the large vertically integrated organisations built up between 1900 and 1975 appeared to be going into reverse. New organisational forms were created to emphasise flexibility and the contracting of non-core functions.

Model 3: In search of excellence introduced private sector concepts about the importance of strong cultures (Peters and Waterman, 1982; Deal and Kennedy, 1982). This could be seen as a humanist reaction against the scientific management approach embodied in Model 1. In its focus on innovation and change, Model 3 emphasises the role of committed product champions, and the entrepreneurial and human processes that are involved in successful change processes.

Model 4: Public service orientation was seen as the least developed of the models in the mid-1990s, but one which drew on private sector concepts such as quality management and the learning organisation. It is characterised by a focus on service quality, requirements of users (rather than customers) and a commitment to a distinctive set of public service tasks and values. Reinventing Government contains elements of this approach and, in Britain, Ranson and Stewart (1994) analysed distinctive characteristics of the 'public domain'.

The typologies developed by Light (1997) and Ferlie et al (1996) help clarify the contradictions that are evident in the NPM systems adopted in the New Zealand public sector. Principles drawn from 'Liberation Management' or 'In Search of Excellence' philosophies have prompted a search for ways to let managers manage free from rule-bound procedures. But a search for efficiencies, cost savings and downsizing has involved scientific management methods of analysing production targets and the separation of thinking and doing functions. Managers have been made to manage the consequences of centrally driven budget reductions and given the 'freedom' to choose how they implement budget cuts. The 'war on waste' has been subsumed in a larger quest for ways of restraining government expenditure. Alongside these pressures has been a continuing commitment to the 'watchful eye' through the emphasis placed on transparency of information and the allocation of funding. Following controversies about managerial bonuses, severance pay, the costs of image building, and the election of a centre-left Government in 1999, the 'public service orientation' has become a strongly debated concept as the Government has sought to establish a new emphasis on public sector standards and values.

Timeline of events

Changing thinking about the control systems of the New Zealand
public management model

Year	Core public service	Wider public sector	Political/economic context
1984			Labour Government elected, July.
1985			Deregulation of finance markets, removal of subsidies.
1986		Restructuring of environmental agencies.	
1987	State Sector Act decentralises employing authorities from SSC to Chief Executives.	State owned enterprises established with major job losses.	Labour Government re-elected, August. Share market crash, October.
1988			
1989	Public Finance Act decentralises financial authorities within accountability framework.		David Lange resigns as Prime Minister, Geoffrey Palmer becomes PM.
1990			National Party elected as Government with a significant majority.
1991	'Logan Review' finds the new model 'basically sound'.		'Mother of All Budgets' of Finance Minister Ruth Richardson cuts spending, particularly in social welfare.

1992	All departments complete moves to accrual accounting.	Ten Crown Research Institutes created from Department of Scientific and Industrial Research.	
1993		Contestable, commercial delivery of health services established, with four purchasing authorities. Housing provided on a commercial model, with subsidies paid to tenants through the welfare system.	National Government re-elected with a very small majority. Voters opt for proportional representation.
1994			Fiscal Responsibility Act requires Government reporting on long-term financial prospects.
1995			First Crown Financial Statements with a full budget/actual comparison.
1996	Review by Allen Schick comments that purchase interests drive out ownership/ capability interests.		First MMP election. National Government retains office only after an unexpected decision by New Zealand First to form a coalition with it.
1997	Michael Wintringham appointed as SSC Commissioner.		
1998	Piloting of Capability, Accountability and Performance (CAP) project, aimed at simplifying reporting requirements.	Health purchasing authorities amalgamated into one. Government efforts to introduce bulk funding for schools increased.	National Party drops Jim Bolger as leader in favour of Jenny Shipley, who brings to an end the coalition with New Zealand First.

1999		Election controversies about bonuses, payouts to managers, hiring of a chartered aircraft by Work and Income NZ. Labour Government elected, pledging to reform excesses of the market model.
2000	Bulk funding to schools ended. Market practices replaced by school zones. Health boards to replace the commercial – competitive model of health enterprises. Housing marketplace curtailed, with income-related rents reintroduced,	
2001	Christine Rankin, CE of Department of Work and Income, loses Employment Court case seeking her reinstatement.	National Party changes leadership to declare a break from past adherence to 'new right' philosophies.
2002	Strengthening the Centre report recommends creation of networks of public service agencies.	General election, July. Labour re-elected as a minority government, in coalition with Jim Anderton's Progressive Coalition, and with support from United Future New Zealand party.

References

Aberbach, J., Putnam, D., and Rockman, B. (1981) *Bureaucrats and Politicians in Western Democracies*. Cambridge, Mass., Harvard University Press.

Advisory Group (2001) *Report of the Advisory Group on the Review of the Centre*. Wellington, State Services Commission.

Agor, W. (1989) *Intuition in Organisations: Leading and Managing Productively*. London, Sage.

Alford, J., and Baird, J. (1997) Performance Monitoring in the Australian Public Service: A Government-wide Analysis. *Public Money and Management* 17(2): 49–58.

Allison, G. (1983) Public and Private Management: Are They Fundamentally Alike in All Unimportant Respects? In Perty, J., and Kraemer, K. (Eds) *Public Management: Public and Private Perspectives*. Calif., Mayfield.

Amabile, T. (1983) *The Social Psychology of Creativity*. New York, Springer-Verlag.

Anthony, R., and Young, D. (1994) *Management Control in Nonprofit Organizations*. Burr Ridge, Illinois, Irwin.

Argyris, C. (1980) Making the Undiscussable and its Undiscussability Discussable. *Public Administration Review* 40(3): 205–13.

Argyris, C. (1990) The Dilemma of Implementing Controls: The Case of Managerial Accounting. *Accounting, Organizations and Society* 15(6): 503–11.

Aucoin, P. (1995) *The New Public Management: Canada in Comparative Perspective*. Montreal, Institute for Research on Public Policy.

Auditor-General (1978) *Financial Management and Control in Administrative Government Departments, 'The Shailes Report'*. Wellington, Office of the Controller and Auditor-General.

Auditor-General (1999) *The Accountability of Executive Government to Parliament*. Wellington, Office of the Controller and Auditor-General.

Auditor-General (2001) *Reporting Public Sector Performance*. Wellington, Office of the Controller and Auditor-General.

Auditors-General, Australasian Council of (2001) *Peer Review of the New Zealand Audit Office*. Wellington, Office of the Auditor-General. http://www.oag.govt.nz/HomePageFolders/Publications/PeerReview/PeerReview.htm. Accessed September 18, 2002.

Ayres, F. (2002) Risk Management in the Shadow of Enron. *The Journal of Business Strategy* 23(4): 36–40.

Bailyn, L. (1985) Autonomy in the Industrial R and D Lab. *Human Resource Management: Special Issue – The Dilemma of Autonomy vs Control in the Management of Organizational Professionals* 24(2): 129–46.

Ban, C. (1995) *How do Public Managers Manage? Bureaucratic Constraints, Organisational Culture and the Potential for Reform*. San Francisco, Jossey-Bass.

Barnard, C. (1968) *The Functions of the Executive*. Cambridge, Mass., Harvard University Press.

Baron, J. (1988) The Employment Relation as a Social Relation. *Journal of the Japanese and International Economies* 2: 492–525.

Baron, J., and Kreps, D. (1999) *Strategic Human Resources. Frameworks for General Managers*. New York, John Wiley.

Barzelay, M. (1992) *Breaking Through Bureaucracy: A New Vision for Managing in Government*. Berkeley, Calif., University of California Press.

Barzelay, M. (1996) Performance Auditing and the New Public Management: Changing Roles and Strategies of Central Audit Institutions. In Shand, D. *Performance Auditing and the Modernisation of Government*. Paris, OECD.

Behn, R. (1991) *Leadership Counts. Lessons for Public Managers from the Massachusetts Welfare, Training and Employment Programme*. Cambridge, Mass., Harvard University Press.

Behn, R. (1995) The Big Questions of Public Management. *Public Administration Review* 55(4): 313–24.

Behn, R. (1996) Public Management: Should it Strive to be Art, Science, or Engineering? *Journal of Public Administration Research and Theory* 6(1): 91–193.

Blau, P. (1963) *The Dynamics of Bureaucracy; A Study of Interpersonal Relations in Two Government Agencies*. Chicago, University of Chicago Press.

Bohte, J., and Meier, K. (2000) Goal Displacement: Assessing the Motivation for Organisational Cheating. *Public Administration Review* 60(2): 173–82.

Bollard, A., and Buckle, R. (Eds) (1987) *Economic Liberalisation in New Zealand*. Wellington, Allen & Unwin/Port Nicholson Press.

Bolman, L., and Deal, T. (1997) *Reframing Organisations: Artistry, Choice and Leadership*. San Francisco, Jossey-Bass.

Borins, S. (1988) Public Choice: 'Yes Minister' Made it Popular, But Does Winning the Nobel Prize Make it True? *Canadian Public Administration* 31(1): 12–26.

Boston, J. (1997) The New Contractualism in New Zealand: Chief Executive Performance Agreements. In Davis et al, 1997.

Boston, J. (2000) The Challenge of Evaluating Systemic Change: The Case of Public Management Reform. *International Public Management Journal* (3)1: 23–46.

Boston, J. (2001) New Zealand: Cautionary Tale or Shining Example? In Rhodes, R., and Weller, P. (Eds) *The Changing World of Top Officials. Mandarins or Valets?* Buckingham, U.K., Open University Press.

Boston, J., Martin, J., Pallot, J., and Walsh, P. (1991) *Reshaping the State. New Zealand's Bureaucratic Revolution*. Auckland, Oxford University Press.

Boston, J., Martin, J., Pallot, J., and Walsh, P. (1996) *Public Management: The New Zealand Model*. Auckland, Oxford University Press.

Brash, D. (1996) *New Zealand's Remarkable Reforms*. London, Institute of Economic Affairs.

Breton, A. (1974) *The Economic Theory of Representative Government*. Chicago, Aldine Publishing.

Brumby, J., Edmonds, P., and Honeyfield, K. (1996) *Effects of Public Sector Financial Management Reform in New Zealand*. Australasian Evaluation Society Conference, 30 August 1996.

Bryson, J. (1995) *Strategic Planning for Public and Nonprofit Organisations. A Guide to Strengthening and Sustaining Organisational Achievement*. San Francisco, Jossey-Bass.

Buchanan, R., and Simpkins, K. (2001) A New Age for Public Auditing. *Chartered Accountants Journal* July: 8–11.

Burns, T., and Stalker, G. (1961) *The Management of Innovation*. London, Tavistock.

Caiden, N. (1998) A New Generation of Budget Reform. In Peters and Savoie, 1998.

Cameron, K., and Quinn, R. (1988) Organisational Paradox and Transformation. In Quinn, R., and Cameron, K. (Eds) *Paradox and Transformation: Toward a Theory of Change in Organisation and Management*. Cambridge, Mass., Ballinger.

Chandler, A. (1962) *Strategy and Structure: Chapters in the History of the Industrial Enterprise*. Cambridge, MIT Press.

Chatterjee, S., Conway, P., Dalziel, P., Eichbaum, E., Harris, P., Philpott, B., and Shaw, R. (1999) *The New Politics: A Third Way for New Zealand*. Palmerston North, Dunmore Press.

Coase, R. (1937) The Nature of the Firm. *Economica* 4: 386–405.

Cohen, S., and Eimicke, W. (1995) *The New Effective Public Manager. Achieving Success in a Changing Government*. San Francisco, Jossey-Bass.

Collins, J., and Porras, J. (1994) *Built to Last – Successful Habits of Visionary Companies*. London, Random House.

Considine, M., and Lewis, J. (1999) Governance at Ground Level: The Frontline Bureaucrat in the Age of Markets and Networks. *Public Administration Review* 59(6): 467–80.

Corrigan, P., and Joyce, P. (1997) Reconstructing Public Management. A New Responsibility for the Public and a Case Study of Local Government. *International Journal of Public Sector Management* 10(6): 417–32.

Davis, G., Sullivan, B., and Yeatman, A. (Eds) (1997) *The New Contractualism?* Melbourne, Macmillan.

Davis, G. (1997) Implications, Consequences and Futures. In Davis et al, 1997.

Davis, S., and Lawrence, P. (1977) *Matrix*. Reading, Mass., Addison-Wesley.

Deal, T., and Kennedy, A. (1982) *Corporate Cultures: The Rites and Rituals of Corporate Life*. Reading, Mass., Addison-Wesley.

Dean, J., and Whtye, W. (1970) How do you know if the informant is telling the truth? In Dexter, 1970.

Deane, R. (1986) Public Sector Reform: A Review of the Issues. From *Purpose, Performance and Profit* – 1986 conference of the New Zealand Institute of Public Administration, Wellington, Government Printing Office.

Denhardt, R. (1992) *The Pursuit of Significance. Strategies for Managerial Success in Public Organisations*. Belmont, Calif., Wadsworth Publishing Company.

Dexter, L. (1970) *Elite and Specialized Interviewing*. Evanston, Ill., Northwestern University Press.

DiLulio, J. (1994) Principled Agents: The Cultural Bases of Behaviour in a Federal Government Bureaucracy. *Journal of Public Administration Research and Theory* 4(3): 277.

DiLulio, J. (1987) *Governing Prisons: A Comparative Study of Correctional Management*. New York, Free Press.

Dixon, J., Kouzmin, A., and Korac-Kakabadse, N. (1998) Managerialism – Something

Old, Something Borrowed, Little New: Economic Prescription Versus Effective Organizational Change in Public Agencies. *International Journal of Public Sector Management* 11(2/3): 164–87.

Downs, A. (1967) *Inside Bureaucracy*. Boston, Little, Brown and Co.

Downs, G., and Larkey, P. (1986) *The Search for Government Efficiency*. Philadelphia, Temple University Press.

Drucker, P. (1964) *The Concept of the Corporation*. (2nd edn), New American Library.

Drucker, P. (1958) *The Practice of Management*. London, Heinemann.

Dunsire, A. (1973) Adminstrative Doctrine and Administrative Change. *Public Administration Bulletin* 15(-): 39–56.

Easton, B. (1997) *The Commercialisation of New Zealand*. Auckland, Auckland University Press.

Easton, B. (2001) *The Nationbuilders*. Auckland, Auckland University Press.

Eccles, R., and Nohria, N. (1992) *Beyond the Hype – Rediscovering the Essence of Management*. Boston, Harvard Business School Press.

Eliassen, K., and Kooiman, J. (Eds) (1993) *Managing Public Organisations*. London, Sage.

Eliassen, K., and Kooiman, J. (1993) Introduction. In Eliassen and Kooiman, 1993.

Feldman, M., and Khademian, A.M. (2000) Managing for Inclusion: Balancing Control and Participation. *International Public Management Journal* 3(2): 149–67.

Feldman, M., and March, J. (1981) Information in Organisations as Signal and Symbol. *Administrative Science Quarterly* 26: 171–86.

Ferlie, E., Ashburner, L., Fitzgerald, L., and Pettigrew, A. (1996) *The New Public Management in Action*. Oxford, Oxford University Press.

Frederickson, H. (1996) Comparing the Reinventing Government Movement with the New Public Administration. *Public Administration Review* 56(3): 263–70.

French, W., and Bell, C. (1984) *Organization development : behavioral science interventions for organization improvement* (3rd edn). Englewood Cliffs, N.J., Prentice-Hall.

Fukuyama, F. (1995) *Trust: the Social Virtues and the Creation of Prosperity*. London, Hamish Hamilton.

Gleick, J. (1987) *Chaos*. New York, Viking-Penguin.

Goldfinch, S. (1998) Evaluating Public Sector Reform in New Zealand: Have the Benefits been Oversold? *Asian Journal of Public Administration* 20(2): 203–32.

Goodin, R., and Wilenski, P. (1984) Beyond Efficiency: The Logical Underpinnings of Administrative Principles. *Public Administration Review* 44(6): 512–17.

Goodman, C. (1999) Motivation of Public Service Chief Executives. *Public Sector* 22(1): 18–21.

Goold, M., and Campbell, A. (1987) *Strategies and Styles: The Role of the Centre in Managing Diversified Corporations*. Oxford, Basil Blackwell.

Gore, A. (1993) *Creating a Government that Works Better and Costs Less*. Washington, D.C., U.S. Government Printing Office.

Gratton, L. (2000) *Living Strategy: Putting People at the Heart of Corporate Purpose*. London, Financial Times/Prentice Hall.

Gray, A. (1998) *Business-Like But Not Like a Business: The Challenge for Public Management*. London, Chartered Institute of Public Finance and Accountancy (CIPFA).

Gregory, R. (1995) The Peculiar Tasks of Public Management: Toward Conceptual Discrimination. *Australian Journal of Public Administration* 54(2): 171–83.

Gregory, R. (1998a) Political Responsibility for Bureaucratic Incompetence: Tragedy at Cave Creek. *Public Administration* 76: 519–38.

Gregory, R. (1998b) New Zealand as the 'New Atlantis': A Case Study in Technocracy. *Canberra Bulletin of Public Administration* 90: 107–12.

Gregory, R. (2000) Getting Better But Feeling Worse? Public Sector Reform in New Zealand. *International Public Management Journal* (3): 107–23.

Gulick, L., and Urwick, L., (Eds) (1937) *Papers on the Science of Administration.* New York, Institute of Public Administration.

Halligan, J. (1997) New Public Sector Models: Reform in Australia and New Zealand. In Lane, 1997a.

Halligan, J. (2001) Politicians, Bureaucrats and Public Sector Reform in Australia and New Zealand. In Peters, G., and Pierre, J. *Politicians and Bureaucrats Under Public Sector reform.* London, Routledge.

Handy, C. (1981) *Understanding Organisations* (2nd edn). Middlesex, U.K., Penguin.

Harmon, M. (1995) *Responsibility as Paradox: A Critique of Rational Discourse on Government.* Thousand Oaks, Calif., Sage.

Hart, J. (1998) Central Agencies and Departments: Empowerment and Coordination. In Peters and Savoie, 1998.

Hayes, R., and Abernathy, W. (1980) Managing Our Way to Economic Decline. *Harvard Business Review* 58(4): 67–77.

Heclo, H., and Wildavsky, A. (1981) *The Private Government of Public Money.* London, Macmillan.

Hennessy, P. (1989) *Whitehall.* London, Secker and Warburg.

Herzberg, F., Mausner, B., and Snyderman, B. (1959) *The Motivation to Work* (2nd edn). New York, Wiley.

Herzlinger, R., and Nitterhouse, D. (1994) *Financial Accounting and Managerial Control for Nonprofit Organizations.* Cincinnati, Southwestern.

Hofstede, G. (1978) The Poverty of Management Control Philosophy. *Academy of Management Review* 3(3): 450–61.

Hofstede, G. (1981) Management Control of Public and Not-for-Profit Activities. *Accounting, Organisations and Society* 6(3): 193–211.

Hoggett, P. (1991) A New Management in the Public Sector? *Policy and Politics* 19(4): 243–56.

Hogwood, B. (1993) Restructuring Central Government: The Next Steps initiative in Britain. In Eliassen and Kooiman, 1993.

Hood, C. (1990) De-Sir Humphreyfying the Westminster Model of Bureaucracy: A new style of governance? *Governance* (3)2: 205–14.

Hood, C. (1991) A Public Management for all Seasons? *Public Administration* 69(1): 3–19.

Hood, C., and Jackson, M. (1991) *Administrative Argument.* Aldershot, U.K., Dartmouth Publishing.

Hood, C. (1998a) *The Art of the State. Culture, Rhetoric and Public Management.* Oxford, Oxford University Press.

Hood, C. (1998b) Individualised contracts for top public servants: Copying business, path-dependent political re-engineering – or Trobriand Cricket? *Governance* 11(4): 443–62.

Hood, C., James, O., Jones, G., Scott, C., and Travers, T. (1998) Regulation Inside Government: Where New Public Management Meets the Audit Explosion. *Public Money and Management* 18(2): 61–8.

Hunn, D. (2000) *Ministerial Review into the Department of Work and Income*, May 8, 2000. Wellington, Office of the Minister of Social Welfare.

James, C. (1992) *New Territory – the Transformation of New Zealand, 1984–92.* Wellington, Bridget Williams Books.

James, C. (2001) With Labour, is it Trust or Control? *New Zealand Herald* 15 August: A13.

Janis, I. (1983) *Groupthink: Psychological Studies of Policy Decisions and Fiascoes.* Boston, Houghton Mifflin.

Jervis, P., and Richards, S. (1997) Public Management: Raising Our Game. *Public Money and Management* 17(2): 9–16.

Jesson, B. (1999) *Only Their Purpose is Mad: The Money Men Take Over New Zealand.* Palmerston North, Dunmore Press.

Johnson, H. (1992) *Relevance Regained. From Top Down Control to Bottom Up Empowerment.* New York, Free Press.

Johnson, H., and Kaplan, R. (1987) *Relevance Lost – the Rise and Fall of Management Accounting.* Boston, Harvard Business School Press.

Kanter, R., and Summers, D. (1987) Doing Well While Doing Good: Dilemmas of Performance Measurement in Non-profit Organisations and the Need for a Multi-constituency Approach. In Powell, W. (Ed.) *Handbook of Non-profit Organisations.* New Haven, Yale University Press.

Kaplan, R., and Norton, D. (1996) *The Balanced Scorecard: Translating Strategy into Action.* Boston, Harvard Business School Press.

Kaplan, R., and Norton, D. (2001) *The Strategy-Focused Organization: How Balanced Scorecard Companies Thrive in the New Business Environment.* Boston, Harvard Business School Press.

Kaufman, H. (1967) *The Forest Ranger. A Study in Administrative Behaviour.* Baltimore, Johns Hopkins Press.

Kaufman, H. (1978) Reflections on Administrative Reorganisation. In Pechman, J. (Ed.) *Setting National Priorities. The 1978 Budget.* Washington, D.C., Brookings Institution.

Kelsey, J. (1993) *Rolling Back the State. Privatisation of Power in Aotearoa/New Zealand.* Wellington, Bridget Williams Books.

Kelsey, J. (1995) *The New Zealand Experiment. A World Model for Structural Adjustment?* Auckland, Auckland University Press/Bridget Williams Books.

Kettl, D. (1993) *Sharing Power: Public Governance and Private Markets.* Washington, D.C., Brookings Institution.

Kettl, D. (2000) *Performance Management: The State of the Field.* Association for Public Policy and Management, 22nd Annual Research Conference, Seattle, Washington.

Keynes, J. (1936) *The General Theory of Employment, Interest and Money.* Cambridge, Cambridge University Press.

Koch, R. (1997) *The 80/20 Principle – The Secret of Achieving More With Less*. London, Nicholas Brealey.

Kohn, A. (1993) *Punished by Rewards. The Trouble with Gold Stars, Incentive Plans, A's, Praise, and Other Bribes*. New York, Houghton Mifflin.

Kravchuk, R., and Schack, R. (1996) Designing Effective Performance Measurement Systems under the Government Performance and Results Act of 1993. *Public Administration Review* 56(4): 348–59.

Lane, J-E. (Ed.) (1997a) *Public Sector Reform. Rationale, trends and problems*. London, Sage.

Lane, J-E. (1997b) Public Sector Reform: Only Deregulation, Privatization and Marketization? In Lane, 1997a.

Lane, J-E. (1999) Contractualism in the Public Sector: Some theoretical considerations. *Public Management* 1(2): 179–94.

Lange, D. (1998) With the Benefit of Foresight and a Little Help from Hindsight. *Australian Journal of Public Administration* 57(1): 19–32.

Lawler, E., Mohrman, A., Mohrman, S., Ledford, G., and Cummings, T. (1986) *Doing Research That Is Useful For Theory and Practice*. San Francisco, Jossey-Bass.

Le Grand, J. (1997) Knights, Knaves or Pawns? Human Behaviour and Social Policy. *Journal of Social Policy* 26(2): 149–69.

Levin, M., and Sanger, M. (1994) *Making Government Work: How Entrepreneurial Executives Turn Bright Ideas into Real Results*. San Francisco, Jossey-Bass.

Lewis, E. (1980) *Public Entrepreneurship – Toward a Theory of Bureaucratic Political Power*. Bloomington, Indiana, Indiana University Press.

Lewis, M. (2000) Exploring Paradox: Toward a More Comprehensive Guide. *Academy of Management Review* 25(4): 760–76.

Light, P. (1997) *The Tides of Reform: Making Government Work, 1945–1995*. New Haven, Yale University Press.

Light, P. (1998) *Sustaining Innovation – Creating Nonprofit Organizations That Innovate Naturally*. San Francisco, Jossey-Bass.

Lindblom, C. (1959) The Science of Muddling Through. *Public Administration Review* 19(1): 79–88.

Lipsky, M. (1980) *Street Level Bureaucracy. Dilemmas of the Individual in Public Services*. New York, Russell Sage Foundation.

Lipson, L. (1948) *The Politics of Equality: New Zealand's Adventures in Democracy*. Chicago, University of Chicago Press.

Lister, P., Rivers, M-J., and Wilkinson, A. (1991) The Management of Change – The Social and Personnel Perspective. In Boston et al, 1991.

Locke, E., Latham, G., with contributions by Smith, K., and Wood, R. (1990) *A Theory of Goal Setting and Task Performance*. Englewood Cliffs, N.J., Prentice Hall.

Logan, B. (1991) The 'Logan Report' *A Review of State Sector Reforms*. Wellington, State Services Commission.

Lucas, J. R. (1976) *Democracy and Participation*. Harmondsworth, U.K., Penguin.

Lynn, L. (1996) *Public Management as Art, Science, and Profession*. Chatham, New Jersey, Chatham House.

Mackenzie, W. (1966) Foreword. In Normanton, E. *The Accountability and Audit of Governments*. Manchester, Manchester University Press.

Mallard, T. (2000) Complying with the new Government's priorities and plans for improving public sector performance and accountability, May 3, 2000. Wellington. URL: http://www.executive.govt.nz/speech.cfm?speechralph=30948&SR=1. Accessed September 18, 2002.

Mallard, T. (2001) Draft Statement of Commitment by the Government to the State Sector, March 2001. http://www.executive.govt.nz/minister/mallard/state/02.htm. Accessed September 18, 2002.

Mant, A. (1997) *Intelligent Leadership*. St Leonards, N.S.W., Allen and Unwin.

Maor, M. (1999) The Paradox of Managerialism. *Public Administration Review* 59(1): 5–18.

Maslow, A. (1954) *Motivation and Personality* (1st edn). New York, Harper.

Matheson, A. (1997) The Impact of Contracts on Public Management in New Zealand. In Davis et al, 1997.

McDonald, H., and Anderson, P. (1997) Case Study on Contracting Out the Functions of the New Zealand Audit Office. In *Contracting Out Government Services*. Paris, OECD.

McGregor, D. (1960) *The Human Side of Enterprise*. New York, McGraw-Hill.

McKevitt, D., and Lawton A. (Eds) (1994) *Public Sector Management. Theory, Critique and Practice*. London, Sage in association with The Open University.

Merton, R. (1957) *Social Theory and Social Structure* (Revised edn). Glencoe, Ill., Free Press.

Meyer, H., Kay, E., and French, J. (1965) Split Roles in Performance Appraisal. *Harvard Business Review* 43(1): 123–29.

Minichiello, V., Aroni, R., Timewell, E., and Alexander, L. (1995) *In-Depth Interviewing: Principles, Techniques, Analysis*. Melbourne, Longman.

Mintzberg, H. (1973) *The Nature of Managerial Work*. New York, Harper and Row.

Mintzberg, H. (1994) *The Rise and Fall of Strategic Planning*. New York, Prentice-Hall.

Mintzberg, H. (1996) Managing Government, Governing Management. *Harvard Business Review*, May–June.

Moore, M. (1995) *Creating Public Value: Strategic Management in Government*. Boston, Harvard University Press.

Mulgan, R. (1992) The Elective Dictatorship in New Zealand. In Gold, H. (Ed.) *New Zealand Politics in Perspective*. Auckland, Longman Paul.

Neustadt, R. (1990) *Presidential Power and the Modern Presidents: The Politics of Leadership from Roosevelt to Reagan*. New York, Free Press.

Nonaka, I., and Takeuchi, H. (1995) *The Knowledge-Creating Company. How Japanese Companies Create the Dynamics of Innovation*. New York, Oxford University Press.

Norman, R. (1997a) *Accounting for Government. How New Zealand built an accounting system that tells the full story about a government's financial performance*. Wellington, VictoriaLink.

Norman, R. (1997b) Past Storms and New Horizons. In Elkin, G. (Ed.) *Human Resource Management in Action*. Palmerston North, Dunmore Press.

Norman, R., and McMillan, R. (1997) Variety and Challenge. Key Motivators for Top Public Servants. *HumanResources*. October: 3–5.

Osborne, D., and Gaebler, T. (1992) *Re-inventing Government. How the entrepreneurial spirit is transforming the public sector*. Reading, Mass., Addison-Wesley.

Osborne, D., and Plastrik, P. (1997) *Banishing Bureaucracy: The Five Strategies for Reinventing Government*. Reading, Mass., Addison-Wesley.

Ouchi, W. (1979) A Conceptual Framework for the Design of Organisational Control Mechanisms. *Management Science* 25(9): 833–48.

Overman, E., and Loraine, D. (1994) Information for Control: Another Management Proverb? *Public Administration Review* 54(2): 193–6.

Pallot, J. (1999) Service Delivery: The Audit Dimension. *Australian Journal of Public Administration* 58(3): 43–9.

Parker, L., Ferris, K., and Otley, T. (1989) *Accounting for the Human Factor*. Sydney, Prentice-Hall.

Patterson, K., Grenny, J., McMillan, R., and Switzler, A. (1996) *The Balancing Act: Mastering the Competitive Demands of Leadership*. Cincinnati, Ohio, Thomson Executive Press.

Perrow, C. (1977) Three Types of Effectiveness Studies. In Goodman, P., and Pennings, J. (Eds) *New Perspectives of Organisational Effectiveness*. San Francisco, Jossey-Bass.

Perry, J., and Wise, L. (1990) The Motivational Bases of Public Service. *Public Administration Review* 50(3): 367–73.

Peters, B., and Savoie, D. (Eds) (1998) *Taking Stock. Assessing Public Sector Reforms*. Montreal, Canadian Centre for Management Development and McGill/Queen's University Press.

Peters, B.G. (1998) What Works? The Antiphons of Administrative Reform. In Peters and Savoie, 1998.

Peters, T., and Waterman, R. (1982) *In Search of Excellence: Lessons from America's Best-run Companies*. New York, Harper and Row.

Petrie, M., and Webber, D. (1999) *Review of Evidence on Broad Outcome of Public Sector Management Regime*. Wellington, the Treasury.

Pfeffer, J. (1992) *Managing with Power. Politics and Influence in Organisations*. Boston, Harvard Business School Press.

Pfeffer, J., and Sutton, R. (2000) *The Knowing-Doing Gap. How Smart Companies Turn Knowledge into Action*. Boston, Harvard Business School Press.

Phillips, E., and Pugh, D. (1987) *How to Get a PhD*. Milton Keynes, Open University Press.

Pollitt, C. (1989) Performance Indicators in the Longer Term. *Public Money and Management* 9(3): 51–5.

Pollitt, C. (1990) *Managerialism and the Public Services: The Anglo-American Experience*. Cambridge Mass., Basil Blackwell.

Pollitt, C. (1995) Justification by Works or by Faith? Evaluating the New Public Management. *Evaluation* 1(2): 133–54.

Pollitt, C. (1998) Managerialism Revisited. In Peters and Savoie, 1998.

Pollitt, C., and Bouckaert, G. (2000) *Public Management Reform. A Comparative Analysis*. Oxford, Oxford University Press.

Pollitt, C., Birchall, J., and Putnam, K (1998) *Decentralizing Public Service Management*. London, Macmillan.

Popper, K. (1976) *Unended Quest: An Intellectual Biography* (Revised edn). London, Fontana.

Porter, M. (1985) *Competitive Advantage: Creating and Sustaining Superior Performance.* New York, Free Press.

Power, M. (1994) *The Audit Explosion.* London, Demos.

Power, M. (1997) *The Audit Society.* Oxford, Oxford University Press.

Pressman, J., and Wildavsky, A. (1973) *Implementation: How Great Expectations in Washington are Dashed in Oakland.* Berkeley, University of California Press.

Pugh, D., and Hickson, D. (Eds) (1996) *Writers on Organisations* (5th edn). London, Penguin.

Pusey, M. (1991) *Economic Rationalism in Canberra. A Nation Building State Changes its Mind.* Melbourne, Cambridge University Press.

Quinn, R. (1988) *Beyond Rational Management.* San Francisco, Jossey-Bass.

Rainey, H. (1997) *Understanding and Managing Public Organizations.* San Francisco, Jossey-Bass.

Rainey, H. (1998) Assessing Past and Current Personnel Reforms. In Peters and Savoie, 1998.

Ranson, S., and Stewart, J. (1994) *Managment for the Public Domain: Enabling the Learning Society.* London, Macmillan.

Rhodes, R. (1994) The Hollowing Out of the State: The Changing Nature of Public Service in Britain. *Political Quarterly* 65(2): 138–51.

Rhodes, R. (1999) Book Review. *Australian Journal of Public Administration* 58(3): 121–3.

Ritchie, J., and Spencer, L. (1994) Qualitative Data Analysis for Applied Policy Research. In Bryman, A., and Burgess, R. (Eds) *Analyzing Qualitative Data.* London, Routledge.

Rittel, H., and Weber, M. (1973) Dilemmas in a General Theory of Planning. *Policy Science* 4(2): 155–69.

Robinson, M. (2000) Contract Budgeting. *Public Administration* 78(1): 75–90.

Robinson, M. (2002) The Public Service and Statements of Intent. *Public Sector* 25(1): 6–9.

Roethlisberger, F., and Dickson, W. (1939) *Management and the Worker: An Account of a Research Program Conducted by the Western Electric company, Hawthorne Works, Chicago.* Boston, Harvard University Press.

Rogers, S. (1999) *Performance Management in Local Government.* London, Financial Times Professional.

Roos, J., Roos, G., Dragonetti, N., and Edvinson, L. (1997) *Intellectual Capital: Navigating in the New Business Landscape.* London, Macmillan Business.

Russell, M. (1996) *Revolution: New Zealand from Fortress to Free Market.* Auckland, Images Ink/Hodder Moa Beckett/TVNZ Ltd.

Sapolsky, H. (1967) Organizational Structure and Innovation. *Journal of Business* 40(4): 497–510.

Schick, A. (1996) *The Spirit of Reform.* Wellington, State Services Commission.

Schick, A. (1998) Why Most Developing Countries Should Not Try New Zealand's Reforms. *The World Bank Research Observer* 13: 123–31.

Schick, A. (2001) Foreword. In Scott, 2001.

Schick, A. (2001a) *Reflections on the New Zealand Model.* Lecture at the New Zealand Treasury, August 28, 2001, Wellington.

Schon, D. (1995) *The Reflective Practitioner. How Professionals Think in Action.* Aldershot, Hants., U.K., Ashgate Publishing.

Scott, G. (1996) *Government Reform in New Zealand.* Washington, D.C., International Monetary Fund.

Scott, G. (1997) The New Institutional Economics and Reshaping the State in New Zealand. In Davis et al, 1997.

Scott, G. (2001) *Public Management in New Zealand. Lessons and Challenges.* Wellington, New Zealand Business Roundtable.

Shapiro, E. (1995) *Fad Surfing in the Boardroom. Reclaiming the Courage to Manage in the Age of Instant Answers.* Sydney, HarperCollins.

Shaw, R. (1999) Rehabilitating the Public Service – Alternatives to the Wellington Model. In Chatterjee et al, 1999.

Sieber, S. (1981) *Fatal Remedies. The Ironies of Social Intervention.* New York, Plenum.

Simon, H. (1946) The Proverbs of Administration. *Public Administration Review* 6(1): 53–67.

Simon, H. (1957) *Models of Man, Social and Rational.* New York, Wiley.

Simon, H. (1976) *Administrative Behaviour: A Study of Decision-making Processes in Administrative Organization.* New York, Free Press.

Simons, R. (1990) The Role of Management Control Systems in Creating Competitive Advantage: New Perspectives. *Accounting, Organisations and Society* 15(1/2): 127–43.

Simons, R. (1991) Strategic Orientation and Top Management Attention to Control Systems. *Strategic Management Journal* 12: 49–62.

Simons, R. (1995) *Levers of Control. How Managers Use Innovative Control Systems to Drive Strategic Renewal.* Boston, Harvard Business School Press.

Simons, R. (2000) *Performance Management and Control Systems for Implementing Strategy.* New Jersey, Prentice Hall.

Sisson, K. (1995) Organisational Structure. In Tyson, S. (Ed.) *Strategic Prospects for HRM.* London, Institute of Personnel and Development.

Skinner, W. (1981) Big Hat, No Cattle: Managing Human Resources. *Harvard Business Review* 59(5): 106–14.

Smith, A., and Norman, R. (1997) *George Hickton. Salesman.* Wellington, VictoriaLink.

Smith, A., and Norman, R. (1998) Margaret Bazley: Change without Trauma. Wellington, VictoriaLink.

Spicer, B., Emanuel, D., and Powell, M. (1996) *Transforming Government Enterprises. Managing Radical Organisational Change in Deregulated Environments.* St Leonards, Australia, Centre for Independent Studies.

SSC (1998) *Assessment of the State of the New Zealand Public Service.* Occasional Paper No. 1. Wellington, State Services Commission.

SSC (1999a) *Improving Accountability: Setting the Scene.* Occasional Paper 10. Wellington, State Services Commission.

SSC (1999b) *Improving Accountability: Developing an Integrated Performance System.* Occasional Paper 11. Wellington, State Services Commission.

SSC (1999c) *Assessing Departments' Capability to Contribute to Strategic Priorities.* Occasional Paper 16. Wellington, State Services Commission.

SSC (2001a) *Annual Report, 2000–2001.* Wellington, State Services Commission.

SSC (2001b) *Human Resource Capability. Survey of Public Service Departments as at 30 June 2001.* Wellington, State Services Commission.

Stace, D., and Norman, R. (1997) Re-invented Government: The New Zealand Experience. *Asia Pacific Journal of Human Resources* 35(1): 21–36.

Stewart, J. (1996) A Dogma of our Times – The Separation of Policy Making and Implementation. *Public Money and Management* 16(3): 33–40

Stewart, T. (1997) *Intellectual Capital.* London, Nicholas Brealey.

Sveiby, K. (1997) *The New Organizational Wealth.* San Francisco, Berrett-Koehler.

Talbot, C. (2000) Performing 'Performance' – A Comedy in Five Acts. *Public Money and Management* 20(4): 63–8.

Taylor, F. (1964) Testimony Before the Special House Committee. In *Scientific Management.* New York, Harper and Row.

The Treasury (1987) *Government Management. A Report to the Incoming Government.* Wellington, the Treasury.

Thomas, P. (1998) The Changing Nature of Accountability. In Peters and Savoie, 1998.

Thompson, G. (1999) What is Wrong With New Zealand's Service Performance Reporting Model. The Case of Public Museums. *Public Management* 1(4): 511–30.

Titmuss, R. (1971) *The Gift Relationship.* London, Allen and Unwin.

Tushman, M., Newman, W. and Romanelli, E. (1986) Convergence and Upheaval: Managing the Unsteady Pace of Organizational Evolution. *California Management Review* 29(1): 29–44.

Ulrich, D. (1997) *Human Resource Champions. The Next Agenda for Adding Value and Delivering Results.* Boston, Harvard Business School Press.

Upton, S. (1995) Contracting in the Science Sector. *Public Sector* 18(4): 2–5.

Upton, S. (1999) Discussion notes for meeting with the Brookings Institution Centre for Public Management, Washington, D.C., 26 April, 1999. Wellington, State Services Commission.

Venter, N. (2000) Are you Listening, Minister? *Dominion,* Wellington, October 4: 11.

Vickers, G. (1965) *The Art of Judgment. A Study of Policy Making.* London, Chapman and Hall.

Vickers, G. (1983) *Human Systems are Different.* London, Harper and Row.

VictoriaLink (1997–2000) Case studies about Public Sector Innovation:
Planning the Unplannable. Ministry of Foreign Affairs and Trade, 1998.
Criminal or Customer? Collections Division, Department for Courts, 1998.
Delivering a Science Business. ESR Ltd, 1999.
Planning for Life. Public Trust, 1999.
Guns and Gold. New Zealand Defence Force, 1999.
Managing the Big One. Earthquake Commission, 1999.
Anchoring the Change. Collections Division, Department for Courts, 2000.
The Heart of the Matter. Education Review Office, 2000.

Waldersee, R. (1999) The Art of Service v the Science of Measurement: Measuring and Managing Service Delivery. *Australian Journal of Public Administration* 58(3) 38–42.

Waldo, D. (1946) Government by Procedure. In Marx, M. (Ed.) *Elements of Public Administration.* New York, Prentice-Hall.

Wanna, J., Forster, J., and Kelly, J. (2000) *Managing public expenditure in Australia.* St Leonards, N.S.W., Allen & Unwin.

Weber, M. (1947) translated (from the German) by A.M. Henderson and T. Parsons *The Theory of Social and Economic Organization.* Glencoe, Free Press.

Weir, J. (1998) *New Zealand Wit and Wisdom. Quotations with Attitude.* Auckland, Tandem Press.

Wheatley, M. (1999) *Leadership and the New Science. Discovering Order in a Chaotic World.* San Francisco, Berrett-Koehler.

Whitehead, A. (1920) *The Concept of Nature.* Cambridge, Cambridge University Press.

Wildavsky, A. (1979) *Speaking Truth to Power: The Art and Craft of Policy Analysis.* Boston, Little, Brown and Company.

Wildavsky, A. (1986) *Budgeting: A Comparative Theory of Budgetary Processes* (Revised edn) New Brunswick, New Jersey, Transaction Books.

Wildavsky, A. (1992) *The New Politics of the Budgetary Process.* New York, HarperCollins.

Williamson, O. (1985) *The Economic Institutions of Capitalism: Firms, Markets, Relational Contracting.* New York, Free Press.

Wilson, W. (1887) The Study of Administration. *Political Science Quarterly,* 2: 197–222.

Wilson, J. (1989) *Bureaucracy: What Government Agencies Do and Why They Do It.* New York, Basic Books.

Wilson, J. (1994) Reinventing Public Administration. *Political Science and Politics* 27(4): 667–73.

Wintringham, M. (2001a) *State Services Commissioner's Annual Report on the State Services, 2000–2001.* Wellington, State Services Commission.

Wintringham, M. (2001b) Opening Address, 2001 annual Public Service Senior Management Conference, *Public Service in a Crowded Age.* Te Papa, Wellington, State Services Commission. http://pssm.ssc.govt.nz/previous/2001/papers/mwintrin.asp. Accessed September 18, 2002.

Wistrich, E. (1992) Restructuring Government New Zealand Style. *Public Administration* 70: 119–35.

Wright, B. (2001) Public Sector Work Motivation: A Review of the Current Literature and a Revised Conceptual Model. *Journal of Public Administration Research and Theory* 11(4): 559–86.

Yin, R. (1994) *Case study research – Design and Methods.* Thousand Oaks, Calif., Sage.

Zifcak, S. (1994) *New Managerialism – Administrative Reform in Whitehall and Canberra.* Buckingham, Open University Press.

Zohar, D. (1997) *ReWiring the Corporate Brain: Using the New Science to Rethink How We Structure and Lead Organisations.* San Francisco, Berrett-Koehler.

Index